HEMINGWAY IN GERMANY

JOSEPH SHUMAN
JOURNALISM COLLECTION

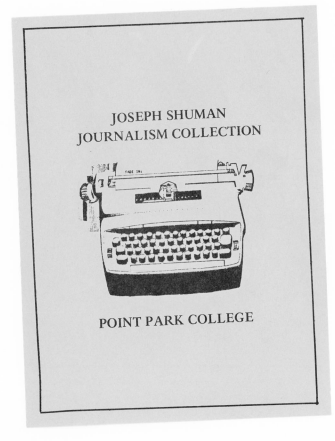

POINT PARK COLLEGE

HEMINGWAY IN GERMANY

The Fiction, the Legend, and the Critics

WAYNE E. KVAM

Ohio University Press: Athens

*This book is dedicated
to my Mother and Father*

© 1973 by Wayne E. Kvam
All rights reserved
Library of Congress Catalog Number LC 79–181689
ISBN 8214–0126–2
Printed in the United States of America by Heritage Printers, Inc.
Design by Hal Stevens

CONTENTS

ACKNOWLEDGMENTS

Quotations from Ernest Hemingway's *Across the River and Into the Trees* (Copyright 1950 Ernest Hemingway) are used by permission of Charles Scribner's Sons and Jonathan Cape Ltd.

Numerous people have given generously of their time and talents to make the publication of this book possible. I am grateful to the late Henry A. Pochmann, who gave me sound criticism and advice during the planning stages. Klaus Schroeter of Saarbrücken, Germany, frequently secured bibliographical information for me; his interest and warm hospitality helped to make my research efforts in Germany both pleasant and profitable. John Stark, my colleague at Kent State, read the manuscript and offered many valuable suggestions. I am deeply indebted to Leanora Sefert for her encouragement and her diligence in helping me with the final manuscript revisions.

The staffs of the university libraries in Madison, Wisconsin, Tübingen, Saarbrücken, Göttingen and Mainz assisted me at various times, and I have continually relied upon the secretarial skills of Mrs. Sallie Saxe. I am also grateful to the Kent State University Graduate School for providing fees for my excellent typists, Harriet Liff and Carolyn Rosenberg.

Finally I should like to thank the editorial staff of Ohio University Press for their kindness, patience, and cooperation.

W. E. K.

Kent, Ohio
January, 1973

INTRODUCTION

No American writer of the twentieth century has exercised a stronger hold on peoples outside his own country. No American writer has so stirred the literary imagination of writers in other languages. This fact—Hemingway's world stature—seems . . . to represent what is most significant historically about Hemingway.

> Norman Cousins in the Hemingway Memorial Issue of *Saturday Review of Literature*, July 29, 1961.

He [Hemingway] was thus a formative element in the spiritual orientation of postwar Germany with its two main streams: the specifically religious and literary-secular.

> Helmut Papajewski in *The Literary Reputation of Hemingway in Europe*, 1965.

The success of American literature in Europe, both among the reading public and literary critics, has attracted considerable scholarly attention during the past fifteen years. This is especially true in the case of the reception of American literature in Germany; see, e.g., Sara Ballenger's "The American Novel in Germany (1945–1957)," 1959; Anne Springer's *The American Novel in Germany*, 1960; Eugene Timpe's *The Reception of American Literature in Germany, 1862–1872*, 1961; and Lawrence M. Price's *The Reception of United States Literature in Germany*, 1966. In an attempt to depart from the broad surveys that characterize these works, the present study is limited to the critical reaction to one writer, Hemingway, during the height of his popularity in Germany. Hemingway's career began in Germany with the publication of two early poems in the magazine *Der Querschnitt* in 1924. Although his works were banned by the Nazis from 1933 to 1945, from the end of World War II until a few years after his death Hemingway captured the imagination of German readers as no other American writer had done. In drawing attention to his artistic skills, German critics contributed significantly to Hemingway's postwar popularity; at the same time their approach to Hemingway, which was frequently different from that of critics in other countries, demonstrates the complexity of literary cross currents, the versatility of Hemingway, and the many-sidedness of a work of art.

For the most part the following study is limited to an examination of critical opinions on Hemingway which appeared in German periodicals, newspapers, and books from 1945 to 1971. The critics consulted are primarily from West Germany. East Germans who are represented are identified as such. In assessing the critical response I have attempted to select representative opinions and to draw conclusions from them. For the sake of convenience and consistency I have translated the quoted material into English. The public reaction to Hemingway was naturally more difficult to determine, and in this study could only be speculated upon.

The critical reactions deal mainly with Hemingway's style, the short stories, and the five major novels. German reactions to *The Torrents of Spring* and *To Have and Have Not* were not significant enough to be included. Hemingway's longer works of nonfiction, *Death in the Afternoon* and *Green Hills of Africa*, are briefly taken into account, but since neither was translated until the 1950's, their reception was ambivalent and perhaps misleading. Responses to Hemingway's posthumous publications are included in the epilogue.

Chapter I provides a brief historical survey of the German reaction to American literature, including the early works of Hemingway, from the time of the first translations until the Nazi take-over in 1933. Emphasis is placed on critical tastes and reactions that paved the way for Hemingway's postwar success. The second part of the chapter is concerned with the immediate postwar atmosphere, and the renewed contacts of the German people with American culture.

The legend of Hemingway is taken up in Chapter II. Following 1945, Hemingway's public image, which had been in the making since the early 1930's, was eagerly adopted by the German press and in turn influenced critical response. Chapter III is divided into six parts dealing with the reactions of specific critics to (1) the Hemingway style, (2) Hemingway's short stories, (3) the two pre-

World War II novels *The Sun Also Rises* and *A Farewell to Arms,* (4) *For Whom the Bell Tolls,* (5) *Across the River and Into the Trees,* (6) *The Old Man and the Sea.* Whenever possible critics are treated chronologically, thereby illustrating the changes in critical tastes and methods. Chapter IV outlines the distinctive traits of both the critics' and the public's reaction and offers an explanation of why Germans reacted to Hemingway in the way that they did. Chapter V describes the reassessment of Hemingway which has been under way during the past six years.

It is hoped that such an analysis will offer a more reliable explanation for Hemingway's popularity in Germany, add further insight into his more controversial writings, and provide a new vantage point from which to assess Hemingway's contribution to world literature.

KEY TO ABBREVIATIONS

The key to abbreviations used throughout the text, footnotes, and bibliography is as follows:

AGR	American-German Review
AR	Amerikanische Rundschau
ASNS	Archiv für das Studium der neueren Sprachen
DB	Deutsche Beiträge
DR	Deutsche Rundschau
DUZ	Deutsche Universitätszeitung
FH	Frankfurter Hefte
GRM	Germanisch-Romanische Monatsschrift
GT	Das goldene Tor
HM	Heute und Morgen (Ost)
JAS	Jahrbuch für Amerikastudien
NA	Neues Abendland
NDH	Neue deutsche Literatur
NR	Neue Rundschau
NS	Die neueren Sprachen
NW	Neue Welt
OW	Ost und West
SF	Sinn und Form
SZ	Stimmen der Zeit
WS	Weltstimmen
WM	Westermanns Monatshefte
WW	Wort und Wahrheit
ZAA	Zeitschrift für Anglistik und Amerikanistik

CHAPTER ONE
AMERICAN LITERATURE IN GERMANY

The recent German critical reaction to Hemingway is a necessary and natural part of the overall reception of American literature in Germany, and of the unusual literary situation that prevailed during the years immediately following World War II. As the ground work of Clement Vollmer[1] and three more recent studies of American literature in Germany by Anne M. Springer,[2] Sara E. Ballenger,[3] and Lawrence M. Price[4] demonstrate, Germans have expressed an early and continued interest in American fiction from the time of the first translation of Charles Brockden Brown's *Ormand or the Secret Witness* in 1802 to the present.

Although German critics and literary historians were slow in recognizing an independent American literature—the first critical work to be devoted entirely to a history of American literature was K. Brunnemann's *Geschichte der nordamerikanischen Literatur* in 1866[5]—the German reading public read American fiction long before their literary historians and critics chose to recognize it. A French translation of Irving's *Bracebridge Hall* was widely read when it first appeared in Germany in 1822.[6] And translations of Cooper's novels *The Pioneers* and *The Spy* became immediate popular successes in 1824;[7] the translation of Harriet Beecher Stowe's *Uncle Tom's Cabin or Life Among the Lowly* went through fifty-eight or more separate editions in Germany after its first publication in 1852.[8] German publishers were aware of the market for American books, for, as Vollmer points out, "there were between ninety and one hundred firms, some of them in Austria and Switzerland, which between 1871 and 1913, published one or more American novel either in the original or in translation."[9] The Bernhard Tauchnitz Verlag alone—one of the most successful firms publishing American novels in the original—"included four hundred and thirty-seven works of sixty-eight American authors" during the same period.[10]

In their selection of American works for translation between 1871 and 1913, German publishers were guided by the taste prevailing among the American public. According to Springer, three types of fiction seemed to appeal most to the average reader: "historical and sentimental romance, the local color story, and social utopia."[11] Of the first type the most popular were Frances Hodgson Burnett's *Little Lord Fauntleroy*, 1887, F. Marion Crawford's *Mr. Isaacs*, 1883, and *A Roman Singer*, 1884, and Kate Douglas Wiggin's *Rebecca of Sunnybrook Farm*, 1904, each of which was published in the original. Local color fiction, interesting to Germans because it described life in the new world, was provided by J. F. Cooper's *Leather-Stocking Tales*; Cooper, the most frequently translated American prose writer, was widely read until the turn of the nineteenth century, when Bret Harte, Jack London, and Mark Twain began to rival him in popularity. Twain, from the first time he attracted attention in Germany in 1874 with *Jim Smileys berühmter Springfrosch und dergleichen wunderliche Käuze mehr; im Silberlande Nevada*, had a large following, both among laymen and literary critics.[12] The novels of social inquiry, such as Edward Bellamy's *Looking Backward 2000–1887* (translated and published in 1889 as *Ein Rückblick 2000–1887*), Frank Norris's *The Octopus*, 1901, and *The Pit*, 1904 (both published in the original), and Upton Sinclair's *The Jungle* (translated and published as *Der Sumpf* in 1906), were aided by the publicizing efforts of the German Socialist Party and by the reception they had had in the United States.[13] Other American literary figures, such as Hawthorne, Thoreau, Melville, Howells, James, and Crane, were for the most part ignored and did not achieve popularity until after World War II.[14]

As the studies of Price[15] and K. T. Locher[16] indicate, a significant change in the attitude of German scholars toward American literature finally took place in works such as E. A. Hopp's *Unter dem Sternenbanner. Streifzüge in das Leben und die Literatur der Amerikaner*, 1887; Karl Knortz's *Geschichte der nordamerikanischen Literatur*, 1891; E. P. Evans's *Beiträge zur amerikanischen Literatur- und Kulturgeschichte*, 1898; Hugo Munsterberg's *Die Amerikaner*, 1904; and Leon Kellner's *Geschichte der nordamerikanischen Literatur*, 1912. Critics began to recognize that America did have an independent literature with its own unique qualities, and they began to discredit the European idea of an uncultured new world. In Kellner's second edition published in 1927, contemporary American novelists—Dreiser, Hergesheimer, and Lewis —appeared in a German history of literature for the first time.

Another pioneer critic in the field was Friedrich Schönemann, who in 1921 urged fellow Germans to discover modern American thought through her literature. A similar approach was taken by Walther Fischer, author of what were once considered "the standard German handbooks of American literature": *Die amerikanische Prosa vom Bürgerkrieg bis zur Gegenwart*, 1926, and "Die englische Literatur der Vereinigten Staaten" in *Handbuch der Literaturwissenschaft*, 1929. Between the wars men like Friedrich Brie, S. B. Liljegren, Wilhelm Dibelius, Alois Brandl, and Theodor Spira, originally known for their work in Anglistics, began to write scholarly interpretations of American literature.[17] Other factors which helped to create a greater interest in American literature after World War I are outlined by Springer: (1) the publication of H. L. Mencken's *The American Language* (1919); (2) the burst of lyrical talent among American poets, including Robert Frost, Edgar Lee Masters, Vachel Lindsay, Carl Sandburg, and Amy Lowell; (3) a declaration of American intellectual independence, especially from Anglo-Saxon Puritanism, which many German critics hastily referred to as the "jung-amerikanische Bewegung." She concludes,

> The enterprising publisher who had initiated and stimulated the taste for the American book long before the first World War, together with a series of histories of literature which in turn attained a fair standard of critical judgment, and finally discussions in the academic and literary magazines on the American language, on American poetry, [and] on American civilization . . . were all factors contributing to the steady growth of German interest in American literature. They were a kind of preparation for the reception and impact of London, Sinclair, Dreiser, Lewis, Dos Passos, Hemingway, Faulkner, and Wolfe, as one after another they became known in Germany.[18]

Springer's study, which focuses on the reception of the above-mentioned novelists in Germany between 1919 and 1932, provides valuable information on the general literary climate into which Hemingway's works were first introduced in the 1920's. Strangely enough it was Jack London who was the most popular American novelist between the wars. Fortunately for London's reputation, he was favored by the Universitatus Verlag in Berlin and by a tireless translator, Edwin Magnus, who supplied a steady flow of translations from 1924 to 1940. Other reasons for London's favorable reception bear a surprisingly close relation to the factors determining Hemingway's reception after 1945: (1) the translation of London's biography into German shortly after its publication in America informed German readers of his varied, fascinating life; like Hemingway he was not the typical "Literat." (2) London appealed to widely diversified tastes; his leftist leanings endeared him to the German Socialist Party, and his adventure stories appealed to youths of all ages. (3) Germany was a nation torn by war, inflation, and political turmoil. The novels of London were associated with the primitive forces of a new continent, which were overtaking a worn and tired Europe.[19] As novelist Walter von Molo remarked in 1927, "We in Germany need Jack London bitterly; his work is like thunderstorms that purify the air."[20] (4) Germans admired the energetic spirit that permeated London's books and, as was later to be the case with Hemingway, the nobility of his fictional characters.[21]

Hemingway, who was well known in Germany before the Nazi regime came to power in 1933, was introduced to the general reading public through magazines. Hemingway himself refers to his early reputation in an episode from *Green Hills of Africa*:

> "Hemingway is my name."
> "Kandisky," he said and bowed. "Hemingway is a name I have heard. Where? Where? O yes. The Dichter. You know the poet?"
> "Where did you read him?"
> "In the *Querschnitt*."
> "That's me," I said, very pleased. "The *Querschnitt* is a German magazine I have written some poems for and published a long story in, years before I could sell anything in America."
> "This is very strange," the man in the Tyrolese hat said, "but it is a pleasure to meet one of the *Querschnitt* group. Tell me, what is Joyce like? I haven't got the money to buy him."[22]

During the 1930's, translations of Hemingway's longer works into German were done exclusively by Annemarie Horschitz; and fortunately Hemingway had as his publisher Ernst Rowohlt, recognized as one of the leading publishers in German literary history. Rowohlt published Hemingway's works in quick succession: *"Fiesta (The Sun Also Rises)* in 1928, *Männer (Men Without Women)* in 1929, *In einem anderen Land (A Farewell to Arms)* in 1930."[23]

Among German *avant garde* critics of the early Thirties Hemingway was considered the biographer of the American Bohemian center in Paris, and they recognized in *Fiesta (The Sun Also Rises)* an expressed kinship with their generation. Others admired the stylistic innovations they found in Hemingway's prose: the art of omission, his ability to capture the intensity of the moment, his primitivism, vitality, and "calculated artlessness."[24] Irene Seligo, writing about Hemingway's influence on younger German writers in the *Frankfurter Zeitung* (1932), asserted that

> Hemingway, at the present moment the most mature and most representative American author, is the first who can claim a definite influence of America back on European literature. . . . No doubt, the young European authors want to write like Hemingway because the simple suggestiveness of his style is too contagious.[25]

Hans Joachim in the *Neue Rundschau* (1930) wrote that Hemingway does not present reality but rather reproduces it; he knows war from firsthand experience, and it is from this experience that he has shaped his writing technique: "Hemingway, who is a great writer, does not narrate. He takes inventory."[26] Hans Fallada, in *Die Literatur* (1931), pointed out that in reading *The Sun Also Rises* or *A Farewell to Arms,* one discovers that Hemingway does not know the art of ornamentation: "Naturally he requires adjectives, but if he says white elephants, he means elephants with white skin, and if he says dark streets, he actually means a street which is dark, and that is all." By omitting feelings and narrating scenically, Hemingway, stated Fallada, only fills in the outline; the rest he leaves to his readers, and the question is whether or not they have something to bring to the story.[27]

The most effusive praise among Hemingway's early critics in Germany came from Klaus Mann, in the *Neue Schweizer Rundschau* in 1931. Hemingway's style, Mann stated, is nothing other than a miracle. One sees afterwards that this is the way one should write and asks the question why we have not done this before. "But this exceptional American," he added, "had to come to show it to us." The feeling of *Angst* which permeates Hemingway's fiction has something in common with Kafka, Mann contended, but Hemingway does not stop at nihilism: "His cynicism is a very healthy protective measure. Life can be unbearable, but on the other hand we do not know anything more beautiful." Hemingway is popular among young Europeans because he combines the best of America with that which Europe has to offer: "He sees this world with the freshness of his young race, and at the same time with the cunning of a European."[28]

In Mann's opinion *Männer* (*Men Without Women*) contained examples of Hemingway's richest prose. Speaking of "Alpine Idyll" and "A Simple Enquiry," individual stories in the collection, he stated: "They are masterworks . . . extracts from life in which each word is loaded with destiny. The essence is bitter, but wonderfully strong." His highest praise was reserved for *A Farewell to Arms*. No other writer of his time, according to Mann, could imitate Hemingway's skill in the concluding scene of the novel. This scene with "its suspenseful reserve which allows the inner events to correspond exactly with the outer, is more characteristic of his art than any other, and it is the most moving scene that Hemingway has written."[29]

Hilde Pieritz in *Hefte für Büchereiwesen* (1932), speaking of Hemingway's reception in Germany following Rowohlt's early translations, stated that "Whoever follows literary criticism knows that he [Hemingway] is a popular topic of discussion; critics debate whether he is a pessimist or nihilist, and draw parallels between his work and that of Hamsun and Joseph Conrad. Some speak knowingly about him, and others misunderstand him completely." Like many of her fellow critics, Pieritz herself praised the objectivity and simplicity she discovered in Hemingway's prose. His honesty, seriousness, and lack of sentimentality would not be likely to appeal to a wide reading public, and thus she feared that Hemingway's popularity in Germany would be superceded by American writers of lesser stature. However, she encouraged those who had discovered Hemingway's extraordinary talent to introduce other readers to his works. By making Hemingway's books available, she stated, city libraries would continue to keep open the avenues to great literature, but above all they would enable the discriminating reader to appreciate the "exceptional experience" of his art.[30]

Max Dietrich, *Hochland* (1933), also drew attention to Hemingway's style, especially his brevity and the staccato effect of his short sentences, which Dietrich considered to be particularly appropriate for Hemingway's subject matter. Like almost all American writers, Hemingway, he stated, is able to portray the fullness and immediacy of real life in his fiction. *A Farewell to Arms* Dietrich considered to be Hemingway's strongest book, for it elevates the individual above the outcome of victory or defeat and does so without decentralizing the plot: "Therefore the book, despite Hemingway's love for truth and sense of reality, is tender and controlled; at no time aggressive or exaggerated, it is filled with the mind of a true writer who is openly committed to peace." In a realistic manner, he concluded, Hemingway could present love as a religious feeling, whereas any German writer would have begun to write a metaphysical novel.[31]

The preceding survey of critical opinions validates the earlier findings of Anne Springer, who concluded that the two main factors determining Hemingway's reception in Germany between the world wars were "a decline of interest in the reportorial novel of social protest and a desire for a new style and technique in novel writing." As Springer pointed out, only among Catholic reviewers was dissatisfaction expressed with Hemingway's accomplishments in fiction. They warned German readers that the times were too grave to be concerned with "the alcohol befogged conversations of the shady Hemingway figures" or with the author himself who chose to treat religion only incidentally.[32] The potential critical debate never really developed, for Hemingway's name was soon placed on the black list of the "Reichsschrifttumsstelle," ending his reception in Germany for the time being.[33]

For the most part the reception of American literature in Germany was over for the ten-year period between 1935 and 1945. However, we can conclude that the way for the burgeoning success of the American novel in postwar Germany had already been paved prior to World War II. The German public may have selected those American writers who could fulfill their particular needs at the time, or simply provide information about the United

States, but German scholars began to recognize the aesthetic value of the new experiments in style and form that characterized the American novel of the 1920's.

After 1933 Germans were at the mercy of the State, and long before bombs set fire to the majority of their bookstores and printing presses, the "cultural policy" of the National Socialists had caused the spiritual death of books and magazines, German as well as American. According to Joachim Joesten, who attempted to keep Americans informed of Germany's literary situation in the Forties, the German press had gained universal prestige during the short time between the world wars. A total of forty-seven hundred newspapers (among them one hundred major ones) were in existence, and Germany could boast a greater number of newspapers per citizen than any other country in the world. However, all this was altered during the twelve-year Nazi rule when the German news media became subjected to Goebbels' Propaganda Ministry.[34] During this period nearly 250 German writers went into exile, and the list of forbidden books numbered nearly thirteen hundred titles by approximately 690 authors.[35]

By the time of the armistice the German literary world had sunk to its lowest point in history. As Heinrich Fischer wrote two years later, in 1947,

> The German scene today, a scene of ruin and chaotic disintegration, is an outward and visible sign of the collapse of the human spirit—the reflection of not six but twelve years of war and terror. Grotesque confusion reigns in the literary life of Germany today. It is so grotesque that one is often scarcely able to distinguish which of the German writers was a criminal accomplice of Hitler, and which was one of Hitler's victims.[36]

A similar situation faced German publishers. Each of the four occupying forces set up rigid censorship regulations, the supply of paper was nearly exhausted, and buildings, machines, and prewar stocks of materials had been destroyed.[37] An intellectually starved people, eagerly awaiting reading material from the outside world in an attempt to make up for twelve years of isolation, were often frustrated in their search for books, magazines, or newspapers. An illustration of the Germans' plight is provided by F. C.

Weiskopf, who included excerpts from personal letters written from the three western zones of Germany in *Books Abroad* (Winter, 1947). A teacher from Bremen: "Bread lines are long . . . but believe me, the lines before book shops and magazine and newspaper stands are longer." A woman in Frankfurt: "You cannot imagine what it means to get a magazine or book from abroad. We are all eagerly waiting for the announced new magazines and books of the licensed publishers. I went to Heidelberg . . . to get some books, but the booksellers have nothing to sell, or they sell only on the black market." A French officer, writing of the book smuggling between Switzerland and the French Zone of Germany: "The demand is extraordinary. The other day I watched an old professor in the University of Freiburg who had to make a difficult choice between a thin Reclam booklet . . . and a copy of the *Linguistic Review*, since the booksellers will sell one item to each customer."[38]

Edward Breitenkamp, who served as an Information Control Officer for the United States Army in Marburg from 1947–1948, has used his experience to examine the effects of censorship on German publications and intellectual life from 1945 to 1949. His study, *The United States Information Control Division and its Effect on German Publishers and Writers*, 1953, provides a useful insight into the gradual recovery of German literature and news media. The Information Control Division, according to Breitenkamp, "was given the mission of destroying Nazistic and militaristic-nationalistic thought in Germany as it might persist in the press and publications, on the stage, in the cinema and in the radio; and to replace Nazi ideology with liberal-democratic ideas such as Americans believe to be characteristic of the American political system."[39]

Thus the ICD, which formerly had been the Psychological Warfare Division, was as "purposive" as Goebbels' Propaganda Ministry; and their encouragement of excellence in German letters and arts was only a secondary goal. The allied armies' control of all existing information services, including publishing houses, libraries, bookstores, and radio stations, isolated Germany as never before. Largely because of the shattered German economy there was a lack of foreign books and periodicals, and those that did cross the border had to pass through the Information Control Division before they were allowed to appear to the German public. International mail service was not available to Germans until one year after the truce, and until 1949 private travel to and from Germany was nearly impossible.[40] Dr. Wilhelm Hoffmann, writing in *German Books*, 1948, expressed the disillusion German intellectuals experienced in the early postwar years:

> It was entirely different than we had imagined it would be. After that unforgettable moment when life came to a standstill in the summer of 1945, we believed that the gates into the world, or better the gates from the world would be opened wide, that literature from without would stream in to fructify our own literature. We believed further that in Germany itself manuscripts would be brought out from the desks and that a long-withheld literature would come to light. Nothing of the sort happened.[41]

The ICD, according to Breitenkamp, promoted the works of German writers who had emigrated, but the internationally known figures, such as the Mann brothers, Hermann Hesse, Franz Werfel, and Arnold and Stefan Zweig, had little possibility of negotiating with German firms and had nothing to gain financially by allowing their works to be published in Germany. Consequently it was the minor writers who were heard from, and those Germans who had expected renewed guidance from their better-known expatriate writers were mostly disappointed.[42] In *Monatshefte*, 1947, Frank Horvay noted that the postwar German literary trend, if one could call it that, was "a kind of memoir and atonement school which consists of concentration-camp diaries, accounts of Nazi persecutions and numerous appeals to bear the present deserved burden with humility and hope."[43]

The Information Control Division dealt directly with the publishers, who in turn were responsible for the political acceptability of the writer. Once the publisher had passed an extremely rigorous examination and received his license, he was provided with a general statement of principles to guide him. According to Breitenkamp, publishers were careful to use safe titles, for they had to please the Control Division to get paper allotments, and violators were threatened by loss of license, fines, and imprisonment.[44] Many settled for re-editions of German classics, and those who had nothing to publish turned to what they thought the occupying powers

wanted to hear. In the American Zone, for example, the first trans-
lation rights sold were for "Carl Sandburg, *Storm over the Land*;
Margaret Mead, *And Keep Your Powder Dry*; . . . Dennis Brogan,
The American Character; Morison and Commager, *The Growth
of the American Republic*; Arthur Hertzler, *The Horse and Buggy
Doctor*; Van Wyck Brooks, *The World of Washington Irving* and
The Flowering of New England."[45]

In spite of these drawbacks, the revival of German publishing
under Allied control proceeded rapidly. Breitenkamp reports that
"By October, 1945, 4,000 book dealers had been registered, compared to 76 licensed newspapers, 17 licensed periodicals, and 35
licensed book publishers."[46] Because of the unstable currency and
acute paper shortage, the book market was first dominated by
brochures and pamphlets. But following the currency reform in
1948, well-printed books in solid bindings began to appear, restric-
tions of the Control Division were lessened, and a normal book
trade resumed.[47] Among the deluge of new periodicals a number
began to distinguish themselves in spite of earlier difficulties: *Die
Wandlung, Hochland, Die Gegenwart, Merkur, Neue Beiträge,
Berliner Hefte, Deutsche Rundschau, Welt und Wort*, and *Die
Sammlung*. And Germans welcomed back old familiar names to
the publishing business, such as Reclam, Insel, Rowohlt, Suhr-
kamp-Fischer, Malik, Cotta, and Herbig.[48]

In the light of Germany's literary situation immediately after
1945, it is easy to see why the time was ripe for the influx of foreign
literature, especially that of America. Germans had been cut off
from foreign influences since 1933 and were eager to have the
world reopened to them. Many of their own writers had emigrated,
and those who remained were under strict censorship control and
for the most part incapable of fulfilling their country's literary
needs. The renewed interest in things American, which had followed World War I, repeated itself after 1945. And as an occupational force the United States was more real to Germans than ever
before.

German critics were quick to point out the implications of this
new confrontation with the American culture and urged their fellow countrymen to prepare themselves. In *Die Neueren Sprachen*,
1952, Horst Oppel wrote that following World War II Germans
were faced with the immediacy of American scientific, political,

and cultural concerns that up to that time they had only super-
ficially investigated. For nearly a generation they had been isolated
from American literature, and consequently, he wrote, "it meant
for the German Americanists that, with the exception of a few
significant studies from the 1920's and 1930's, they would have to
begin over again."[49]

Rudolph Hartung, recalling in *Welt und Wort*, 1946, the limited
freedom of artists to experiment and explore under the National
Socialists, and their consequent isolation from changes in physics
and psychoanalysis, speculated on the new type of literature that
would thrive in postwar Germany:

> The literature of the future must no longer overlook the
> reality of our altered world and our transformed image of
> man; it must strive to represent them. In this task the well
> developed realism in Anglo-Saxon literature will certainly
> be an encouragement to us.[50]

Karl Geyh in his article "Prophetisches in Dichtungen und
Kunstströmungen," *Welt und Wort*, 1946, claimed that Germans
were experiencing the overwhelming significance of America in
their lives as never before. The "neue Sachlichkeit," which, he
said, was an "early manifestation of America's influence on the
European and especially the German world," was daily confronted
through radios, magazines, and newspapers. Like Hartung, he
mentioned the "magische Realismus" or "Surrealismus," which
would characterize literature of the future: "Now it is also possible
for artists in Germany to achieve a synthesis of 'neuer Sachlichkeit' and 'magischem Realismus.' Perhaps this will enable them to
anticipate events in the future, from which we hope will come a
real peace."[51]

An overwhelming number of American books in translation did
flood the German book market shortly after the war, and the trend
continued even after the Information Control Division was no
longer in existence and native German writers were heard from
again. According to a publication of the United States Information
Service, *Verzeichnis amerikanischer Bücher in deutscher Übersetzung Erschienen seit 1945*, a total of 3,097 volumes were translated into German between 1945 and 1956; of these 1,443 were
volumes of American prose fiction.[52] In addition to the large num-

ber of translations were the Overseas Editions and Armed Services editions of American works in the original. Pocket Books Inc. was founded in 1939, and soon afterwards cheap paperback editions of American fiction with good print and striking covers began selling in Germany for 1,25 DM per copy.[53]

The contributions of publishing companies were supplemented by various American agencies, which, according to Sigmund Skard, "began spreading knowledge of the United States through a system of Information Offices, press bureaux, newspapers, and reviews, and a large-scale program of lectures, film performances, and exhibitions. A main instrument in this activity," stated Skard, "was the net of Amerika-Häuser, which were set up in the main cities of all the occupied zones of Western Germany; most of them were equipped with splendid libraries covering all fields of American Civilization."[54]

German scholars responded to the influx of American books with a revitalized critical approach to the American language and literature. Ballenger provides a summary of the main contributions during the early postwar years:

> In fact, the first, Friedrich Schönemann's *Die Vereinigten Staaten*, was published as early as 1943. Two years later Walter Schirmer's excellent study *Kurze Geschichte der englischen Literatur von den Anfängen bis zur Gegenwart* appeared. This volume contained discussions of several American writers, although they were not treated separately from their British confreres. An anthology, *Amerikanische Erzähler*, was edited by Fritz Güttingen in 1946, and Augusta Bronner's *Amerikanische Literaturgeschichte* was published that same year. *Hauptströmungen des modernen amerikanischen Schrifttums* by Walther Fischer came out in 1948. Four important works arrived on the scene in 1949: Karl Friedrich Frahne's handbook, *Von Franklin bis Hemingway*, Julius Bab's *Amerikanische Dichter*, Hildegard Blomeyer's *Grundriss der amerikanischen Literatur*, and Heinrich Stammler's *Amerika im Spiegel seiner Literatur*, which was followed in 1950 by his *Amerikanische Literaturgeschichte im Überblick*. In 1953 Heinrich Lüdeke's *Geschichte der amerikanischen Literatur* was published.[55]

The German Association for American Studies, which encourages scholarly investigations of an interdisciplinary nature, was founded in 1953; and soon there appeared two serial publications devoted entirely to research in American literature and civilization: *Jahrbuch für Amerikastudien* and *Mainzer amerikanistische Beiträge.*[56]

Another result of the awakening interest in the United States was the revived interest of German secondary schools and universities in American Studies (*Amerikakunde*), which had come to a standstill during the Nazi period. In the first postwar decade there was an average of four specialized courses in American Studies for each West German university (twice the prewar number), and a growing tendency to give American literature separate status within English departments.[57]

The prominence of American culture, although generally welcomed in West Germany, did not meet with unanimous approval. On the extremely conservative side was Curt Hohoff, who in nationalistic fashion claimed that Germany had novelists and philosophers superior to Hemingway and Sartre, and that the "fatal attraction of things foreign" prevented the proper recognition of contemporary German writing.[58] John R. Frey, one of the first Americans to study the impact of American literature in postwar Germany, noted that in the early issues (November and December, 1950) of *Das literarische Deutschland*, the official organ of the "Deutsche Akademie für Sprache und Dichtung," the question of foreign literature was considered under the appropriate title "Befruchtung oder Überschwemmung." In that discussion a more liberal viewpoint was expressed by Karl Friedrich Boree, who stated that the influx of foreign books was necessary at that time, but it should be a matter of concern to both reader and publisher, for Germans, although they had the right to escape their depressing surroundings through the reading of foreign literature, must come to terms with their own country's past and present.[59]

For the most part German writers welcomed their country's renewed contact with foreign literature, especially those of the middle generation, such as Elizabeth Langgässer, Hermann Kasack, Ernst Kreuder and the young authors associated with the loosely organized "Gruppe 47."[60] This group, listing among its original members Hans W. Richter, Walter Kolbenhoff, Walter Jens, Heinrich Böll, Hans J. Soehring, Ernst Schnabel, Wolfdietrich Schurre, and Ilse Aichinger, expressed in their periodical *Der Ruf* a skeptical attitude toward the provincialism and lack of social awareness among Germany's older generation of writers. Deliberately remaining aloof from German *Innerlichkeit*, they encouraged an "engaged literature" and looked to foreign models for guidance in their creative efforts.[61] Postwar German writers were drawn to three main elements in contemporary American fiction: (1) the way in which American writers approached all sides of life realistically and yet managed not to be overcome by the sordid; (2) the powerful spirit or vivacity, often referred to as American optimism, that permeated their fiction; (3) the creative talent and technical skill that made Americans masters of adventure stories as well as longer epic narratives. Like their writers and critics, the postwar reading public in Germany also turned to the American novel, but for slightly different reasons:

> The discriminating as well as the average readers could not help marveling at the world that was again opened up to them after the war: intact, basically stable, and reassuringly coherent; a world anchored firmly enough to afford an essentially generous view of things, meaning wholesome naturalness, tolerance, vitality and humor. These qualities and the corresponding absence of weighty *Weltanschauungen* and pretentious intellectualism have made American literature so welcome, aside from its informational worth, which is always so avidly looked for.[62]

During the early postwar period Germans recognized that America was producing a literature that was equal to that of any of the European countries. Friedrich Schönemann warned fellow Germans that although their European traditions would often cause them to find currently successful American books primitive or superficial, they should not allow this to prejudice them against a distinctive prose style which had elevated American fiction to the status of world literature within the last fifty years.[63] The majority of German critics were aware that because of the recent destruction of their country they could not be cultural leaders in the immediate future, and they looked freely to foreign influences. As author-critic Friedrich Sieburg remarked in 1949, "We allow ourselves to be led by movements which include no German names, but names such as Thornton Wilder, Thomas Wolfe, and Sartre. No German influences our writing style as strongly as the American Hemingway does."[64]

The reception of American fiction in Germany, which had continued to increase steadily since the mid-nineteenth century in spite of serious, but temporary, interruptions and distortions, reached a new level of intensity immediately after 1945, and it is against this background that the present investigation begins. Wolfe, Wilder, Faulkner, and Steinbeck, writers who had been known briefly in Germany before World War II, together with Caldwell, Saroyan, and war novelists Mailer, Jones, and Shaw have gained a wide following among Germans during the postwar years. However, the most prominent among them, both as a literary force and a living legend, has been Hemingway. Critics such as Robert Pick, who compared the impact of Hemingway upon his generation in Europe with the Werther-fever after 1770,[65] or Broder Carstensen, who suggested that Hemingway's vitality and revolutionary prose style have left a permanent stamp on the age,[66] may have exaggerated somewhat, but to confirm Hemingway's popularity in Germany, one need only consider the frequency with which Germans translated and published his works after 1945. As the following investigation of the German critical reaction to Hemingway will indicate, his writings attracted not only a wide public audience, but also the attention of Germany's foremost scholars and literary critics.

NOTES

[1] Clement Vollmer, *The American Novel in Germany 1871–1913* (Philadelphia, 1918).

[2] Anne M. Springer, *The American Novel in Germany: A Study of the Critical Reception of Eight American Novelists Between the Two World Wars* (Britannica et Americana), VII (1960).

[3] Sara E. Ballenger, "The Reception of the American Novel in German Periodicals, 1945–1957" (Unpublished Ph.D. dissertation, Department of Comparative Literature, Indiana University).

[4] L. M. Price, *The Reception of United States Literature in Germany* (Chapel Hill, 1966).

[5] *Ibid.*, p. 46.

6 *Ibid.*, p. 81.

7 *Ibid.*, p. 85.

8 *Ibid.*, p. 100.

9 Vollmer, p. 47.

10 *Ibid.*, p. 41.

11 Springer, p. 23.

12 See E. H. Hemminghaus, *Mark Twain in Germany* (New York, 1939).

13 Springer, pp. 23–24.

14 Ballenger, p. 15.

15 Price, pp. 44–50.

16 K. T. Locher, *German Histories of American Literature* (Chicago, 1955), p. 113.

17 Springer, p. 28.

18 *Ibid.*, pp. 29–30.

19 *Ibid.*, pp. 32–35.

20 As quoted by Springer, p. 39, from *Books Abroad* (July, 1927), p. 80.

21 Springer, p. 35.

22 As quoted by Springer, p. 80, from "The Man with the Tyrolese Hat," *Der Querschnitt* (January 16, 1936). The quoted passage also appears in Ernest Hemingway, *Green Hills of Africa* (New York, 1935), pp. 7–8.

23 Springer, p. 80.

24 *Ibid.*, p. 81.

25 Irene Seligo, "Mr. Hemingway und der Tod," *Frankfurter Zeitung*, 969–70 (1932) as quoted by Springer, p. 83.

26 Hans Joachim, "Romane aus Amerika," *Neue Rundschau*, XLI (1930), 405–6.

27 Hans Fallada, "Ernest Hemingway oder Woran liegt es?" *Die Literatur*, XXXIII (1931), 672–74.

28 Klaus Mann, "Ernest Hemingway," *Neue Schweizer Rundschau*, XXIV (1931), 272–74.

29 *Ibid.*, pp. 225–26.

30 Hilde Pieritz, "Ernest Hemingway und sein Werk," *Hefte für Büchereiwesen*, XVI (1932), 314–16.

31 Max Dietrich, "Ernest Hemingway," *Hochland*, II (1933), 90–91.

32 Springer, pp. 81–83.

33 Germans living under the Nazi regime did hear from Hemingway again, even though his books had been banned. "Rede an das deutsche Volk (1938)," printed in *Die Weltbühne* of August 25, 1946, and reprinted in the issue of July 19, 1961, was a radio address first delivered by Hemingway himself over the Deutsche Freiheitssender in November of 1938. After commending those Germans who continued to read his works and had the courage to stand up against Nazi tyranny, Hemingway added, "your destiny has made me sad, German people." He recalled the cruel attacks of German bombers in Spain during the Ebro offensive, but he also remembered the heroic efforts of other Germans, such as those of the Thälmann battalion, in giving relief aid to the Spanish victims. "They were the true, noble Germans," he concluded; "Germans, as we love them; Germans, who we are certain number in the millions."

[34] Joachim Joesten, *The German Press in 1947* (New York, 1947), p. 3.

[35] Bayard Q. Morgan, "The Literary Underground in Germany," *Books Abroad* (Summer, 1947), p. 283.

[36] Heinrich Fischer, quoted in "German Writers of Today," *Books Abroad* (Summer, 1947), p. 283.

[37] Ballenger, p. 22.

[38] F. C. Weiskopf, "German Publishers Have Their Problems," *Books Abroad*, XXI (Winter, 1947), p. 9.

[39] Edward Breitenkamp, *The United States Information Control Division and Its Effect on German Publishers and Writers* (Grand Forks, 1953), p. 1.

[40] *Ibid.*, pp. 2–6.

[41] Wilhelm Hoffmann, *German Books*, 1948, as quoted by Breitenkamp, p. 6.

[42] Breitenkamp, pp. 91–92.

[43] Frank Horvay, "Book Publishing in Germany in 1946," *Monatshefte*, XXXIX (1947), 134.

[44] Breitenkamp, p. 34. See also David A. Randall, " 'Dukedom Large Enough': II. Hemingway, Churchill, and the Printed Word," *Bibliographical Society of America Papers*, LVI (1962), 346–53. Randall describes the erroneous charges brought against a German publisher for alleged anti-Semitism in a translated edition of *The Sun Also Rises*.

[45] *Ibid.*, p. 69.

[46] *Ibid.*, p. 38.

[47] *Ibid.*, p. 93.

[48] Victor Lange, "Notes on the German Literary Scene 1946–1948," *Modern Language Journal*, XXXIII (1949), 3.

[49] Horst Oppel, "Forschungsbericht der deutschen Amerikanistik," *Die Neueren Sprachen* (1952), 292–302.

[50] Rudolph Hartung, "Zur Situation Unserer Literatur," *Welt und Wort*, I (1946), 142.

[51] Karl Geyh, "Prophetisches in Dichtungen und Kunstströmungen," *Welt und Wort*, I (1946), 142.

[52] Ballenger, pp. 25–27.

[53] F. Schönemann, "Das amerikanische Buch in Deutschland," *Die Lebenden Fremdsprachen*, III (1951), 168.

[54] Sigmund Skard, *American Studies in Europe*, II (Philadelphia, 1958), pp. 292–324. "At its peak the system had branches in almost 50 German cities; in 1955 there were still 22. Some of these libraries numbered between 20,000 and 30,000 volumes and contained much material of a purely scholarly character" (p. 331).

[55] Ballenger, pp. 32–33.

[56] Hans Galinsky, "American Studies in Germany," *American Studies in Transition*, ed. Marshall W. Fishwick (Philadelphia, 1964), pp. 234–35.

[57] Sigmund Skard, *The American Myth and the European Mind* (Philadelphia, 1961), p. 102.

[58] John R. Frey, "Postwar German Reactions to American Literature," *Journal of English and Germanic Philology*, LIV (1955), 175.

[59] *Ibid.*, p. 176.

[60] *Ibid.*, pp. 173–74.

[61] John R. Frey, "Gruppe 47," *Books Abroad*, XXVI (Summer, 1952), 238. See also Kurt Opitz, "Negative 'Bilanz'? German Literary Reconstruction," *Books Abroad* (Summer, 1963), pp. 275–79.

[62] Frey, "Postwar German Reactions," p. 185.

[63] Schönemann, p. 170.

[64] Friedrich Sieburg, "Bücher von Heute," *Gegenwart*, LV (March 1, 1949), 19.

[65] Robert Pick, "Mit europäischen Augen: Amerika im Spiegel der europäischen Literaturkritik," *Der Monat*, II (1950), 662.

[66] Broder Carstensen, "Evelyn Waugh und Ernest Hemingway," *Archiv für das Studium der Neueren Sprachen*, CXC (1954), 193.

CHAPTER TWO
THE HEMINGWAY LEGEND

As the American critic John A. Jones has pointed out, Hemingway's public legend has always remained in the shadow of his own works, and often "critics have written about their own attitudes toward the legend rather than about their dispassionate critical interest in Hemingway's fiction." The legend began as early as 1925, with Burton Rascoe's review of *In Our Time* in *Arts and Decorations*. Rascoe offered general comments about Hemingway's art, but placed major emphasis on his active life, masculinity and love of adventure. Hemingway himself contributed to the legend in *Death in the Afternoon*, 1932, by expressing scorn for artists such as Jean Cocteau, Aldous Huxley, and El Greco, who he felt did not display manliness in their works. This led to his confrontation with reviewer Max Eastman in the office of Maxwell Perkins on August 11, 1937, and soon Hemingway's tough-man image developed.[1]

Clifton Fadiman's article, "Ernest Hemingway: An American Byron" appeared in *Nation*, January 18, 1933 (it was translated in *Querschnitt* in April, 1933), and according to Jones, "the image of Hemingway as a democratic, proletarian Byron became more current."[2] Fadiman pointed out that Hemingway received more publicity than any other American writer because he represented a new kind of romanticism:

> Hemingway is the hero thrown up by the American ferment, as, in a different way on a profounder level, D. H. Lawrence was thrown up by the industrial ferment of England. Hemingway is the modern primitive, who makes as fresh a start with the emotions as his forefathers did with the soil. He is the frontiersman of the loins, heart, and biceps, the stoic Red Indian minus traditions, scornful of the past, bare of sentimentality, catching the muscular life in a plain and muscular prose. He is the hero who distrusts heroism; he is the prophet of those who are without faith.

Hemingway, Fadiman suggested, was like Lord Byron in that both were defiantly romantic, focusing on the disillusion, turmoil, and bitterness during a postwar era: "Like Byron, he expresses the aspirations of that portion of his generation which genuinely feels itself lost and is eager to admire a way of life which combines lostness with courage and color." Both have a sense of fatality, "the courting of violence, darkness, and even death," which "is a kind of splendid, often very beautiful, disease of the imagination noticeable during periods of social decay."[3]

From 1933–1936 Hemingway contributed twenty-five articles on hunting, fishing, and traveling to *Esquire* magazine. As Jones has indicated, these, too, enhanced the legend: "Frequently photographs of the author, smiling as he posed with a dead marlin, kudu, or lion, accompanied his articles. He always posed himself as a symbol of the masculine and healthful and the critics (or anybody he did not like) as symbols of the puerile and the abnormal." Hemingway's longer works of the Thirties, *Death in the Afternoon, Green Hills of Africa, To Have and Have Not,* and *The Fifth Column* were all "expressions of Hemingway the popular personality rather than Hemingway the artist." The poor reception of *Green Hills of Africa* in the United States, Jones explained, "must be attributed to Hemingway's attacks upon contemporary critics and writers, and to the widespread, unfavorable impression of the Hemingway legend on reviewers and critics, rather than to his avoidance of themes which critics thought important."[4]

Although Hemingway published nothing of significance between 1941 and 1948, he remained continuously in the news, as a bearded hunter of German submarines off the coast of Cuba and as a war correspondent and guerrilla leader in France. This prompted an article by Malcolm Cowley in *Life*, January 10, 1949 (translated in *Der Monat* in December, 1954), which was "a heroic and flattering write up of Hemingway's personality and those of his habits and attitudes that were bound to be attractive to the public." According to Jones, the publication of *Across the River and Into the Trees* in 1950 began the last phase of critical concern with the public legend, and by the time *The Old Man and the Sea* appeared two years later it had almost disappeared.[5]

The legend of Hemingway outlined above continued to thrive

in postwar Germany and to influence German reactions to Hemingway's fiction. Like American critics of the 1930's, German critics of the post-World War II era cultivated a romantic notion of a "lost generation" and considered Hemingway as its most significant representative. As Gotthilf Dierlamm wrote in *Sprache und Literatur Englands und Amerikas,* 1952,

> The American [Hemingway], is enthusiastic about hunting and fishing, indeed, about all dealings with nature. Inspired by a love of adventure which leads him, as a soldier, war reporter, and sportsman, to foreign battlefields and distant countries, he returns home from his travels deeply disillusioned. He gives up his home; he cuts the ties which bind him to society. The values of his contemporaries he considers shallow. Thus he becomes the spokesman of the 'Lost Generation.'

Dierlamm reflected the influence of Fadiman's article when he compared the figure of Hemingway moving about from country to country to that of a wandering Childe Harold, still suffering from "Weltschmerz." "Lord Byron," he concluded, "has awakened again."[6]

For the remainder of his life the German news media eagerly contributed to the growing legend surrounding Hemingway. Frequently in postwar news articles there was a deliberate effort to link the author with his fictional heroes, and journalists engaged freely in romanticizing Hemingway's private life. As a result he was restored to an even greater prominence than he had enjoyed earlier among German readers. One of the first noted critics to attempt an explanation for the cult Hemingway inspired among Germans shortly after the war was Ursula Brumm (*Weltstimmen,* November, 1950). After summarizing Hemingway's adventuresome youth, she wrote that the title *In Our Time* had significance for all his works because it was the immediate that he was concerned with: "He has never written about events which he has not seen." Hemingway, "driven by an urge to witness things firsthand," participated in and wrote about four large-scale wars, two of which had been central to the lives of twentieth-century Germans. He had been subjected to the depths of terror and fear that came with war, and Germans found in him a fellow sufferer. Also they looked

to Hemingway as a model for living; in spite of his personal set-
backs and near brushes with death, he never allowed them to overcome his desire for a full, adventuresome life:

> He is a writer who has gripped our time by its horns and has
> wrestled with its demons. . . . Thus, he is a prototype of one
> who lives his life to the fullest. His crude directness and his
> extravagances have been pointed out by many. His human
> qualities—helpfulness, courage, honesty and humor—have
> been affirmed by all those who know him.[7]

In 1954, four years after Brumm's article appeared, Hemingway's fame in Germany reached a peak. By this time his most recent novels *Across the River and Into the Trees* (1950) and *The
Old Man and the Sea* (1952) had been translated and widely read.
His name appeared in international headlines at two different
times during the year; in January when he survived two airplane
crashes in Africa and in the fall when he received the Nobel Prize
for literature. Philip Young's influential study *Ernest Hemingway*
(1952) was translated into German in 1954. And Malcolm Cowley's "Mister Papa," the first of many articles describing Hemingway's life and writing habits in Cuba, appeared in translation in
Der Monat in November of the same year.

The news coverage of Hemingway's two plane crashes, as *Der
Spiegel* (February, 1954) cleverly illustrated, reveals the Germans'
tendency to romanticize when writing of Hemingway. The day
after the first of the two mishaps, January 24, headlines in Hamburg's *Bild* newspaper read, "Ernest Hemingway Missing in Deepest Africa" or "Airplane Crash—Little Hope." The Frankfurt
Abendpost (also January 24) featured an emotionally heightened
obituary "Helfgen: Hemingway and His Belief in God" by Heinz
Helfgen, a reporter who, seven months earlier, had spent three
days at Hemingway's home in Cuba. The article implied that
something fateful occurred one calm, starlit night when the reporter stood looking out upon the Caribbean Sea and Hemingway
said, "I believe in God because he must be so infinitely big and
beautiful." Helfgen added ominously, "That was two days before
his trip; his destination was Africa."[8]

Many reporters yielded to the temptation of drawing exaggerated parallels between Hemingway and his fictional hero of "The Snows of Kilimanjaro." On January 25, radio station NWDR of Hamburg postponed its regularly scheduled program to broadcast a reading of "The Snows of Kilimanjaro." While stressing the similarities between the supposed real event and fiction, the announcer overlooked the fact that Hemingway crashed 850 kilometers from the famous mountain. An article appearing in the *Hamburger Anzeiger* the same night intimated that Hemingway could have written "The Snows of Kilimanjaro" with premonitions of his own death in mind: "Hemingway made Kilimanjaro a symbol for the flight into eternity. Have the events which he described in his story come true for himself, a short distance from the 'White Mountain'?" A commentary in *Die Welt* which still had first page status by Tuesday, the day after Hemingway had been rescued, almost expressed remorse because the course of events did not parallel the story: "If his airplane had crashed over Uganda and if he had disappeared in the African jungle, would not this event itself have joined together his life and works?" The conclusion of the article was written in the same questionable vein: "Ernest Hemingway lives. That is consoling. It shows that destiny still has plans for him." The *Spiegel* journalist concluded that Hemingway would enjoy reading his own obituaries; and "Then he will discover just how sentimental the admirers of his hard-boiled, tearless prose are."[9]

Another article reflecting the tendency to fuse Hemingway the man with Hemingway the writer appeared in the periodical *Gegenwart* in January of 1954. The author (anonymous) referred to Hemingway as one of the most fascinating writers of modern literature and added that good fortune had allowed him to survive a near tragic accident and to continue his writing career. At the site of the plane crash, this critic wrote, one could imagine a desolate area filled with crocodiles, elephants, buffalo, and lions, and then recalling some of Hemingway's short stories which tested the heroes' courage and endurance, one could imagine how the man and his wife would bravely accept the challenge of the wilderness and would have survived this test of mettle. Some have thought that a crash ending would have been the appropriately stylistic way for Hemingway to die but, the writer added, the "stilvolle" death was reserved for Francis Macomber and Manuel

Garcia ("The Short Happy Life of Francis Macomber" and "The Undefeated"), not for the author. If fate had chosen to end his life in this dramatic fashion Hemingway, like Harry in "The Snows of Kilimanjaro," would have had reason to complain of untimeliness, the article concluded, for he still would like to live long enough to write three more novels and twenty-five short stories.[10]

In a similar vein was the article "Der Schreck am Kilimandscharo" by Julius Bab, which appeared in the Berlin newspaper *Die Zeit*, February 4, 1954. Bab was visiting in the United States and reported that all of New York was aroused by Hemingway's airplane crash. The "most astounding thing," according to Bab, was that the accident occurred in the vicinity of Kilimanjaro: "And to think that the creator of the story had met the same fate which he had described in his fiction; that was a sinister, unnerving thought which was enjoyed to the fullest." The news of Hemingway's second plane crash began to sound like fiction to Bab, but, he concluded, "this colossal man actually experiences such things. His expressions of manliness, which so easily disturb those of a weaker constitution, are sincere. . . . In any case one can say that this man Hemingway is one of God's exaggerations."[11]

Malcolm Cowley's "Mister Papa," published by *Der Monat* in November, the same month in which Hemingway received the Nobel Prize, provided the first biographical account of Hemingway in Cuba. Cowley, like many of the German critics, looked forward to the major novel of the Second World War that Hemingway supposedly had been working on for twelve years. Hemingway, he informed German readers, was eminently qualified to write such a book, and he included a summary of Hemingway's activities in World War II: his service for Naval Intelligence off the coast of Cuba (1942–1944), his connection with the 3rd U.S. Army and the 4th Infantry Division during the European invasion, his camaraderie with the allied soldiers, who good-naturedly referred to him as "Kraut-Jäger," "old Dr. Hemingstein," or his favorite name "Papa," as he was called in Cuba. Cowley supplied a minute description of Hemingway himself, of his villa Finca Vigia, and the variety of guests entertained there (somewhat romanticized): "They all have . . . in common physical or moral courage and reliability. They are men who are not afraid of danger—for this reason the mortality rate among them is extremely high." The description also included an anecdote of the kind Germans liked to associate with Hemingway. If one sits in Café Florida in Havana and orders a Daiquiri, Cowley wrote, he will be asked "Como Papá?"—and if the answer is yes the customer receives a double Daiquiri without sugar. From Cowley Germans also learned of Hemingway's high school days at Oak Park, Illinois, his early journalistic experience, his participation in World War I, his sporting activities, complex marital affairs, disciplined writing habits, and literary accomplishments from the early Paris days to the present.[12]

By the end of the year Hemingway was known well enough in Europe to become the subject of the following anecdote (a variation of an old Mark Twain story) appearing in the "Personality" section of the December *Spiegel*.

> Ernest Hemingway, 56, American writer, received a postcard a short time ago from friends who had forgotten his address (Cuba). The outside of the card read:
> "To Mr. Ernest Hemingway, God knows where." The Nobel Prize winner wrote them back:
> "He knew it."[13]

Following Hemingway's headline-making activities of 1954, it was *Der Spiegel*, rapidly developing into West Germany's leading news magazine, that was largely responsible for keeping Hemingway before the public eye during the last seven years of his life. One of the earliest of the *Spiegel* articles "Der grosse Killer" (November, 1954), announcing the publication of Philip Young's book in translation, featured the typical picture of Hemingway sitting alone in a bar before a half-filled glass of wine. In a recent bar brawl, Hemingway, according to the article, had defended himself admirably against an unprovoked attacker, thus disproving the rumor that his strong man image was in reality a fraud. With Hemingway's image still intact, *Der Spiegel* went on to provide a clear outline of Young's book, introducing German readers to the controversial trauma theory, which was to have a significant influence on later German and American criticism.[14] Now even the casual reader of Hemingway's fiction could be made aware of the autobiographical parallels between Nick Adams and the author, of the gradual education of Nick in the stories of *In Our Time*, of the code that Hemingway himself and his later heroes adopted, of Hemingway's use of the primitive as a defense against fear, and of the reasons behind his continual courting of danger and the prominence of death in his fiction.[15]

The following year in *Der Spiegel* (November, 1955), appeared excerpts from an interview in which Hemingway recalled his plane crashes in Africa. Here the author and his interviewer collaborated to present to the public the Hemingway image that had become so familiar: a very serious man, but one with a ready wit and captivating sense of humor, one who readily courted danger but maintained an easy sense of detachment in the face of death. According to the report, Hemingway reacted to the two near-fatal crashes in the same casual, unsentimental way that he wrote his novels: "Miss Mary . . . had never seen an airplane burn before. That is a rather impressive picture—except when one is sitting inside it."[16] Similar to Cowley's "Mister Papa," *Der Spiegel* article supplied the minute details of Hemingway's work day at Finca Vigia in Cuba; his habits of standing up while writing early in the morning, faithfully counting the words written for every day, and ending the session with a glass of gin and mineral water. Hemingway stopped writing only when he knew how he would continue the next day, and he willfully forgot his work when not actively engaged in it, thus, according to his own theory, preserving energy and freshness, while allowing his subconscious to work ahead on the subject. The *Spiegel* journalist, like Cowley, dutifully claimed that Hemingway was working on a new, longer novel, but explained that his financial situation allowed him to finish when he pleased.[17]

The colorful descriptions of Hemingway at his home in Cuba were continued in *Merkur* (1959) in the form of an interview which the author George Plimpton had originally published in *The Paris Review* a year earlier. Plimpton again gave the German reader a thoroughly detailed description of the interior of Hemingway's home, including a list of knick-knacks, trophies, souvenirs, and titles of books on the shelves. He repeated the well-worn account of Hemingway's personal writing habits, his theory of omissions and the iceberg principle, the authoritative statement on Jake's wound, Hemingway's refutation of Young's theory, and a list of writers that Hemingway said had had a lasting influence upon him.[18]

Another biographical article accompanied by pictures of Hemingway was "Der Unbesiegte" ("The Undefeated"), published in the popular *Westermanns Monatshefte* in November of 1956. The author, Hermann Boekhoff, expanded still further on Hemingway's legendary novel of the land, the sea, and the air, and speculated that possibly it was the fifth and final act of the powerful "Lebenstragödie" that began with the somber early short stories, led to a heroic melancholy, and culminated in a "mythischer Urszene" with Santiago in *The Old Man and the Sea*. In the brief biography which followed, Boekhoff made the familiar comparison between Hemingway and his fictional characters. Germans know them all, he wrote, "For those qualities which he requires in his heroes, he has long before adopted for himself, and none of his books, despite their variety and adventuresome fullness, measures up to the novel of his life." The Germans' feeling of kinship with Hemingway and his heroes was explained by Boekhoff when he said that the heroes, too, were isolated from former values and traditions and thus stood "auf dem Nullpunkt im leeren Raum." They were drawn from among "the solitary, the wounded and the lost," and aware that each must face his own type of crucifixion, they lived in the twilight of spiritual and physical catastrophe. Yet Boekhoff found in them the same guidelines for living that Ursula Brumm had written of earlier. Secretly Hemingway's characters carried with them values from past experiences, e.g., brotherly love for the oppressed or dependability among close friends. Only when death approached did the testing moment appear; then the preserved values were suddenly recalled and the hero faced firmly the circumstances that life had prepared for him. Thus, according to Boekhoff, Hemingway's recurring theme, "Man can be destroyed, but he must not give up," corresponded to "the same 'Zeitgefühl' and the same faith in the potential of man" that one finds expressed in the works of Kafka, Camus and Eliot.[19]

A similar fascination for Hemingway was expressed by Günter Blöcker in his book *Die neuen Wirklichkeiten*, 1957. He wrote that although most people assumed that an artist was two persons, one who lived and the other who created, there was no division for Hemingway. For him intellectual daring was identical with physical adventure; he lived his own life in accordance with the hard, adventuresome world of his novels. This, according to

Blöcker, was one of the reasons for Hemingway's world-wide appeal. With his fictional soldiers, fishermen, matadors, boxers, and globetrotters he was able to renew the old type of fictional hero, because he himself lived according to their laws. But, Blöcker warned, Hemingway's popularity could lead to many false conclusions about his artistry, for there was much more to Hemingway than manliness and robust vitality. Blöcker, like many of his fellow German critics, found behind the apparent primitivism something tender, intellectual and refined.[20] Relying heavily on Philip Young's thesis, he claimed the real Hemingway could be found more easily in his short stories than in his more famous novels. Stories like "Ten Indians" and "In Another Country" illustrated that courage meant not the absence of fear, but the conquering of it; and hardness meant not the lack of feelings, but the necessary protection of a wounded mind. We come to see the importance of individual standards outside those of society—standards which depend on a strong, self-willed order. Hemingway's idea of style and discipline, he concluded, insured "the protection of form, the certainty and distinction of a directed . . . life."[21] In this way Hemingway served as a guide, whether it was for writing, bullfighting, boxing, a job ethic, or simply achieving a sense of humor.

Similar to Blöcker's commentary on Hemingway was that of Wilhelm Grenzmann (*Weltdichtung der Gegenwart*, 1961) which began with a reference to the legendary Hemingway as "currently the most successful and the most frequently read author of the United States." Hemingway himself, he wrote, contributed to the legend that grew up about him by presenting himself to the public as one who led a daring life, disregarding the worst of dangers, a primitive man who despised his own culture and society. Like Blöcker, Grenzmann accepted Young's thesis that Hemingway's traumatic wound caused his continual fear of death and his need to overcome it by repeatedly putting himself near danger. But this did not detract from his fascination with Hemingway himself or his fictional heroes, for it was this ability to construct a firm defense against the disorders of life and "to persevere in the face of nothingness" that Grenzmann most admired.[22]

In September of 1958 *Der Spiegel* publicized another incident from Hemingway's private life for the benefit of the German public. The article concerned Hemingway's threatened court action against *Esquire* which, in celebrating its twenty-fifth anniversary, planned to publish a collection of stories by well-known writers who were either first published in *Esquire*, or who had stories published in *Esquire* that were never published elsewhere. In spite of Hemingway's protest, the magazine planned to include three of his stories that had been written in 1938 and 1939. The dispute was finally settled out of court (*Esquire* agreed to use only one), but a debate arose over whether or not a writer should be allowed to detach himself from his earlier work. The most interesting viewpoint was expressed by Willy Haas, literary critic of the Hamburg daily newspaper *Die Welt*. His defense of Hemingway, which sounded much like a defense of the German past at the same time, demonstrates the tendency of Germans to identify with the man himself. Haas said there had been much hate recently in the world and many in good conscience had taken a position which they no longer defended. And as long as one was not guilty of murder, we should not keep bringing up things that he might have said or written in the distant past. *Der Spiegel*, however, took a more objective view of the matter and said Hemingway was not satisfied with these particular stories and wanted to rework them for publication in a collection of his own.[23]

Hemingway was projected into the news again in November of 1960 when *Der Spiegel* prematurely announced the forthcoming publication of *The Dangerous Summer*, and accompanied the article with a large picture of Hemingway drinking among friends in a Spanish bar. Refusing to entertain the suspicion that Hemingway's writing talent was waning, the journalist explained that he was still working on his great novel about World War II and that the present work, part of which had already appeared in *Life* magazine, was only a "Gelegenheits-Intermezzo." The primary emphasis of the new book was to be on the rivalry of two matadors, Luis Dominguin and Antonio Ordoñez, which developed during the summer of 1959. *Der Spiegel* explained that Hemingway had returned to his favorite themes, the ones with which he achieved fame and the ones which provided the central motifs for his fiction: death, fear, struggle, bravery, and pride. Judging from what was written about the work itself, however, it appears that *Der Spiegel* was more interested in continuing the Hemingway legend than in criticizing his writing. In his new book, wrote the journalist, Hemingway lives up to his reputation among literary historians "als ganzer Kerl": "Hard-boiled and sportive as ever he hunts and swims, plays football . . . or shoots cigarettes out of the mouths of his friends." To show that time had not dimmed "Papa's" lust for living, the article also recorded an incident which Hemingway said occurred during his stay in Pamplona. He and matador Ordoñez took two pretty, young American girls prisoners, and *Der Spiegel* quoted suggestively, "They remained good and loyal prisoners . . . until the end of the month."[24]

Hemingway's public image, cultivated by the American and German press, could also be found in works which professed scholarly objectivity. Hermann Stresau, in an effort to give his critical biography of Hemingway (1958) a colorful beginning, recorded two stories of Hemingway's World War II activities. Hemingway, wrote Stresau, left his correspondent's duties with General Patton's army to join a tank division, and later led his own guerrilla band into Paris before the French and American armies arrived. When a member of his group asked him why he was not a general, he replied: "Young man, that is very simple . . . I would have been a general a long time ago, but I can neither read nor write." On another occasion (during the battle at Hürtgenwald) Hemingway was eating dinner close to the front lines when the German artillery began bombing the regiment's quarters. The candles suddenly went out and the soldiers inside threw themselves to the ground. As everything quieted and the candles were lit again, Hemingway was found at the table, still calmly eating.[25] Stresau himself believed the story, for he later wrote in connection with Hemingway's adventuresome life, "The man who, in acute danger of losing his life, calmly continues to eat while his comrades seek protection, 'knows' somehow that he is going to be spared."[26]

One of the most significant contributions to the Hemingway legend in Germany, although an inferior work of scholarship, was *Hemingway: eine Bildbiographie* (1960) by Hermann Lazar, who wrote under the pseudonym Leo Lania. Like the previously mentioned *Spiegel* articles, the book contained numerous pictures of "Papa" Hemingway, a gray-haired, wistful-looking old man, at his Cuban villa among friends, hunting trophies, house pets, and shelves of books. Complementing these were the usual pictures of Hemingway of the late 1950's, at bullfights, sidewalk cafes, or crowded bars. Oddly enough, the most prominent position was given to the pictures from films of Hemingway's works. Thus German readers could associate America's best-known film stars with characters from Hemingway's fiction: Humphrey Bogart in *To Have and Have Not*, Spencer Tracy as Santiago in *The Old Man and the Sea*, Rock Hudson, the Frederic Henry of *A Farewell to Arms*, Tyrone Power and Ava Gardner as Jake and Brett in *The Sun Also Rises*, Burt Lancaster in "The Killers," Gregory Peck and Susan Hayward in "The Snows of Kilimanjaro," and Gary Cooper and Ingrid Bergman in *For Whom the Bell Tolls*.

The German reader could also get a glimpse of Hemingway's boyhood through the pictures of his home and high school at Oak Park, which featured Hemingway, the high school journalist, the football player, and the swimmer. Hemingway, the lover, is shown with full-page pictures of his four wives, including one with Hemingway and Martha Gellhorn drinking martinis at the Stork Club. There is Hemingway, the father, pheasant hunting with his sons; the soldier, sitting in a wheel chair in a Milan hospital in 1918, or receiving a medal following the Normandy invasion of 1944; the correspondent, covering the Greece-Turkey encounter of 1922; the young writer, posing with acquaintances Sylvia Beach, Archibald MacLeish, and James Joyce. Lania thus presented the sides of Hemingway that fascinated German readers. They felt a kinship with him because he knew suffering (Lania carefully documented this: 227 steel splinters removed from a leg wound incurred on the Italian front, shell wounds in both feet, knees, and hands, ten concussions, six broken ribs, three serious car accidents, and two plane crashes);[27] in spite of his ills, Hemingway continued to lead a full and daring life and at the same time perfected his creative talents through an intense self-discipline. Lania's book is valuable mainly for its pictures; the critical commentary on Hemingway's fiction is often superficial and unreliable, such as the following example from his discussion of *The Sun Also Rises*: "Overnight boys and girls at Colleges and Universities spoke like his leading characters and assumed their way of life—their outward behavior, melancholy nihilism, drinking, and loving."[28]

Hemingway's death in July of 1961 prompted a new flood of articles in German news and literary publications, ranging from obituaries, to speculation on the reasons behind his suicide, re-evaluations of his fiction, and explanations for his popularity. The most significant of these in terms of public appeal was the July issue of *Der Spiegel* which printed Hemingway's picture on the cover and in the lead article on his life included the familiar photographs of Hemingway as sportsman, world's traveller, lover, and writer.

Der Spiegel took a very skeptical attitude toward Mary Hemingway's claim that her husband died as the result of an accident, and informed its readers that Hemingway had been undergoing treatments at the Mayo Clinic and that years before his father had also ended his life by shooting himself. Hemingway's death, according to *Der Spiegel*, if not consistent with his own self image was at least consistent with the image the world had of him, and the colorful life he led served to publicize his person even more than his books did.[29]

Like Lania's biography, *Der Spiegel* presented the sides of Hemingway that his German readers would find most appealing. An example is the account of Hemingway's dealings with Ernst Rowohlt, who first published *Fiesta* (*The Sun Also Rises*) in Germany in 1928 and later almost all of Hemingway's books. A very close friendship developed (both were "bullig gewachsen, lebenskräftig, und trinkfreudig," *Der Spiegel* explained) which continued in spite of the war. To illustrate this, the letter Hemingway sent to Rowohlt in 1946 was reprinted:

> You certainly had a hell of a war . . . and I am happy that you were not killed by us in the Schnee-Eifel or in Hürtgenwald. Please don't believe that I'm speaking as an arrogant victor, for God knows you certainly have killed many of our boys too—I am glad that the two of us didn't do away with each other at the same time.[30]

In opposition to the charge of naiveté or primitivism, leveled against Hemingway especially after Lillian Ross's unflattering report published in *The New Yorker* in 1950, *Der Spiegel* described him as a man who killed animals for sport, and yet loved them and lived with six dogs and thirty-eight cats in his villa in Cuba. Although his working habits were strictly disciplined and involved rising before dawn every day and writing for at least six hours, he was a gracious host, and matadors, generals, boxers, and film stars were among his many guests. He enjoyed the luxury of nine servants, a private tennis court and a swimming pool, but he had also endured extreme hardship through three separate wars.[31]

Der Spiegel still believed that Hemingway's "great book" on World War II had been written, at least in part, and suggested that it could be the most valuable of his unfinished writings. Repeating its statement of the previous year, *Der Spiegel* concluded that the main appeal of his projected book *The Dangerous Summer* would be in the picture it presented of "Papa" himself as "a real man": "hunting, swimming, drinking, hard-boiled and sportive."[32]

Manfred George, writing in *Universitas* (October, 1961), shared the hope that Hemingway's posthumous publications would include the large project of "the land, the sea, and the air" that he had often referred to, and, like so many Germans, he expressed awe at Hemingway's accomplishments apart from his writing. Though at times it seemed as if Hemingway were misdirecting his energy, he knew his own values and acted in accordance with them. To support his claim, George repeated an anecdote concerning Marlene Dietrich, a good friend of Hemingway's and one dear to the hearts of most Germans. Miss Dietrich called Hemingway in Cuba, asking his advice about accepting a new contract, and he counseled: "Don't do anything that you would not like to do in earnest. Never confuse movement with action." Hemingway himself, according to George, never confused the two, and always tried to link "his writing and his life through the vast energy and power of his personality."[33]

A more emotional response came from Wolfgang Koeppen, whose article appeared in the *Frankfurter Allgemeine*, July 4, 1961, two days after Hemingway's death. Hemingway's diverse talents and unceasing curiosity, he wrote, put him in the same category as Homer:

> We all have him to thank! He presented the world to his readers, the world the way it is, and the way one with a heightened sensitivity, a strong hunger and a tireless curiosity pictures it as being: the way Homer has pictured it from his time up to the present.

Koeppen agreed with Elio Vittorini, who referred to Hemingway as the Stendhal of the twentieth century. Next to Proust and Stendhal, Hemingway, Koeppen stated, will find his place in the "Himmel der Dichter."[34]

Wieland Schmied (*Wort in der Zeit*, July, 1961), wrote that a violent death was suitable for a man of Hemingway's stature, "A death with which the writer Hemingway would have sympathized." Perhaps Hemingway appeared so great, he speculated, because he lived his entire life as one about to face death; as if he despised death and triumphed over it. Hemingway's courage, self control, and vitality, according to Schmied, shaped an attitude towards death that is distinctively American:

> Hemingway has set an example for the Americans. He is the embodiment of this attitude, an archetype of American conduct in the face of sickness and death. I know of no picture taken of Hemingway in a hospital—and he was often in hospitals—that does not show him smiling.[35]

Schmied linked Hemingway with the Hollywood actors who had played the roles of his fictional heroes. Clark Gable, Gary Cooper, Humphrey Bogart, Tyrone Power, and Errol Flynn, he wrote, all shared Hemingway's attitude and faced death bravely. Now the author himself had joined his old friends, "zur letzten Fiesta, in einem anderen Land."[36] Schmied concluded his sentimental eulogy by expressing the kinship that many Germans felt for Hemingway, the man and writer: "His own end has indeed come. His life has had no twilight, no slow extinction of power, no gruesome old age. Hemingway is dead. We need not be ashamed of our sadness. He was more than a great writer. He was our comrade."[37]

A tribute from H. M. Ledig-Rowohlt, heir to the Rowohlt Publishing Company, appeared in *Die Zeit* a few days after Hemingway's death. Ledig-Rowohlt described the friendship that had developed between the elder Rowohlt and Hemingway and released for the first time excerpts from two letters which Hemingway had sent to Ernst Rowohlt in the 1930's. "His [Hemingway's] life and his works," Ledig-Rowohlt stated, "have left a greater impact on the world than any other writer of this century. He has become the model for an entire generation, a legend of the manly life."[38] Walter Jens in his article "Zum Tode Ernest Hemingways,"

Merkur, 1961, also mourned the loss of the writer who had served as the model, the spokesman for his age: "Exactly for this reason we have a feeling of great sadness at the end of his life. With the exception of Sartre and Faulkner, what writer still lives who would be in the position to set standards, to determine a fixed point on which youth can orient themselves, and to defend a position which must in turn be attacked by them?"[39]

Hemingway continued to make news in Germany even after the astonishment over his death had faded. Seven months after its lead article prompted by Hemingway's suicide, *Der Spiegel* (February, 1962) again proclaimed that he died just like one of his own heroes, and in doing so confirmed and completed the legendary picture the world had already made of him. The subject of the article was the Hollywood filming of *The Adventures of a Young Man*, and *Der Spiegel* warned its readers that the combination of Hemingway's biography, the early Nick Adams stories, and A. E. Hotchner's additions, though appearing to be a film biography of the young Hemingway, was really not.[40] A second *Spiegel* article appearing in July, 1962, commented on the Hemingway literature that had sprung up in the United States immediately following his death. At least ten books had appeared in addition to an article by Hemingway's sister published in the *Atlantic Monthly*, and a biography by his brother Leicester, *My Brother, Ernest Hemingway*. The remainder of the article quoted from Leicester Hemingway's book, and Germans learned still more about the life that continued to fascinate them: Hemingway's rebellion against his family at Oak Park, his parading of war wounds after his return from Italy in 1918, and his friendships with famous personalities, such as André Malraux, Jean Paul Sartre, and Simone de Beauvoir.[41]

American critics of Hemingway, as John Jones[42] and Ben R. Redman[43] have pointed out, were adversely affected by what they saw as the public image of Hemingway emerging in such works as *Death in the Afternoon*, *Green Hills of Africa*, and *Across the River and Into the Trees*. In Germany, however, the situation was reversed. Postwar Germans were fascinated by Hemingway the man and welcomed contributions to the legend that surrounded him. Especially in the first years of reconstruction people of all classes found in Hemingway and his fictional characters a guide for living, heroes with whom they could identify. This attitude, as we shall see, also played an important role in the German critical reaction. Critics were often most favorably impressed by those works in which they felt Hemingway had projected his own opinions or his public image. Instead of criticizing him for lack of detachment, as American critics often did, they praised him for his honesty and forthrightness.

NOTES

1 John A. Jones, "The Critics and the Public Legend," *Western Humanities Review*, XIII (Autumn, 1959), 387–90.

2 *Ibid.*, p. 390.

3 Clifton Fadiman, "Ernest Hemingway: An American Byron," *Nation*, CXXXVI (January 18, 1933), 63–64. Translated into German in *Querschnitt*, XIII (April, 1933), 235–40.

4 Jones, pp. 392–94.

5 *Ibid.*, p. 397.

6 Gotthilf Dierlamm, "Der moderne amerikanische Roman als Spiegelbild geistigen Austausches zwischen USA und Europa," *Sprache und Literatur Englands und Amerikas*, ed. Carl A. Weber (Tübingen, 1952), 178–79.

7 Ursula Brumm, "Hemingways Neuer Roman," *WS*, XX (1950), 50–51.

8 "Grosses Tamtam," *Der Spiegel*, VIII (February 3, 1954), 25.

9 *Ibid.*, pp. 26–27.

10 "Von den Löwen träumen," *Gegenwart*, IX (January, 1954), 69.

11 Julius Bab, "Der Schreck am Kilimandscharo," *Die Zeit*, February 4, 1954, p. 4.

12 Malcolm Cowley, "A Portrait of Mister Papa," *Der Monat*, VII (December, 1954), 205–6. First published in *Life*, XXV (January 10, 1949), 86–101.

13 "Personalien," *Der Spiegel*, VIII (December 1, 1954), 40.

14 Young contended that Hemingway suffered an early spiritual wound and during the rest of his life administered permanent self-therapy through autobiographical repetition of the fundamental experience.

15 "Der grosse Killer," *Der Spiegel*, VIII (November 3, 1954), 36–38.

16 "Romane im Safe," *Der Spiegel*, IX (November 23, 1955), 59.

17 *Ibid.*, pp. 59–60.

18 George Plimpton, "Gespräch mit Ernest Hemingway," *Merkur*, XIII (1959), 526–44. First appeared in English in *Paris Review*, V (Spring, 1958), 60–89.

19 Hermann Boekhoff, "Der Unbesiegte," *WM*, II (1956), 48–53.

20 Günter Blöcker, *Die neuen Wirklichkeiten* (Berlin, 1957), pp. 241–42.

21 *Ibid.*, p. 246.

22 Wilhelm Grenzmann, *Weltdichtung der Gegenwart*, 3rd ed. rev. (Bonn, 1961), 417–18.

23 "Das nie Gedruckte," *Der Spiegel*, XII (September 17, 1958), 54.

24 "Papas Fiesta," *Der Spiegel*, XIV (November 9, 1960), 75–77.

25 Hermann Stresau, *Ernest Hemingway* (Berlin, 1958), p. 5.

26 *Ibid.*, p. 28.

27 Leo Lania [Hermann Lazar], *Hemingway: A Pictorial Biography*, trans. Joan Bradley (London, 1961), p. 25. The original was published in Munich in 1960 as *Hemingway: eine Bildbiographie*.

28 *Ibid.*, p. 29.

29 "Wem die Stunde schlägt," *Der Spiegel*, XV (July 12, 1961), 45.

30 *Ibid.*, p. 49.

31 *Ibid.*, pp. 50–51.

32 *Ibid.*, p. 52.

33 Manfred George, "Ernest Hemingways Nachlass," *Universitas*, XVI (1961), 1130–31.

34 Wolfgang Koeppen, "Wie David vor Saul: Zum Tode Ernest Hemingways," *Frankfurter Allgemeine*, July 4, 1961, p. 16.

35 Wieland Schmied, "Der Tod war sein Thema: Ernest Hemingway, Mann ohne Dämmerung," *Wort in der Zeit*, VII (Autumn, 1961), 2–4.

36 *Ibid.*, p. 3.

37 *Ibid.*, p. 5.

38 H. M. Ledig-Rowohlt, "Der Tod am Morgen," *Die Zeit*, July 7, 1961, p. 12.

39 Walter Jens, "Zum Tode Ernest Hemingways," *Merkur*, XV (1961), 799.

40 "Als ob," *Der Spiegel*, XVI (February 7, 1962), 84–85.

41 "Big Brother," *Der Spiegel*, XVI (July 4, 1962), 63–64.

42 Jones, pp. 387–410.

43 Ben R. Redman, "The Champ and the Referees," *Saturday Review of Literature*, XXXIII (October 28, 1950), 15–16, 38.

CHAPTER THREE

THE GERMAN CRITICAL REACTION

Part I: The Hemingway Style

A list of the most popular German fiction for the period immediately following the war (Thomas Mann's *Lotte in Weimar*, 1939; Hermann Hesse's *Das Glasperlenspiel*, 1943; Ernst Wiechert's *Der Totenwald*, 1945 and *Die Jerominkinder*, 1945; Theodor Plievier's *Stalingrad*, 1946), indicates that Germans favored literature which reflected a sense of cultural and historical crisis. Hermann Kasack's *Die Stadt hinter dem Strom* (1947), a symbolic novel of a world in turmoil, appealed to a German reading public naturally preoccupied with death and destruction. Ernst Jünger's novel *Auf den Marmorklippen* (1939) was an example of the "magic realism" which postwar Germans felt characterized contemporary fiction. And according to Victor Lange, it was Jünger's interest in the "phenomonology of death, the representation and interpretation of areas of human failure and of the triumph of nonhuman power and organization" that especially fascinated German readers and writers. On the other hand, a novel such as Thomas Mann's *Dr. Faustus* (1946) with its Christian humanist assumptions, middle-class values, and elegant prose style did not suit the tastes of the postwar readers, for they had endured the holocaust and were not attracted to what must have appeared to them as a bystander's intellectual commentary.[1]

Against this background, one can understand the appeal of Ernest Hemingway when he reappeared on the German literary scene after World War II. Death, disjointedness, and destruction which played such a prominent role in recent German history and in postwar German fiction were themes of his major novels, and it is not surprising to find that *A Farewell to Arms* was reissued as early as 1946, *The Sun Also Rises* in 1947, and *For Whom the Bell Tolls* in 1948.[2] Hemingway's fiction corresponded to the prevailing mood in the early postwar years, for it was skeptical and at times metaphysical; yet it illustrated how the individual, pitted against an overwhelming collective force, could endure through an inner sense of pride and stoic courage. Hemingway, unlike Mann, had not only participated in World War II, but also in two previous wars, and he knew firsthand what it meant to suffer, to face death, and to lose one's sense of values and security. His style, while achieving the type of symbolic realism that Germans were to look for, was not artfully elegant, but simple, direct, and consequently powerful.

As the preceding survey of German criticism between the world wars has already made clear, Hemingway's style attracted considerable attention before the Nazi regime came to power. In 1933 Max Dietrich had written that one received a strange, almost bizarre impression from the passionate "commitment to truth," which inspired Hemingway's prose.[3] Similarly, many postwar German critics, even before they understood what Hemingway was attempting to do with his stylistic innovations, were drawn to a writer who rejected the illusions which he claimed society and tradition had foisted upon him, and focused only on that which he could experience firsthand.

Rudolf Rohlinger, writing of Hemingway's postwar impact in *Das Auditorium*, 1947, stated, "People talk about him; not only individually, not only among scholars, but in all the prestigious journals of our day his name is mentioned in heated discussions. . . . Even new writing courses are concerned with him." A brochure by the name of "Objektivismus," which was circulating in Germany in 1947, claimed to have discovered the proper technique for writing objectively: "It ["Objektivismus"] analyzes style and composition, formulates rules and regulations, and illustrates thereby how even in Germany 'Hemingways' can begin their careers." Erich Kästner, Rohlinger reported, felt that the gravest danger for the future of German writing was that a generation of disciples imitating Oscar Wilde and Ernest Hemingway could arise.[4]

An illustration of the renewed interest in Hemingway's style is provided by the following answer to a questionnaire concerning literary models, circulated among young German writers in the late 1940's:

Once before, at a time of which we barely have any conscious memories, the accounts were subjected to balancing after a

catastrophe. . . . It was then that a writer, Ernest Hemingway, re-established in the human consciousness the recognition of the simple, real and true in life. All emotions, ideas
and principles were stripped of any and all embellishments,
and people were startled. But to those seeking to understand
life, the naked and ever quivering human heart became visible, like a miracle in the midst of a sober and desolate
world. . . . —We of a later generation did not until twenty
years after have the experience of making his discovery, now
as then the only one about whose existence we, perforce
grown skeptical, need have no doubt. We are afraid that even
that might slip away from us, wherefore we try either timidly
or vigorously, but at any rate awkwardly, to hold on to it.
We know that our aim must be set higher than the aim of
the generation that directed the world's eyes to the bare
human heart. We should like to protect it and to make it
secure.[5]

In the early postwar years, however, Germans were more interested in knowing what this forceful, captivating man of the world
stood for, than they were in discussing the technicalities of his
style. Their fascination with the public image of Hemingway was
obvious, and Hemingway, the man, was often confused with Hemingway, the artist. Consequently, the early criticism was subjective
and often superficial. Because their need for spiritual guidance
was so great, Germans often emphasized qualities in Hemingway's
writing which were only vaguely present: the transcendental, the
existential, the orthodox Christian. Similarly, Hemingway's theoretical statements, e.g., "A writer's job is to tell the truth," often
taken with a grain of salt by American critics, were treated very
seriously by the critics in a country which had seen its literary
standards destroyed during the twelve-year period of the Nazi
regime. In German criticism after 1955 the American influence
becomes evident, but Germans, from the time of their first discovery of the new prose style in the 1920's, have admired Hemingway's sincerity as an artist. As they began to read his works more
objectively, they discovered for themselves the complexities that
go into making the Hemingway style what it is.

Both a sense of identification with Hemingway and hope for
a new direction in prose style are evident in Fritz Knöller's statement in *Welt und Wort*, 1952: "As the result of his participation
in World War I, Hemingway lost many of his former illusions and

gained a new respect for honesty and simplicity in self-expression. Recognizing the fatal errors of his predecessors, he offered an alternative scale of values." Although *Death in the Afternoon* (1932) and *Green Hills of Africa* (1935) were not available in German translation until the 1950's, Knöller, like many of his fellow critics, was familiar with Hemingway's statements on the writer's approach to truth which these two works contain. Germans admired the sincerity of a writer who said he was attempting to write a prose without tricks and deception, one that would survive the test of time. Knöller offered no detailed analysis of Hemingway's style, but nevertheless saw it as a return to objectivity and honesty: "Enemy of all big words, enemy of similes and metaphors, enemy of superfluous ornamentation, he economizes like a thrifty housewife." Hemingway, according to Knöller, limits himself to colloquial speech and has a keen ear for sound and accent, thus allowing his characters to be identified by their speech patterns. However, instead of illustrating Hemingway's skill in dialogue, Knöller chose to become metaphorical himself: Hemingway's style has the roughness of a surgeon's instrument, but also its precision; the cool smoothness of a streamlined building, but also its fullness; the limited function of a machine, but also its dexterity. Hemingway, he added, was the first of the contemporary writers who equaled the technical developments of the age with an artistic achievement.[6]

As German critics began to emerge from their extended period of isolation, the words "Wahrheit," "Wirklichkeit," and "Realismus" echoed through their pleas for a new type of literature to re-educate the German reader. Ernst Berndt, writing in *Das Goldene Tor*, 1947, claimed that the enthusiasm raised for American literature immediately after the war was not totally due to Germany's previous isolation:

> On the contrary, one has continually a stronger impression that something is being stated [in American literature] which contributes significantly to a clarification of the human predicament, including the predicament facing Germans today. More than anything else, we await a clarification of our situation,—we who find ourselves in the middle, between the nihilism of the East and the existentialism of the West.[7]

Wolfgang Grözinger (*Hochland*, 1952) urged publishers to choose works for translation according to Germany's needs, and to revise their definition of world literature if necessary; for in the immediate postwar situation, he wrote, "the quality of foreign literature is much less important to us than its usefulness. We need literature which can help us create a new European culture and way of life."[8]

Similarly, Friedrich Knapp (*Welt und Wort*, 1947) called for guidance from contemporary writers when he stated that the chaotic state of the intellectual and physical world during the postwar years "demands order." Necessary for a restoration of order was a knowledge of reality or at least a searching for it, and he warned that in the past Germans had been subjected to over-simplifications of reality through pseudo-myths and false ideologies. Since the time of Fontane, Knapp continued, German literature had moved from realism to romanticism, expressionism and a photographic naturalism. This flight from reality resulted in a naive, often misunderstood "Innerlichkeit" and prevented the exploration of the diversity that life presents. The antithesis of this "Innerlichkeit" on the part of German writers can be found in "Realismus," which, according to Knapp, was the "challenge of the hour!" "Realismus," he explained, not only involves close attention to exterior details, but also includes breaking through the superficial to the transcendent. This requires both creative imagination and rational analysis; the artist has the responsibility to integrate new scientific knowledge into a world view, thus shaping the world anew for disillusioned mankind:

> Only by combining the perception of the transcendent . . . with a sharply critical observation of external reality can present and future literature direct man back to his rightful "place," and thereby liberate him.[9]

Knapp concluded that an ideal writer for Germany must be an acute observer of contemporary political and sociological events; a contemporary who has lived and suffered along with the German people; an artist with mystical insights which allow him to perceive spiritual essences; a universalist, and at the same time a humorist, for whom the basis of humor is the destruction of illusion through the presentation of reality. Knapp included Hemingway in his list of writers who could provide "a new conception of reality and the forcefulness necessary to give it expression."[10]

According to Ernst Berndt it was in American literature that this new kind of realism was to be found; a realism which portrayed "the divine, the transcendent, the vital" indirectly. Berndt pointed out the timelessness which was allowed to break into the time sequence in Hemingway's *For Whom the Bell Tolls*; the "Allgemeingültigkeit" or concern with universal manhood in the works of Steinbeck, Hemingway, Dreiser and Dos Passos; and the "glimpses of immortality" in Thornton Wilder's *Our Town*.[11] Critics such as Berndt and Knapp were extremely vague in their approach to what they labeled "transcendental realism" and seemed to understand it only as being deceptively complex and carefully formulated:

> In this literature, which occasionally is a literature of the supernatural, one sentence leads into the next just as in reality one minute follows another with enforced mathematical exactness. It resembles a mechanical process, and is only referred to as literature because of its consistency and refinement.[12]

One of the reasons Hemingway was associated with this new type of realism, as Germans defined it, can be traced to Malcolm Cowley's article "Hemingway at Midnight," which appeared in the *New Republic* in 1944 and was translated in the German *Umschau* in 1947. According to Cowley, Hemingway, because of his insistence upon seeing things truly and writing accurately, was received in the 1920's as a naturalist, the new Dreiser of the lost generation. But actually, he explained, Hemingway was aligned with another tradition, that of Poe, Hawthorne, and Melville: "the haunted and nocturnal writers, the men who dealt in images that were symbols of an inner world." In a story, such as "Big Two-Hearted River," Cowley pointed out, external details are in the foreground, but it is in the background, in Nick's inner world, that another drama unfolds. When seen in this light, the events and external details, presented so vividly by Hemingway, become metaphors or symbols, and there is the sense of depth and of moving forward on different levels which is characteristic of poetry. In addition to the symbolic and the ritualistic, Cowley also drew attention to the mythological characteristics of Hemingway's fiction when he pointed out Hemingway's own version of the "Wasteland" myth in *The Sun Also Rises*. Although Hemingway may not be as affirmative as many critics felt he should be, Cowley concluded, Hemingway was an artist who wrote as he must: "like Poe and Hawthorne, and Melville he listens to his personal demon, which might also be called his intuition or his sense of life."[13]

Cowley's approach to Hemingway's style is also reflected in later German criticism, as is illustrated by Hanns Effelberger's article in *Die Neueren Sprachen* in 1957. It is often the case, he explained, that modern American literature is set apart from the "aesthetic-idealistic position" of European literature by virtue of its "brutalen Realismus." Although the term "Realismus" may be applied to novels which draw upon documentary material, such as Norman Mailer's *The Naked and the Dead*, in the case of Hemingway the term must be seen as a convenient label rather than as an accurate description of style. The simple prose of *The Old Man and the Sea*, for example, presents only the exterior side of the events. More important is the emotional upheaval the old man experiences during the fishing trip. The narrative, according to Effelberger, is hardly an example of brutal realism; rather, "the simple facts of the story are so ordered, that they permit the reader to see through them to the spiritual essences on the other side." Similarly, in *Across the River and Into the Trees* "the external facts only create an inner space in which the spiritual events take place." A spiritual event occurs when the colonel purges himself of the horrors of war by confessing them to Renata; the confession has nothing to do with a religious rite, but is "a spiritual release which he accomplishes himself." And it is this, rather than the external details surrounding the colonel's last three days in Venice, that is the most significant part of the novel and yet it has nothing to do with "brutal realism."[14]

As Hemingway's literary fame in Germany continued to grow in the early 1950's, a number of critics attempted to link his style to what they thought was Hemingway's philosophy or Weltanschauung. Wolfgang von Einsiedel in *Merkur*, 1950, wrote that it was difficult to recall the excitement Hemingway aroused as spokesman for the Americans of the "lost generation" (which von Einsiedel called a masochistic honorary title coined by young

American expatriates). His tightly compressed, sparse language, which gave originality and manliness to his works, seemed at that time to announce a new era of literary expression. The surprising thing, according to von Einsiedel, was that this tone also came through in translation, and in almost all European countries Hemingway influenced the diction of writers and to some extent the language of films: "At that time Hemingway was considered to be the leading figure of the literary *avant-garde.*"[15] Although some critics claimed that the distinct characteristics of Hemingway's style came from Midwestern speech patterns, and others found in his prose equivalents of the British understatement, von Einsiedel argued that it was rather the "Tonfall" of the disillusioned intellectual that marked Hemingway's style. What remained honest, true, and positive for Hemingway in a disillusioning, self-destructive world were his sensual perceptions, apart from abstract thought: "the brief, animalistic sensations with which existence, in its pain and joy, reaches its highest intensity." His characters were thus reduced to the functionary role of reacting to such sensations, and their language had to be stripped of all artistic or conventional elements. This stylized manner of expression linked the undeveloped and the refined in one common denominator and gave new immediacy to Hemingway's realistic prose.[16]

In 1951 Helmut Papajewski wrote in *Anglia* that the inclusion of the banal in Hemingway's fiction was a fundamental part of "Existenzanalyse," which began in American literature with Edgar Lee Master's *Spoon River Anthology* in 1915 and continued to have much in common with the modern "Existenzphilosophie" in Europe: "An idea which the analysts of modern 'Existenzphilosophie' in Europe had introduced in philosophic terms—that of reducing human existence to a kind of 'Nullpunktsexistenz'—was promoted independently in America by the use of banality in literature."[17] According to Papajewski, the reduction to "Nullpunktsexistenz" ("life at the point of zero," an expression coined by Kierkegaard and used frequently by German existentialists) plays an important role in the fiction of Hemingway and is intimately connected with his theory of style. Drawing on one of Hemingway's statements from *Death in the Afternoon*, "Prose is architecture, not interior decoration," Papajewski explained that the starkness and plainness of Hemingway's prose is the result of a

reduction process similar to that in "Existenzphilosophie." In the
end both are limited to only the essential.[18]

It is indicative of Hemingway's prominence in Germany during
the early postwar years that Bishop Hanns Lilje, the leading
spokesman for the protestant church in West Germany, should
publish a critical article on Hemingway's fiction. Such an article
was justified, Lilje felt, for he saw in Hemingway a crystallization
embodying the spiritual fate of an entire generation. Like Papajewski, Lilje saw existential characteristics in Hemingway's fiction
in that his characters find themselves "at the edge of existence,"
and consequently they react to life about them with "unusual intensity." Consistent with the predicament of his characters, Hemingway's language allows for no illusions, abstract ideologies, romantic posturing, mystical or mythological reflections. Rather it
takes place on an unmistakably realistic plane. Up to this point
Lilje is in agreement with existentialist critics of Hemingway's
style, but in going one step beyond this, he comes surprisingly
near the proponents of symbolic or transcendental realism, such
as Knapp and Effelberger. For Lilje claimed that although Hemingway focuses on the immediate present, he does not ignore that
which is not immediately perceptible. In fact, "the terse, low-keyed
diction is intended to illustrate, without the aid of emotionally
loaded, sentimental . . . reflections, that a reality so precisely described *cannot have meaning* in itself." [19]

Lilje claimed that this deliberate sense of incompleteness in
Hemingway's descriptions of the finite left the way open for the
emergence of the infinite. Hemingway's style, therefore, is not
seen as realistic or even symbolically realistic, but as a prose style
which is deliberately flat in order to indicate in a negative way
that there is a greater reality beyond that which is described. Inti-
mations of this greater reality, according to Lilje, come in the form
of questions among Hemingway's fictional characters concerning
guilt, fate, and death. Even if the answers are incomplete and
vague, the questions themselves have served a purpose: "For they
illustrate that Hemingway's fictional world is not limited to an
inflexible, finite reality." [20] Going still one step farther, Lilje compared Hemingway's "Existenzverständnis" to that expressed in the
New Testament. These authors also relied upon precise, concrete
diction: "The facts surrounding the life, death and resurrection of

Christ are reported in the most precise detail in order to illustrate that the *decisive* event in *world history* has taken place."[21]

A more objective approach to Hemingway's style began with critics like Gotthilf Dierlamm and Werner Ross. Dierlamm, writing in *Sprache und Literatur Englands und Amerikas*, 1952, stated that Hemingway learned his prose style from Gertrude Stein and Ezra Pound in Paris in the early 1920's. The style of the mature Hemingway "appears to be very similar to colloquial speech patterns; in reality it contains numerous subtle artistic effects." To demonstrate this, Dierlamm chose to examine the stylistic qualities of "The Snows of Kilimanjaro," which he said were both realistic and symbolic (the corpse of the leopard, the vultures, and the hyena) and allowed Hemingway to achieve a convincing blend between interior monologue and stream of consciousness. Another skill Hemingway possesses, according to Dierlamm, is his artistic control over prose rhythm; to illustrate this Dierlamm analyzed a passage from *For Whom the Bell Tolls* according to prose rhythm:

> Then they were together/so that/as the hand on the water moved,/unseen now/they knew/that nothing could ever happen to the one/that did not happen to the other,/that no other thing could happen more than this;//that this was all and always;//this was/what had been/and now/and whatever was to come.// This,/that they were not to have,/they were having.//They were having now/and before/and always/and now/and now/and now.//Oh, now,/now,/now,// the only now,/and above all now,/and there is not other now/but thou now//and now is thy prophet.[22]

Dierlamm recognized that a passage such as this lost its impact in translation and that one must read it aloud and observe the caesuras to get the full artistic effect. But he concluded somewhat questionably that in passages like the above, Hemingway's language had become an expression of existential thought. Instead of following this up, as later German critics were to do, Dierlamm quoted John Peale Bishop, who claimed that perhaps the best characteristics of Hemingway's prose stemmed from his careful observation of Spanish bullfighters; and this led Dierlamm from an objective examination of Hemingway's style to the author's private life. The "inner conduct" Hemingway learned from engaging in war or dangerous sporting adventures, he found confirmed in the matadors that he examined so closely: "The stoical bearing of these men in the face of grave danger aided him in preserving his own composure during the crises of his life."[23]

In spite of Dierlamm's disjointed approach to Hemingway's style, he did isolate certain passages of Hemingway's prose for analysis and pointed out that the style itself involved more than a close attention to detail and physical sensation. The more sophisticated critics of Hemingway's style became increasingly aware of the complexity of his artistic effects. Werner Ross in *Hochland*, 1953, quoted a passage from *A Farewell to Arms* which describes Henry's actions outside Catherine's hospital room at the end of the novel. Although it appears simple enough to be an elementary school composition, Ross stated, one must know what is going on in the background in order to understand the style. While Catherine lies in an adjoining room near death, Hemingway expresses the inexpressible feelings of Henry through his outward movements, his eating, reading, and waiting in the darkened room. Hemingway's style operates on different levels simultaneously and also gives a sense of immediacy to the events and characters that he describes. Reading Hemingway, one is not simply amused by the characters that he sets in action but is made to share their sensations: "Dramatization rather than explanation is the goal of Hemingway's narrative art and at the same time the secret of his success." Through his use of colloquial diction and simple, carefully formulated sentences with precise details, Hemingway is able to present the most unpoetic scenes with exactness and clarity. The reader, according to Ross, feels as if he is looking backwards through a set of binoculars.[24]

A response to Ross came from Hans Blumenberg, who included a brief commentary on style in his general discussion of Hemingway in *Hochland*, 1955. Blumenberg claimed that although Hemingway always tried to avoid rhetoric, and in fact protested against it, his anti-rhetorical style was capable of developing into a rhetoric of its own:

> There is the mistaken belief that the most climactic events are hidden behind the detached precision of his prose. However this is not true, for Hemingway finds it necessary to say so much in describing these situations, that a kind of erotic rhetoric develops in his writing.

Blumenberg contended that if one looked closer one would see that Hemingway's characters are often speaking in monologue. They have little to say to each other and when they try to speak they understand each other even less. Thus dialogue often becomes a means whereby Hemingway's characters can keep others at a distance.[25]

By far the most penetrating critical approach to Hemingway's style was that of Nikolaus Happel, who from 1954–1957 published four articles in German periodicals, exploring in detail Hemingway's stylistic accomplishments. Happel explained that one of the reasons for the postwar boom of American fiction in Germany was that it counteracted so effectively the war propaganda which Germans had been subjected to in their recent past: "Hemingway and the younger generation of writers do not want to beautify or to conceal plain reality. They present things just as they really are." Hemingway, he claimed, was the foremost representative of the truth-seeking American novelists:

> For Hemingway the first principle of writing is the presentation of truth. Therefore he attempts to give an accurate reproduction of reality. Hemingway describes life in all of its crassness, just as it is without its illusions.[26]

Happel, like many German critics, admired Hemingway's frequent assertions that the absolute sincerity with which a writer presented reality would determine the lastingness of his works and the success of the writer himself. Happel implied that this was especially applicable to the German situation:

> Even if a country engages in war with an external enemy, it cannot dispense with the principle of truth. If a writer betrays this principle, if he violates "his one complete obligation" to the truth, he must forfeit his right to future success.[27]

Hemingway, according to Happel, had his own version of T. S. Eliot's "objective correlative." To illustrate this he cited "Big Two-Hearted River," which, although it describes no significant events, "presents details with such accuracy and directness that the reader experiences them for himself." Though German critics recognize Hemingway's kinship with the naturalistic school in his close attention to realistic detail, it is, as we have seen, Hemingway's ability to go beyond this, to seek a deeper truth in reality that Germans admire most. This is one of the reasons why they found later war novelists, such as Norman Mailer or James Jones, inadequate and why they accepted Hemingway's remarks about a possible fourth or fifth dimension in prose. Happel, like many other Germans, felt that Hemingway honestly fulfilled his stated goal as a prose writer: to raise the observation of the factual to the level of absolute truth.[28]

In his second article discussing Hemingway's style published in *ASNS*, 1955, Happel focused on a single paragraph—Chapter V from *In Our Time* (the execution of six Greek cabinet ministers)—which he felt illustrated Hemingway's statement that "Prose is architecture." Happel, who did not attempt to fit Hemingway's style to any preconceived philosophy, successfully showed how the perfect combination of content and style resulted in a "classical form." As Carlos Baker had done in *Hemingway: The Writer as Artist* (1952), he isolated Hemingway's use of realistic symbols, e.g., pools of water, the wet, dead leaves and the rain, the nailed shutters and the wall, and then proceeded to analyze the rhythm, word choice, and sentence length. The plainness and directness of the language, Happel said, correspond to the brutality of the event, and the constant, even rhythm of the sentences suggests mechanical inevitability and increases the feeling of hopelessness. The prominent place given to exact figures of measurement stresses the accuracy in the description and emphasizes the precision in the execution and the failure of the human element. This type of approach to Hemingway, although infrequent among German critics, shows that in spite of translation difficulties they were aware of the intricacies in Hemingway's style: the much discussed ironic undertones, the realistic symbols, and the subtle use of simple sentence rhythms.[29]

In 1956 Happel undertook a similar analysis of *The Old Man and the Sea*, which he felt was particularly important in Hemingway's development. Philip Young had written (his book, *Ernest Hemingway*, was translated into German in 1954) that Hemingway's style was the fullest expression of his content; Happel added that the style was also the goal and purpose of the man. No matter what his limitations might be, Hemingway, Happel claimed, offers a perfect unity of man and writer, of theme and presentation. Going a step farther than he did in his article on Chapter V of *In Our Time*, Happel pointed out Hemingway's careful use of the antithetical in this longer prose work: (1) the tattered sail of the boat forecasts defeat, but Santiago's eyes look undefeated; (2) the ocean is beautiful and kind, but also cruel; (3) Santiago loves and respects the fish, but he must kill him. From this Happel concluded that Hemingway does not regard life as harmonious, but rather as a juxtaposition of opposites, whereby the pleasant and unpleasant, the good and the evil, intertwined as they are, set up a tension integral to the book.[30]

Another stylistic trait in *The Old Man and the Sea* noted by Happel is the frequent use of repetition, especially that of the dream which becomes a leitmotiv. This Happel interpreted as a sign of the old man's longing for his happy boyhood and as an intentional contrast with the tragic events and sufferings of his old age. All the main ideas of the novel are repeated often enough, Happel noted, to assume the stature of leitmotivs: loneliness, suffering, killing, luck, hope, resolution, and defeat. In this way it becomes impossible for the Hemingway reader to lose sight of the theme. Happel was in full agreement with Philip Young, who earlier had written that the novel was classic in its theme of courage, pride, honor, and death, in its limiting concentration on fundamental subjects, its purity of construction, its struggle of man against superior powers. Through a careful examination of style, said Happel, one can see that discipline is the classical form-giving principle for Hemingway's writing:

> *Discipline*, or training, is therefore the first requirement for the creation of form; . . . this we have learned from our investigation of style. It allows Hemingway to achieve *simplicity*, *clarity*, and accuracy in word choice and sentence structure.[31]

Happel is typical of a number of German critics who were fascinated by Hemingway's sense of discipline, not only in his style, but in his attitude towards working, writing, and living in general. They knew through various biographical accounts of Hemingway's personal habit of rising at dawn, writing until noon, and faithfully counting the words he had written every day. Hemingway's statement, "What I had to do was work . . . to work was the only thing, it was the one thing that always made you feel good," was given special attention, and as Happel explained, Hemingway's exemplary attitude pertained to more than his writing: "Discipline is the necessary principle for creating order in one's life."[32] It was this combination in Hemingway that Germans so admired—his ability to live fully and adventuresomely combined with his capacity for persevering self-discipline, both in his private life and in his writing style.

In his fourth article on Hemingway, "Ein Beitrag zur 'discipline' in Hemingways Stil," published in *NS*, 1957, Happel claimed that Hemingway's reliance on discipline resulted in a moral accomplishment and manifested itself stylistically in the following ways:

> the regulated, paratactic sentences, the frequency of coordinating conjunctions, the rare use of adjectives for ornamental purposes . . . the avoidance of abstract language and the emphasis on concrete perceptions, the frequent crassness in expression, the use of antithesis and repetition, the brevity and directness in dialogue, the principle of omission . . . and the corresponding rhythmic effects of his prose.[33]

As he had done in his article on Hemingway's style in *The Old Man and the Sea*, Happel focused on the antithetical, this time in the short story "Soldier's Home." This story of the young soldier returning home, understandably a favorite with German readers, focuses on the bourgeois life of the Krebs' home and the soldier's inability, following his war experience, to find anything worthwhile in its routine formalism. Happel illustrated Hemingway's technique of building tension through carefully planned use of the antithetical: "Krebs went to the war—from a Methodist college in Kansas"; or "The men from the town who had been drafted had all been welcomed elaborately on their return. There had been a great deal of hysteria—Now the reaction had set in. People seemed to think it was rather ridiculous for Krebs to be getting back so late, years after the war was over."[34] Also included in Happel's analysis are the photographic descriptions, Hemingway's repeated use of the *ing* verb form, the car motif, the leitmotiv in the phrase "too complicated," all shown to be part of the antithetical basis of the story. In explaining the ending, in which Hemingway gives no solution to the disharmony he has so carefully set up, Happel claimed that most of Hemingway's stories rely not so much on what he calls an architectural construction, but on the impressions that they give of life, determined by their total atmosphere: "They do not offer a carefully constructed plot with a denouement, but rather they present a psychological portrait or recreate a mood with varying degrees of intensity." In concluding, Happel contradicted a review of *The First 49 Stories* (*Frankfurter Allgemeine*, 10. 3. 1951), which stated that in spite of their masterful style, the stories did not go beyond the level of literary experiment. It was Hemingway's masterful style, according to Happel, which transformed his stories into subtle works of art.[35]

Happel's criticism reflected the influence of the two foremost American Hemingway critics, Baker and Young, but in analyzing Hemingway's use of antithesis, leitmotivs, and realistic symbols, and demonstrating how these corresponded to Hemingway's theoretical statements concerning a writer's primary goal, Happel marked a new step forward in objective, independent criticism of Hemingway's style.

NOTES

1 Lange, "Notes on the German Literary Scene 1946–1948," pp. 8–12.

2 Ballenger, p. 94.

3 Dietrich, pp. 89–90.

4 Rudolph Rohlinger, "Ernest Hemingway," *Das Auditorium*, I (1947), 40–41.

5 As quoted by Frey, "Postwar German Reactions to American Literature," p. 191.

6 Fritz Knöller, "Hemingways Weltbild und Werkform," *Welt und Wort*, VII (1952), 411–12.

7 Ernst Berndt, "Neue Dichtung in Amerika," *Das Goldene Tor*, II (1947), 151.

8 Wolfgang Grözinger, "Roman zwischen Dichtung und Reportage," *Hochland*, XLIV (1951–1952), 555.

9 Friedrich Knapp, "Realismus in der zeitgenössischen Literatur," *Welt und Wort*, II (1947), 159–59.

10 *Ibid.*, p. 159.

11 Berndt, pp. 152–56.

12 *Ibid.*, p. 157.

13 Malcolm Cowley, "Hemingway at Midnight," *New Republic*, CXI (August 14, 1944), 190–95. German translation in *Umschau*, II (1947), 542–50.

14 Hanns Effelberger, "Probleme der modernen amerikanischen Literatur," *Die Neueren Sprachen*, VI (1957), 319–20.

15 Wolfgang von Einsiedel, "Ein Komet verblasst," *Merkur*, IV (1950), 1220–21.

16 *Ibid.*, p. 1222.

17 Helmut Papajewski, "Die Frage nach der Sinnhaftigkeit bei Hemingway," *Anglia*, LXX (1951), 187.

18 *Ibid.*, pp. 189–90.

19 Hanns Lilje, "Gnadenlosigkeit und Gnade im Werke Hemingways," *Zeitwende*, XXIV (1953), 5–8.

20 *Ibid.*, p. 10.

21 *Ibid.*, p. 12.

22 Dierlamm, pp. 176–78.

23 *Ibid.*, p. 178.

24 Werner Ross, "Der amerikanische Roman der Gegenwart," *Hochland*, XLVI (1953–54), 155.

25 Hans Blumenberg, "Die Peripetie des Mannes. Über das Werk Ernest Hemingways," *Hochland*, XLVII (1955–1956), 223–25.

26 Nikolaus Happel, "Äusserungen Hemingways zur Darstellung der Wirklichkeit und Wahrheit," *ASNS*, CXC (1954), 204.

27 *Ibid.*, p. 205.

28 *Ibid.*, pp. 206–10.

29 Nikolaus Happel, "Chapter V aus Hemingways Kurzgeschichtenband *In Our Time*," *ASNS*, CXCI (1955), 324–25.

30 Nikolaus Happel, "Stilbetrachtung an *The Old Man and the Sea*," *Die Neueren Sprachen*, V (1956), 74.

31 *Ibid.*, pp. 76–78.

32 Nikolaus Happel, "Ein Beitrag zur 'discipline' in Hemingways Stil," *Die Neueren Sprachen*, VI (1957), 583.

33 *Ibid.*, p. 584.

34 *Ibid.*, p. 585.

35 *Ibid.*, p. 587.

Part II: Hemingway's Short Stories

During the twenty year period after the war's end, at least six-
teen separate volumes of Hemingway's short stories were published
in German translation. Often German publishers used their own
discretion in grouping the stories, and the best-known, such as
"The Snows of Kilimanjaro," "The Short Happy Life of Francis
Macomber," "The Killers," and "The Undefeated," were issued
under separate cover.[1] Supplementing the individual volumes were
short story anthologies and the English editions of Hemingway's
works made available to German readers by the Albatross and
Tauchnitz Publishing Companies.

In spite of the frequent appearance of Hemingway's short fiction, German critics as a rule were not familiar with the short story
form, and it was not until the mid 1950's that they rather grudg-
ingly admitted that the short story was indeed an independent
literary genre. Early reviewers of Hemingway's *In Our Time*
(translated into German in 1932), such as Max Dietrich[2] and Hans
Fallada,[3] praised the contrapuntal arrangement of chapters and in-
terchapters, the detached objectivity of the author, the intensity of
the plain style, the realism, brutality, and "epic breadth" in the
description of a soldier's fortune, but they made little attempt to
determine what were Hemingway's main achievements within the
short story form.

Because of its foreign origin, the short story did not fare well
during the Nazi reign, and consequently, as we shall see, the German critical reaction to the first Hemingway short stories translated soon after World War II was very general and often superficial. One of the earliest major investigations of the short story
form was Edgar Mertner's "Zur Theorie der Short Story in England und Amerika," published in *Anglia*, 1941. Characteristically,
Mertner did not evaluate the short story as a unique genre, but
compared it unfavorably with the *Novelle*. By accepting Poe's early
definitions, Americans, he claimed, exaggerated the importance of
mechanics, technique, and formula. Mertner discouraged focus on
technique and reliance on what he called the vague terms *plot*,

theme and *setting.* Rather he favored a greater emphasis on the truly poetical elements ("wahrhaft Poetischen") of the *Novelle.*[4]

Such an approach, Mertner pointed out, would give deeper meaning to Poe's definition of unity of effect, for attention is directed to "fateful situations" which are of a spiritual nature and offer a "sudden perception of the supernatural." The *Novelle,* as Mertner defined it, possessed the symbolic or transcendental realism that German critics were to look for in their discussions of American literature in the late 1940's and early 1950's:

> it appears to be the two-sidedness of the *Novelle,* a combination of the concrete-realistic and the mystifying-supernatural, which always dominates the genre, and in the German *Novelle* leads to the presentation of man's tragic involvement with destiny.[5]

Another advantage the *Novelle* has over the short story, according to Mertner, is in its reliance on the "Rahmenerzählung" or framework device. This he felt gave the writer a definite point of view from which to describe events that had occurred in the past; at the same time it provided for the necessary epic distance between the reader and the subject material. The *Novelle* has the greater potential for expressing the tragic, for at its turning point it "provides a subtle, unexpected insight into the tragic nature of the human predicament." Only the best short stories, Mertner concluded, offer similar possibilities.[6]

The first of Hemingway's short fiction to appear in translation after 1945 was contained in a volume entitled *Der Schnee vom Kilimandscharo,* which included the title story, "The Killers," "The Undefeated," and "Big Two-Hearted River." In reviewing the stories in *Welt und Wort,* 1949, Hanns von Krannhals pointed out their "solid compactness," praised Hemingway's skill in making the atmosphere of a situation or event threateningly real, and added that it was not necessary to repeat that Hemingway was "a great writer." But instead of analyzing or defining the "economical and, literarily speaking, invisible means," which he claimed Hemingway employed, von Krannhals appeared content to remind Germans of the author's "epic personality." "The Snows of Kilimanjaro," he concluded, was the most realistic of the stories, "The Undefeated" the most suspenseful, and "Big Two-Hearted River" the most stylistically beautiful. The translation of "The Killers" suffered, von Krannhals added, because of the lack of slang equivalents in German.[7]

On a similar plane is the review of the same collection by a critic with the initials E. F., writing in *Neues Abendland*, 1949. According to this critic Hemingway still represented "the best in American writing," and the distinctiveness of his style ("seine ungeheuer eindringliche Art des Erzählens") was clearer in his stories than in the novels. In discussing the individual stories, E. F. was concerned with content rather than technique. After summarizing "The Snows," he concluded that Harry's insights during the last hour of his life were "fearful"; the atmosphere of "The Undefeated" and "The Killers" he described as "oppressing and gloomy." "Big Two-Hearted River," E. F. pointed out, was so simple that it could almost be considered an experimental piece in which Hemingway practiced his stylistic talent; however, beneath "the surface of a detailed fishing trip" was a "philosophical attitude," which this critic claimed was related to existentialism or heroic nihilism. Instead of stressing Hemingway's connection with contemporary European existentialists as later critics were to do, E. F. concluded simply that this was an aesthetic attitude, one apart from good or evil.[8]

In 1950 the Rowohlt Publishing Company issued a translation of Hemingway's *First 49 Stories* (the original publication date was 1938), including the stories which had appeared in magazines and newspapers prior to 1938, and those in the volumes *In Our Time* (1925 and 1930), *Men Without Women* (1927), and *Winner Take Nothing* (1933). Unfortunately German critics were still not in the position to do justice to Hemingway's fiction, and critical commentary remained on the same level as that of von Krannhals and the critic E. F.

Reviewing *49 Stories* in *Westermanns Monatshefte* in 1951, Barbara Bühler wrote that the development of narrative technique which led to Hemingway's art could be traced in painting; and she added somewhat vaguely that the field was currently dominated by "a bold meaninglessness" and that the opposition of elemental unities out of form and color had become the sole purpose and means of a new expression. Bühler said little about Hemingway's technique, except that he rarely provided exposition for his stories and often began immediately with dialogue; and when this threatens to run out, Hemingway "very unconcernedly stops." The dry, witty dialogue ends prosaically as almost everything in life, "with brutal dullness and simplicity." Bühler admired Hemingway's variety of characters and settings, and his cosmopolitanism, but what was missing, she felt, was the spiritual substance which Hamsun (according to Bühler and a number of others, the founder of a realistic style) knew how to instill into his works. Hemingway's short stories, she concluded, were only experiments preceding his more successful novels.[9]

The same superficial approach to *49 Stories* was taken by Clara Menck, whose review appeared in *Welt und Wort* in 1951. Menck considered Hemingway to be a representative of the "lost generation" and pointed out that as soon as his discipline slackened, the melancholy behind his fictional world of hunters, soldiers, and boxers resulted in sentimentality or cynicism. At times, she claimed, the melancholy came very near despair and left one with the same feeling of Pilar in *For Whom the Bell Tolls*: "with the taste of death in one's mouth." Menck concluded that the further Hemingway detached himself from his melancholy tone, the more exemplary his stories became. His skill in making a country, a mood, or a relation between humans come to life with indirect, banal language and deceptively simple sentences enabled a number of the stories to become classic examples of the genre.[10]

In an article published in the *Frankfurter Hefte* in 1950, the critic Engelbert Kirchner drew attention to the numerous short stories of high quality which were published in American magazines and attempted to explain their basic form to German readers. According to Kirchner, the ground work for the short story was provided by writers like Hemingway, Faulkner, and Steinbeck, and the form itself was distinctly American in its sense of directness and immediacy. It left the writer no opportunity to gradually prepare his audience for an event:

> They [the stories] have no introductions, no symbols, no climaxes and no conclusions. If the author's bold psychological grasp does not immediately succeed in capturing the reader's interest . . . the story will be a bad one even if the author speaks with the tongue of an angel.[11]

The short story, Kirchner claimed, is not only concrete and immediate, but it is also the most human form of expression in contemporary literature. Unlike the characters in a novel or a play, the characters in a short story are not prototypes, but commonplace individuals. Americans, he stated, still have a valid image of the "decent," "honest" man, and this allows for his sympathetic treatment in American fiction. The commonplace individual is only a beginning, but through him doors are opened to the heights and depths of humanity. Because these doors no longer exist in war-torn Europe, Kirchner explained, there is little interest in the short story form among European writers.[12]

In 1953–1954 a series of events occurred which brought about a dramatic change in the German critical approach to the short story, and especially to the short story art of Ernest Hemingway. The first of these was the publication of the ground-breaking work of Klaus Doderer, "Die angelsächsische Short Story und die deutsche Kurzgeschichte," and *Die Kurzgeschichte in Deutschland*, both in 1953, and Johannes Klein's *Geschichte der deutschen Novelle von Goethe bis zur Gegenwart*, 1954, which treated the short story as an independent literary genre. In 1954 Philip Young's *Ernest Hemingway* appeared in German translation and provided a critical guide to Hemingway's short fiction; in the same year Hemingway received the Nobel Prize and was at the peak of his popularity in Germany.

In his article published in *Die Neueren Sprachen* in 1953, Doderer explained that the word *Kurzgeschichte* (short story) was coined in the 1920's when well-known American writers made the form popular, and consequently both the word and the form were still relatively young in Germany. Originally "Kurzgeschichte" was discussed in connection with firmly established literary genres, e.g., the *Novelle*, anecdote, or sketch, but later it became associated with inferior literature in magazine and newspaper publications. Since the word was notably foreign and new, and connected with England and Anglo-Saxons, it was subject to certain prejudices in German literary circles. Doderer supplied a much-needed discussion of form and genre when he explained that the short story had unique characteristics which set it apart from other genres, the first of these being the "Schicksalsbruch" or epiphany and the typical open ending. The short story, Doderer argued, is separated from the sketch in that "The action which takes place in either the foreground or background of the short story reduces the atmosphere (of primary concern in the sketch) to a secondary position." Its intricate composition separates the story from a narrative report, and it is different from the anecdote in that it requires neither a historical background nor a definite climax. The short story may have many variations, but "Common to all is a decisive experience presented as an epiphany, which alters the story's development."[13]

Up to this time, Doderer pointed out, German critics had almost totally ignored the short story, because they did not understand its basic structure and regarded it simply as an "inferior magazine sickness" or a "passing novelty." On the other hand, Doderer claimed, American critics failed to recognize the *Novelle* as a genre and confused the development of the short story themselves. In tracing the history of the short story in both Germany and the United States, Doderer stated that the contributions of Hemingway had been as important as those of Poe more than a hundred years earlier. Hemingway introduced a new, concrete prose to the short story, and by turning his focus inward on his characters, de-emphasized the role of the plot. This is what distinguishes the short story from the *Novelle*. A story "Hills Like White Elephants," for example, "relies upon an epiphany and is, with its open ending and its emphasis upon atmosphere, removed . . . from the logical progression of the *Novelle*." This is the reason, Doderer explained, that it is a commonly held opinion in Germany that Hemingway discovered the short story form.[14]

In his book-length study *Die Kurzgeschichte in Deutschland*, 1953, Doderer stressed the influence of technological advancement on the development of the short story and explained that literature was needed "which through terseness and clarity could accurately portray man's problems even amid the confusion of urban life." But contrary to prevailing critical attitudes in Germany, Doderer maintained that this did not restrict the short story to America. In fact, he claimed, Germany had its own history of the short story, which could be divided into three stages: the first under the influence of naturalism in the nineteenth century resulted in a sketch-like form; a reaction against this prompted the second, the strictly epic; the third, or the objective type, attempted to present a slice of life and therefore played down the plot and the role of the author, while relying on dialogue rather than elevated descriptive prose. It is on the third of these that American writers, especially Hemingway, exerted the strongest influence. German writers, Doderer explained, admired the vivacity with which Americans sought to present the truth, to combat prejudice and illusion. Hemingway was among the most popular for he attempted to achieve "without falsehood and exaggeration, a precise and poetic naturalness." His influence can be clearly seen in the works of Elizabeth Langgässer, Wolfgang Borchert, and Ernst Kreuder.[15]

Following Doderer's studies, the stature of the short story in Germany continued to increase as more German critics became familiar with the form. Johannes Klein in his *Geschichte der deutschen Novelle von Goethe bis zur Gegenwart,* 1954, attempted to separate the short story from the *Novelle* by tracing their separate origins.[16] Siegfried Unseld, in his review of Wolfgang Borchert's second volume of short stories in *Akzente,* 1955, outlined the distinctive characteristics of the short story and traced its history from Poe and Gogol, through Joyce and Anderson to Hemingway. According to Unseld, Hemingway's *49 Stories* "provided the entire world with a new form of literature, which influenced and inspired a whole generation of writers."[17] In a special issue of *Der Deutschunterricht,* 1957, Helmut Motekat, Ruth Lorbe, and Hermann Pongs discussed the origin and form of the short story and compared it to the German "Kurzgeschichte."[18] In the same year Franz Link in his article "Tale," "sketch," "essay," and "short story" (*Die Neueren Sprachen,* 1957) summarized the previous criticism of Mertner, Doderer, and Klein and concluded with a final definition of the short story as an independent genre:

> The tale develops into the short story by placing less emphasis on the plot and by focusing on the passive behavior of the hero, or upon the hero's helplessness in the face of circumstances which govern his fate. The hero's predicament, which determines the inner form of the story, reflects a new outlook: man has lost the ability to understand his world. Such a loss is not yet apparent in the fiction of Dickens, but it emerges in Hawthorne's conflict with the religious beliefs of his puritan ancestors, and develops fully for the first time in the works of Poe.[19]

A new interest in the history of the American short story became evident in studies such as Hanns Effelberger's "Probleme der modernen amerikanischen Literatur" (*NS*, 1957),[20] and Adalbert Schmidt's *Literaturgeschichte: Wege und Wandlungen moderner Dichtung*, 1957.[21] In his article in *Die Pädagogische Provinz* (1959) Hans-Joachim Lang, to counteract the commonly-held opinion in Germany that the short story originated with American realistic writers of the 1920's, traced the history of the short story back to Irving, Poe, and Hawthorne. Since the short story is more compact than the novel, he added, it is therefore more consciously artistic and more carefully constructed. A comparison of early stories with those of contemporary writers, such as Hemingway or Katherine Mansfield, he concluded, would show the progress that has been made in the use of dialogue, colloquial tone, and realistic narrative.[22]

Paralleling this new seriousness in the German attitude towards the short story was the search by German teachers and critics for representative American stories for literary study in the classroom. Theodor Wolpers in his article "Die amerikanische *short story* in der Schule: Gesichtspunkte und Vorschläge für eine representative Auswahl," (*Die Neueren Sprachen*, 1956), recommended Hemingway as the most representative American short story writer. Reflecting the influence of Philip Young, Wolpers stated that Hemingway's Nick Adams stories were often stories of initiation, and if "A Day's Wait," "My Old Man," and "The Killers" were read in order, they would show the gradual development of the hero. In fact, as did many Germans, Wolpers saw an overall progression emerging in all of Hemingway's fiction, from young boyhood, to the achieving of manliness in "The Undefeated," and finally the culmination in *The Old Man and the Sea*, which combined bravery, wisdom, love, and a final affirmation of life. Although he concluded that "The Snows of Kilimanjaro" and "The Short Happy Life of Francis Macomber" were too difficult to be taken up on the secondary school level, Wolpers judged them to be Hemingway's best stories. Hemingway's search for lasting values, he pointed out, was most clearly demonstrated in these two works in which characters discover that in moments of crisis survival depends on the adoption of a heroic code, similar to the one followed by bullfighters, boxers, and hunters. Hemingway's prose, according to Wolpers, is emphatically unsentimental and concise, but nevertheless extremely expressive and rich in nuances. Hemingway, he added, established the model for contemporary fiction:

> the scenic method which permits the speakers to characterize themselves through their dialogue, the art of subtle allusions and symbolic correspondences, the use of fictional characters as narrators, and the consequent open ending.[23]

In the same issue of *Die Neueren Sprachen* Karl Krebs reported on a teachers' conference held in Düsseldorf during which Dr. Stader of Bonn used Hemingway's short story "The Killers" to illustrate the methods of new criticism. Stader pointed out to the German teachers of English Hemingway's technique of building suspense, his skillful use of dialogue and significant details, his detached objectivity which forced the reader to participate, and the main themes which he developed in the story. As the status of the short story increased in Germany, critics were becoming more aware of the complex artistry that the form demanded. Krebs himself concluded: "One example convincingly illustrated that a method of interpretation which follows this new way can elucidate a subtle and concentrated work of modern art such as the short story 'The Killers.' "[24]

Philip Young's *Ernest Hemingway* (1952) provided German critics with valuable information concerning Hemingway's early short stories, especially those dealing with Nick Adams. Previously Germans had not known enough of Hemingway's early life to connect the author with his fictional hero. Young placed the stories that deal with Nick's initiation and development in a definite chronological order, explaining that Nick, the fisherman alone in northern Michigan in "Big Two-Hearted River," was the same one who had been severely wounded during World War I and was trying to find himself again by returning to an area he had known many years before.[25] Malcolm Cowley in his article "Hemingway at Midnight," translated in the German periodical *Umschau*, had pointed this out as early as 1947,[26] but as we have seen in their reactions to Hemingway's style, German critics immediately after the war were not in a position to deal objectively with Hemingway's fiction. But by 1954 the short story had taken on added importance in German critical circles, and Hemingway was at the peak of his popularity; consequently Germans were much more responsive.

Dieter Wellershoff, for example, wrote in *Der Gleichgültige: Versuche über Hemingway, Camus, Benn, und Beckett* (1963) that a story such as "Big Two-Hearted River" was more than the precise, factual description of a fishing trip. The surface details reflect Nick's "controlled fright" as he performs a series of rituals in order to protect himself from his own memories of war experiences. Wellershoff could now make the connection that German critics had not perceived earlier: that what is occurring with Nick in "Big Two-Hearted River" takes place in a more subtle and varied way with Jake in the San Sebastian episode of *The Sun Also Rises*.[27] Or as Günter Blöcker pointed out in *Die neuen Wirklichkeiten* (1957), after properly crediting Young's book, Nick's trip is a deliberate return to the primitive, a simpler means of existence which allows one to concentrate only on sensual experience. Nick, Blöcker explained, is not one individual fleeing from his wound (also a form of mental illness), but he is the representative of an entire generation. All of Hemingway's heroes, he pointed out, find themselves in a scorched landscape like Nick Adams; and like Nick they attempt to make themselves at home in it by building their own tent, biting their teeth together, and struggling with the desolation. Blöcker agreed with Young that the overcoming of spiritual trauma became a necessary characteristic of Hemingway's writing. And he echoed the American critic in stating that Hemingway's defense against his own weakness is perhaps his greatest theme.[28]

Young's influence is also reflected in Wellershoff's discussion of the story "Indian Camp," in which the young Nick witnesses violent birth and death among the Indians in northern Michigan. According to Wellershoff, these events occur to every human, and behind them stands a myth—the ordering of Adam out of paradise. Nick's last statement (that he was still convinced he would never die) is an attempt to regress, but his initiation has already begun and from now on the return is only possible in the form of a brief flight into nature. The myth, Wellershoff stated, is the American dream of a new Adam in a new land, the innocent, utopian experience of the pioneers. Hemingway found something that corresponded to this in northern Michigan, and this became the "Urbild" for the rehabilitating refuge of his heroes in later fiction.[29]

Hermann Stresau's monograph on Hemingway published in 1958, although it often did little more than summarize the content and point out the autobiographical elements in Hemingway's fiction, performed a valuable service in that it supplied important chronological information concerning Hemingway's publications of short stories. Hemingway's first printed work, Stresau told his fellow Germans, was *Three Stories and Ten Poems*, published in Paris in 1923. "Up in Michigan," the first of Hemingway's stories, contained the psychological conflicts which were to become typical of his later work, and in the other two stories of the first volume, "Out of Season" and "My Old Man," Stresau pointed out that Hemingway employed the art that he was later to perfect: "allowing the most important events to occur silently beneath the detailed surface of his prose." In addition Stresau explained that the volume of short stories *In Our Time*, first translated in Germany in 1932, contained the vignettes of *in our time* (published in Paris in 1924) used as inter-chapters to supply a factual background for the later stories and to express the meaning of the title —that in our time such things are possible.[30]

But besides emphasizing the autobiographical elements in the Nick Adams stories in *In Our Time* and in *The Fifth Column and the First Forty-nine Stories*, and explaining the underlying meaning of the ritual Nick follows in "Big Two-Hearted River," as Philip Young had already done, Stresau offered little detailed analysis of Hemingway's writing technique. He stated only that "this technique is responsible for the uniqueness of the short story." Stresau recognized that the narrator's role was altered in the American short story, but he was extremely vague in explaining it: "he brings together the various qualities of a relationship or an impression and he develops them as a writer develops his themes, only these themes are of a different kind."[31]

Typical of Stresau's approach to individual stories is his discussion of "The Snows of Kilimanjaro" which, he claimed, reflects Hemingway's early dissatisfaction with himself. The disillusioned Harry is not an exact replica of the author, "but the elements of his life, his experiences, are the elements in the author's life; his preoccupation with death is a subject especially close to Hemingway." The leopard on the mountain side, Stresau explained, stems from the symbolic tradition of the Middle Ages and embodies worldly joy and desire: "It is the symbol for the purification of the soul, which death makes possible." And the howling of the hyenas supplies the story with the same kind of dissonance provided by the shot in "The Short Happy Life of Francis Macomber." Stresau speculated that Hemingway, in revealing the inner consciousness of Harry, was striving for the fourth and fifth dimension in prose which he mentioned in *Green Hills of Africa*. But he concluded that no matter what Hemingway intended by the terminology, he succeeded in breaking through to a deeper conception of man and at the same time perfected his writing technique and the short story form.[32]

The publication of Philip Young's book, although it supplied guide lines for the Germans' renewed approach to Hemingway's short stories, hindered independent investigations on the part of German critics, such as Wellershoff, Blöcker, and Stresau. It was not until 1957 that the earlier critical debates concerning the stature of the short story began to bear fruit in terms of independent scholarly investigations of Hemingway's work. Among the first of these was an article by Werner Hüllen in *NS*, October, 1957, which examined Hemingway's use of dialogue in "A Day's Wait" and "Cat in the Rain." Hüllen traced in the two short stories the existential experience as outlined by Karl Jasper's *Einführung in die Philosophie* (1953). Jaspers explained that man in his desire for communication turns in upon himself and in this way achieves the purpose of all philosophy: "the perception of being, the illumination of love, the completion of peace." According to Hüllen the transcending of one's own isolation to reach the communion of the self with the self ("Gemeinschaft des Selbstseins mit dem Selbstsein") is no longer in the province of Hemingway's story. But, he added, the fact that Hemingway chose as his characteristic theme the lack of meaningful exchange in human dialogue is proof that he saw in this the cardinal failure of his and our time. The finding of the seeds of recovery in sickness itself and making virtue out of necessity, he concluded, have always shaped Hemingway's attitude toward the heroic.[33]

In his discussion of the first story, which involves a boy's mis-

taken belief that he is suffering from a fatal disease, Hüllen focused on the nuances and ironic overtones in the dialogue between
the boy and his father. This Hemingway achieves, he explained,
by having the two thought processes meeting on the banal level of
speech, but diverging underneath. After the boy's revealing question, "About what time do you think I'm going to die?" Hüllen
convincingly demonstrated that all previous conversation between
father and son must be seen in a new light, for they all have double meanings: "(1) I'd rather stay awake, (2) No, I mean you don't
have to stay if it's going to bother you, (3) You mustn't get what
I have, (4) I don't worry, but I can't keep from thinking, (5) I'm
taking it(!) easy, (6) Do you think it will do any good?" From his
study Hüllen emerged with a new appreciation for Hemingway's
artistry:

> One admires the skill with which commonplace details, in-
> deed banalities, are given such subtle ambivalence. Two
> separate ranges of ideas exist in the sentences, and because
> they never are united, they preserve that suspenseful tension
> which makes "A Day's Wait" a tightly structured short
> story.[34]

The second story Hüllen chose to analyze, "Cat in the Rain,"
also focuses on two characters, a married couple isolated geo-
graphically in an Italian resort hotel and at the same time isolated
from each other. The position of both indicates separation, boredom, and emptiness—she staring out the window, and he reading
on the bed. Because it is raining they lack diversion and escape,
and boredom is at its heaviest. It is this situation which causes the
woman to take up the insignificant task of protecting a stray cat
from the rain, and to give vent to her subconscious desires. The
cat itself, Hüllen pointed out, is important only in that it prompts
a cry for help from a disconsolate human; the woman is unable to
find a satisfactory purpose in her life or in the "Beziehungslosig-
keit" of the marriage. She does get a cat, but at the moment of the
literal fulfillment of her wish she knows with crushing finality that
no one has understood her. Up to this point Hüllen was mainly
concerned with the content of the story, and with uncovering key
secondary meanings in the Hemingway dialogue, as he had done
in his discussion of "A Day's Wait." However, in drawing the two

stories together, Hüllen joined a number of German critics who concentrated on the existential qualities of Hemingway's fiction.[35]

In these two stories Hemingway, according to Hüllen, intends more than simply to dramatize modern lack of communication; he also deals with destructive misunderstanding that emerges from a "fateful sense of loss." In the case of the boy the misunderstanding throws him back upon himself ("Auf-sich-selbst-Angewiesensein"). Facing alone a decisive existential problem, the boy achieves the miracle of self-evaluation, and by the strength of his will, conquers his fear of death. Only when this fear is no longer present does he revert back to being a nine-year-old boy who cries easily and enjoys reading pirate books. Hüllen claimed that a similar experience occurs with the American woman in "Cat in the Rain." She, too, is thrown back upon herself: "At this point one sees a heroic, loving human being emerge from a state of fear and disillusioning boredom." As Hüllen saw it, projecting an existential framework on to "A Day's Wait" and "Cat in the Rain" did not distort the stories, but rather elucidated their philosophic background:

> Both [the boy and the American woman] were able to find only themselves because they were alone in their own depths ("ihren eigenen Tiefen"), and because that which Karl Jaspers calls communication did not take place. Applying the existential framework to Hemingway's fiction, it means that the characters' communication with their fellow human beings took place only on the surface and did not develop into a true dialogue.[36]

The failure to establish a true dialogue is both a sickness and a cure, for only in being alone ("Alleinsein") is man thrown back entirely upon himself; here is his deepest misery, but also the beginning of his deepest fulfillment. Never, said Hüllen, is this thrust into one's essence ("Vorstossen in die Wesentlichkeit") in vain, even if the results are not immediate. Even at the end of "Cat in the Rain" as the wife looks out the window, the sun begins to break through.[37]

The marked change in the German critical approach to Hemingway's short stories which began with articles like Hüllen's continued into the 1960's. Titles of the following critical articles, for example, "Das Zeitmoment und einige charakteristische Motive in Ernest Hemingways Kurzgeschichte 'The Killers,'" "Beharrende Strukturzüge im Wandel eines Jahrhunderts amerikanischer Kurzgeschichte . . . ," "Kontrast und Parallelität in den Kurzgeschichten Ernest Hemingways," " 'The Gambler, the Nun, and the Radio': Untersuchung zur Gestaltungsweise Hemingways," illustrate the increased emphasis on structural or stylistic devices in individual stories. No longer were the short stories grouped together and treated as Hemingway's apprenticeship work; they were singled out as separate artistic achievements, and German criticism took on a new objective tone in explicating them.

Serving to encourage the detailed explication of individual short stories was *Insight I: Analyses of American Literature* (1962), a collection of critical studies of American fiction edited by John V. Hagopian and Martin Dolch. According to the editors, the purpose of the book was "to encourage and improve the study of American literature in the German schools."[38] The critical interpretations, which were also intended to publicize the methods of new criticism, relied heavily upon textual analysis and stressed the unity of form and content in the individual selections. The works of Hemingway dealt with in the collection were "Cat in the Rain," "A Canary for One," "The Killers," "A Day's Wait," "A Clean, Well-Lighted Place," and *The Old Man and the Sea.*

Among the first German critics to apply the methods of new criticism to the Hemingway short story was Broder Carstensen in his study of "The Killers" (*Jahrbuch für Amerikastudien*, 1959). The aim of the study was to illustrate the way in which Hemingway gives a realistic basis to the story and at the same time unifies it dramatically through references to the clock or to time. As Carstensen pointed out, the main action which takes place in the cafe covers two hours and consists of eleven pages, eighty per cent of which is dialogue. Contrasting attitudes towards time are established as soon as the gangsters Al and Max enter the cafe at 5:20 p.m. and begin their wait for Ole Andreson. When George mentions that the clock is twenty minutes fast, one of the gangsters answers, "to hell with the clock." Time means nothing to them, for only their task is important; this sets them apart from Nick, George, and Sam, representatives of the normal world regulated by the clock. Between 5:20 and 7:10 Hemingway makes frequent references to time, but after it becomes certain that Ole is not going to appear, he is no longer concerned with exact chronology. This indicates, according to Carstensen, that the fate of Ole is clear and will be carried out regardless of time.[39]

The first part of the time scheme is realistic, for in thirty to forty-five minutes the gangsters have spoken with three people, tied up two of them, eaten and drunk. From 6:00 to 6:15 p.m. Hemingway provides only thirty-two lines of dialogue, but he makes this acceptable by the ominous tone which indicates long silences between speeches. The description of George's frequent head movements as he glances at the clock makes the reader aware of the slow passing of time. After the entrance of the streetcar driver at the time Ole should likely appear, the reader knows that Ole, if he does come, will be late, and that the length of Al and Max's wait becomes a matter of suspense. Between 6:20 and 6:55 only five lines of dialogue appear, but Hemingway remains on a realistic level by saying that two other people had been in the lunchroom and George made a sandwich to go. By manipulating the action this way, Carstensen explained, Hemingway reminds the reader of the tense quietness that would pervade the cafe as the killers continued to wait. The next time-reference ("We'll give him ten minutes more") is vague, thereby indicating the timelessness of the final act. Two more references to the clock follow, and Carstensen pointed out that Hemingway is employing his "Visual-technik" in making the reader aware of the exact movement of the hand on the clock and of the slow moving time which relates to the condition of the prisoners, the feelings of the gangsters, and the hopelessness of Ole: "The hand of the clock forces the reader into a visual participation."[40]

Carstensen, like many of his fellow German critics, began paying closer attention to the seemingly insignificant in Hemingway's style, to the qualities that set him apart from early American realists and many of his later imitators. In "The Killers" Carstensen pointed out Hemingway's skillful use of telling details, e.g., the gangsters' gloves which they leave on during the story, or the bulging sawed-off shotgun under Al's coat. Another technique of Hemingway's, Carstensen explained, is "to only allude to a subject and leave the details for the reader to fill in." A good example of this is in the way Hemingway presents the theme of despair and hope-lessness in connection with Ole. We are given only a visual im-pression which we see in Ole's eyes and in his single movement towards the wall, but with this movement Ole shows his submis-sion to unavoidable death. Similar visual effects serve to indicate new turns in the plot, e.g., Al's smoothing his coat with his gloved hand suggests that the exposition has ended and the action is about to begin, or George's wiping the counter after Nick returns shows his disgust with the whole affair and indicates that he wishes to have nothing more to do with it. By linking style and technique so closely with the content of the story, Hemingway, Carstensen suggested, may have achieved the possible fourth or fifth dimension that he felt a writer was capable of. Hemingway has illustrated his principle of writing truly "and having found what is true, to project it in such a way that it becomes a part of the experience of the person who reads it." [41]

In an attempt to place Hemingway in a historical perspective and to clarify the tradition of the short story in America, Hans Ga-linsky, one of Germany's foremost scholars in American literature, compared the structural devices in Edgar A. Poe's "The Masque of the Red Death" and Hemingway's "The Killers" (*Amerikanische Dichtung in der höheren Schule*, 1961). It is the intricate structural principles operating in stories such as the above, according to Galinsky, that qualify the short story as an independent genre. In "The Killers" Galinsky examined Hemingway's careful build up of the opposing appearance-reality planes, his use of ironic over-tones, symbolic repetition, and leitmotivs. The dialogue, in which the denotative meaning belongs to the banal and the connotative to the symbolic plane, prepares the reader for similar combina-tions of the realistic and the symbolic ("realistisch-symbolischen Doppelsinn") in the story. [42]

The structural pattern, according to Galinsky, is embodied in Hemingway's description of the men in the scene. Here the char-acters in a symbolic setting (as Carstensen pointed out) are wit-nessing an event which is at the same time symbolic and universal: the entrance of the gangsters who come as ambassadors for the anonymous power of death. The actual or anticipated moment of deadly confrontation between human and superhuman power, Galinsky saw as governing the structural principles of both Poe's and Hemingway's stories. In emphasizing the artistry of "The Killers" Galinsky drew attention to its kinship with Greek tragedy: the Negro Sam has the role of the Greek chorus; the messenger is Nick and the hero, Ole. Hemingway's analytical method which allows truth to come to light bit by bit, as well as the inevitability of fate and death, is reminiscent of Sophocles's *Oedipus*. This "realistic-symbolic" method is not new with Hemingway in the 1920's, for already in the mid-nineteenth century, Galinsky pointed out, Poe and Hawthorne had developed similar structural principles. The inspiration for this type of structure in the American short story Galinsky found in America's Calvinistic background which encouraged solitary introspection and soul searching, and predisposed nineteenth century writers towards symbolism. Galinsky concluded that since the actual or expected appearance of death is the structure-determining event in both "The Masque of the Red Death" and "The Killers" and since death carries with it "something of supernatural power," this proves the continual religious source of American symbolism. Though secularized in the twentieth century, it is the same tradition that Galinsky felt could be traced to James, Eliot, O'Neill, Faulkner, Hemingway, and Williams.[43]

One of the few studies of Hemingway's influence on German writers was made by Horst Kruse, whose article "Hinrich Kruses *Weg un Ümweg* und die Tradition der Short Story Ernest Hemingways" was published in the *Germanisch-Romanische Monatsschrift*, 1962. According to Horst Kruse, Heinrich Kruse's volume of short stories in low German shows striking similarities to Hemingway's *In Our Time*. In his discussion of individual stories Kruse was influenced strongly by Philip Young and Carlos Baker and consequently offered little that was new to Hemingway criticism. But as Stresau had done in his monograph in 1958, Kruse discussed the organizational pattern of the stories and provided Germans with valuable guidelines for approaching Hemingway's early work. Kruse (as Young had done earlier) also pointed to the development of Nick Adams as the unifying device in the volume and explained that the chronology of his experiences determines the order of the stories within the collection. Although Nick is not mentioned in seven of the stories, he can be considered implicitly as a witness. The chronology indicates that the seven stories take place during his wartime experiences (after "The Battler" and before "Big Two-Hearted River") and they show Nick progressing to the role of writer that he assumes in "Fathers and Sons," the last story of *Winner Take Nothing*.[44]

Kruse's most significant contribution to Hemingway criticism came in his discussion of the symbolism in the story "Cat in the Rain." Like Carstensen and Galinsky, Kruse pointed out that the short story depends on a concentrated, associative expression and therefore symbols take on an added importance. As Galinsky had done in his study of "The Killers," Kruse focused on the central symbolic situation which he felt controlled the structure of the story: in this case the wife's attempt to rescue a cat out of the rain, which represents her wish for a child. All other events, Kruse stated, are subordinated symbolically to this central one. Like Galinsky, Kruse maintained that symbolism is an important structural element in Hemingway's short stories, but he argued that Hemingway's symbols do not grow out of any tradition. They function only in the context of the individual story.[45]

Another of the recent, more objective approaches to Hemingway's short stories was the explication of "A Clean, Well-Lighted Place," which appeared in the anthology *Zeitgenössische amerikanische Dichtung* (1964), edited by W. Hüllen *et al.* Although brief, the article is objective and penetrating in its exploration of Hemingway's concise form, the art of omission, and the deceptively casual method by which the revelation or illumination is brought about in the dialogue of the two waiters. Yet Hüllen and his fellow editors indicated that the story, in spite of its nihilistic tone, is not entirely pessimistic, for it is the distraught older waiter who wants to keep the restaurant open for those who need a light during the dark hours: "Here, in the concern expressed for others, something positive emerges: the humanistic response."[46]

Increasing independence and originality is evident in Franz Schulz's lengthy study "Der nordamerikanische Indianer und seine Welt in den Werken von Ernest Hemingway und Oliver La Farge," which appeared in the *Mainzer amerikanistische Beiträge* in 1964. Along with his discussion of Hemingway's treatment of Indians in his fiction, Schulz offered a close analysis of structure, theme and stylistic devices in Hemingway's earliest short stories and in the often neglected novel *The Torrents of Spring* (1926). Schulz was familiar with American criticism of Hemingway, but his subject was restricted enough to allow him to escape from the standard clichés. In his discussion of "Indian Camp," for example, he began by explaining Hemingway's artistic treatment of Indians. The suggestive repetition of the word *Indians* in the beginning of the story prepares the reader for the elemental human experience in the primitive surroundings of the Indian camp. And the Indians' silence in turn emphasizes that intellectually and spiritually they are different from the white doctor.[47]

After Nick's father has performed the Caesarian operation, he says, in referring to the Indian woman's husband, "I must say he took it all pretty quietly." This misconception further reveals the breach between the thinking and feeling of the Indian and the doctor, and sets up the appearance-reality poles in the story:

> The apparent calmness and patience of the Indian are understood by the white man to be signs of indifference. At the same time the factual statements of the doctor, "her screams are not important. I can't hear them because they are not important," remain incomprehensible to the Indian, who has been so tormented by his wife's screams that he commits suicide.[48]

Schulz found evidence of the same type of symbolic realism in "Indian Camp" that Carstensen and Galinsky pointed out in "The Killers." The statement "The husband in the upper bunk rolled over against the wall," which is repeated after the doctor's operation, has the same symbolic meaning as the similar movement of Ole Andreson in "The Killers," and is typical of Hemingway's method of allowing the gestures of his characters to speak for their feelings. In another passage the experience of Nick is projected symbolically into nature: "The sun was coming up over the hills. A bass jumped, making a circle in the water. Nick trailed his hand in the water. It felt warm in the sharp chill of the morning." According to Schulz we see here the power of ever-continuing life in cosmic nature (the sun), in the animal world (fish), and in human existence (Nick's sensitivity to bodily warmth), together with the circle in the water which symbolizes the "lastingness in change."[49]

In a second initiation story, "Fathers and Sons," Schulz pointed out that Nick is exposed to another fundamental aspect of life, this time through a young, primitive Indian girl. Hemingway's description of Nick's first sexual encounter, Schulz explained, involves a careful counterpointing between the setting and the event itself:

> At first one is offended by the juxtaposition of an almost romantic description of the "pure," "cool," calming atmosphere of the "virgin forest" and the abrupt introduction to a sexual union. However, if one examines the text more closely, one discovers that the lavish description of nature and the straightforward questions which lead to sexual intercourse, are given equal weight through the use of paratactic sentence constructions. The parataxis allows the youthful love-making to appear exactly as natural, as obvious and as unreal as the paradisaical description of the "virgin forest."

The simplicity of the narrative sections, Schulz explained, parallels the tone and idiom of the dialogue, corresponds to the educational level of the participants in the story, and as a conscious "principle of art," explains and justifies the sparse, one-sided presentation of the Indian world.[50]

Schulz's discussion of "The Doctor and the Doctor's Wife" is significant for the independent critical opinion it expressed, and it provided another example of the way in which German critics of the 1960's not only took American or English criticism into account but also ventured out on their own. According to Schulz, this story, which uncovers the hidden tension between Nick's father and mother, indicates that all Hemingway's characters are not "tough people," as James Hart had claimed in the *Oxford Companion to American Literature* (1956); equally doubtful is the statement of George Hemphill (in McCaffery's *Ernest Hemingway: The Man and his Work,* 1950) that Doctor Adams is "the spiritual father of all the good people in Hemingway." As he had already done in the previous story, "Fathers and Sons," Schulz took issue with Leslie Fiedler's claim in *Love and Death in the American Novel* (1960) that Hemingway's women were "mindless, soft, subservient, painless . . . seed-extractors." The charge was unjust, Schulz argued, because Hemingway did not intend to develop his female characters fully, but instead gave them a functional status.[51] Indians are used in "The Doctor and the Doctor's Wife," Schulz explained, as a means of uncovering the hidden tension existing between the doctor, who knows of the brutal reality of the world, and his wife, who closes her eyes before the whole truth. Nick is gradually drawn away from his mother's to his father's point of view, but the secondary conflict (between the white civilized world and that of the primitive Indian) which Schulz claimed had been overlooked by previous critics, demonstrates that the doctor, in addition to his wife, does not want to face truth directly.[52]

Another German who has made original contributions to Hemingway criticism is Gerhard Hoffmann, who published two penetrating articles on Hemingway's use of contrast and parallelism as structural principles in his short stories. According to the second of Hoffmann's two articles, "Kontrast und Parallelität in den Kurzgeschichten Ernest Hemingways" (*Anglia*, 1965), the modern short story no longer requires a definite plot with exposition, complication, climax or definite character development:

> Instead of a dynamic conflict there is frequently a static episode which represents a slice of daily life. The "plot" often consists of an innocent character's experience in complex reality.[53]

A central theme in Hemingway's stories, according to Hoffmann, is the contrast between conventional thinking and real understanding—the latter coming only with the loss of security and with personal suffering. To develop this dualistic conception of reality Hemingway employs the structural principles of parallelism and contrast, which allow the narrative to proceed on two separate planes simultaneously:

> The external events are both counterpointed and complemented by the internal: numerous references direct one from the external to the internal, from the apparent to the real. They create such a tight web of relationships that both aspects of reality are presented at the same time.[54]

"The Gambler, the Nun, and the Radio," a story in which Hemingway employs both structural patterns, Hoffmann analyzed in detail in his first article which appeared in *GRM*, 1965. Hemingway, Hoffmann explained, reveals his "Schein-Sein-Thematik" on various planes of consciousness through different characters and their behavioral patterns. The story is full of carefully developed contrasts which Hoffmann outlined: beginning with the stoical conduct of the wounded Cayetano and the fearful, self-pitying Russian, the contradictions increase as Frazer (Hemingway's spokesman) questions the Mexicans sent to the hospital by the police, and reach a climax in Cayetano's speech with Frazer. We learn that for Cayetano gambling is not only a profession, but at the same time a necessary "game of chance" (or an "existentielle Notwendigkeit"), which makes him subject to luck and the unknowable. Here, Hoffmann explained, Hemingway plays on the double meaning of *gamble*, for at the end of the speech when Frazer calls him a philosopher, we see "the disparity between conventional thinking and the existential attitude."[55]

Similar contradictions Hoffmann found in Sister Cecilia: she prays for meaningless things such as a football game, about which she knows little, and yet expresses an intense sympathy for the "bad ones." This reflects an inner tension which becomes clear in her ambition to be a saint, and at the same time it links her to Cayetano. For both the nun and the gambler know that they will not reach their individual goals (luck and sainthood), and it is this knowledge which causes their inner turmoil and allows them to appear "strange" or "crazy" to people around them. In linking such diverse characters, Hemingway establishes a definite pattern of correspondences supported by the parallel revelation scenes with (1) Frazer-Sister Cecilia and (2) Frazer-Cayetano.[56]

Added to these two parallel cases is that of Frazer, who at first appears the most rational character, but at the end of the story is overcome by what Hoffmann calls the existential predicament. Leading up to Frazer's final outburst, the appearance-reality theme continues through Frazer's imagining what the "morning revellers" on the radio really look like, his attempts to create real pictures of the city from its nightly radio broadcast, and his distortions of reality implicit in his preference for the view from his room or for certain types of songs.[57]

Similar incongruities which appear at other moments in the story are isolated by Hoffmann: (1) the man who wounded Cayetano is not a hoodlum, but a fine guitar player; (2) it is not he who has lost money to Cayetano, but it is the others who come to visit; (3) the visitors are not friends of Cayetano, but friends of the man who shot him, and they do not come of their own accord, but at the request of Sister Cecilia and the police. These revelations of the absurd or the incongruent can also be found in the fate of the other hospital patients—the rodeo rider, the carpenter, and the farm boy—who find that their lives have been interrupted and altered.[58]

The hospital, Hoffmann explained, becomes a microcosm, and the physical wounds imply the spiritual hurts of the occupants. The main characters represent different ways of living: Sister Cecilia (traditional religion); Cayetano (self-developed code of behavior); Frazer (withdrawal into self without religious, social, or ethical consolation). Yet what they all have in common is a striving for something absolute, whether it be in terms of immortality, or in human exchange, or in the private region of existential knowledge. But it is to Frazer alone that the full knowledge of the opposites of appearance and reality comes. It is this that brings forth his nihilistic utterances, and Hoffmann claimed Frazer is consequently nearest to Hemingway's own attitude: "Only Frazer presses forward to the extreme consequences of existential stress, where all values become valueless . . . and where only suicide or deliberate deception remain as alternatives."[59]

Yet, according to Hoffmann, the presence of other views makes Frazer's relative; in the same way the story sets up tension between itself and abstract reality which it simplifies and represents only partially. Even the title is more complex than at first it appears. "The Gambler, the Nun, and the Radio" suggests occupations— play, worship, entertainment—but all three, according to Frazer are "opium of the people": "thus the relativity of human perception and the possibilities of confusion in one's consciousness are already alluded to in the disparate elements linked in the title." As Hoffmann explained it, the title and contrasting elements in the very beginning, in addition to the thematic motifs, the contrapuntal dialogue, and Frazer's final outburst, reveal Hemingway's purpose in writing the story: "to reveal two levels of existence ("die Doppelbödigkeit der Wirklichkeit") by opposing appearance and reality."[60]

Hoffmann's approach to the symbolic in Hemingway's fiction was more promising than that of many earlier German critics. Instead of attempting to relate isolated symbols to a literary tradition, Hoffmann drew attention to the important functional role of natural details and events in Hemingway's stories. In "The Three Day Blow," for example, the wind as a "Naturmotiv" demonstrates how quickly love can disappear; at the end of the story it makes way for Nick's freedom and the desire for something new. The same is true in "The End of Something" in which the introductory descriptive passages—concerning the fate of the town Horton's Bay —reflect the break up of Nick and Marjorie. In a similar manner Hemingway is able to elevate seemingly inconsequential natural events or observations to important functional devices, as in "The Battler"; the appearance of fire in the beginning and the end of the story serves to emphasize what went on in between—Nick's introduction to human sorrow and evil.[61]

These external details with a thematic function operate as a limited type of symbolism, severely restricted to specific stories, situations, or characters. Hoffmann illustrated this in his analysis of "A Canary for One," in which the conviction of the lady (that non-American males should not marry American girls) is reflected ironically through external parallel events throughout the story, e.g., (1) the blindness of the woman (she refuses to look out the window); (2) the burning farmhouse; (3) the group of Negro soldiers and the white sergeant on the train platform; (4) the carefully tended forest through which the train passes. In the same manner Hemingway's use of the color white in "The Snows of Kilimanjaro" and "Hills Like White Elephants" carefully avoids cliché and allows for a multiple interpretation. The symbol is always an integral part of the story:

> In Hemingway's fiction the symbolic always grows out of the very realistic description of external things, especially the landscape. The symbols pertain to individual situations, and they are frequent enough so that the transitions (between detail and symbol) are smooth and varied.[62]

Contrast and parallelism are not only important structural devices in Hemingway's stories, according to Hoffmann, but they can also be used for character development as in "Hills Like White Elephants," in which the opposition of two people, developed through a conscious use of ambivalent language, is at the basis of the story. Or contrast effects may be used with understatement or exaggeration, as in the fishing speech of "A Way You'll Never Be" or in the connotative description of the swamp in "Big Two-Hearted River." At the same time the principles of contrast and parallelism put forth a fundamental conception of the world:

> What stirs Hemingway and his heroes is the impossibility of uniting the ideal and the real, the awareness that there are no simple truths, but only paradoxes, and the distressing knowledge that we live in a world in which each man must find his own code of behavior.[63]

In his final analysis Hoffmann joined Hüllen and Wellershoff in classifying Hemingway as an existentialist. The loss of objective values, the discovery of the subjectivity of all truth, the "primary experience" of existential fear are all characteristic of the Hemingway hero, according to Hoffmann. This, he said, stems from Hemingway's own war experience and also reflects the "Grundkonzeptionen" of his time, which found its own philosophical expression in existentialism. Contrast and parallelism, according to Hoffmann, offer Hemingway an adequate means to represent this new "Zeitgefühl"; contrast allows him the opportunity to set the hero against conventions, superficialities, and lies, while paralleling characters, such as Cayetano and Frazer, allows him to take nihilistic experiences from individual, subjective experience and make it a condition of all sensitive men.[64]

Distinctive in the most recent German critical approach to Hemingway was the emphasis critics placed on the existential framework, the complex structural principles, and the naturalistic symbols that they found in individual stories. These critics pointed out that Hemingway's stories frequently achieved a perfect balance between form and content; by demonstrating this in their criticism, they made important contributions to an understanding of his art. It is significant that Walter F. Schirmer in his 1949 edition of *Geschichte der englischen und amerikanischen Literatur* had no separate division for the short story; the 1967 edition, however, set the short story apart as an established genre and traced its development from the 1920's to the present. It was Hemingway, according to Schirmer, who played a major role in the development of the modern American short story, for through his use of laconic dialogue, sparse narrative, and diverse undertones, he elevated the naturalistic-concrete to the symbolic level, and thereby developed the early sketch into an art form.[65]

NOTES

[1] With the exception of an early German version of "The Undefeated," all of the short story translations were done by Annemarie Horschitz. Following World War II her name was changed to Horschitz-Horst.

[2] Dietrich, pp. 89–91.

[3] Hans Fallada, "Ernest Hemingway oder Woran liegt es?" *Literatur*, XXXIII (September, 1931), 672–74; "Gespräch zwischen Ihr und Ihm über Ernest Hemingway: *In Our Time*," *Literatur*, XXXV (October, 1932), 21–24.

[4] Edgar Mertner, "Zur Theorie der Short Story in England und Amerika," *Anglia*, LXV (1941), 188–97.

[5] *Ibid.*, pp. 197–98.

[6] *Ibid.*, pp. 202–5.

[7] Hanns von Krannhals, *Welt und Wort*, IV (1949), 248.

[8] E. F., "Romane—Stories—Erinnerungen," *Neues Abendland*, IV (1949), 350–51.

[9] Barbara Bühler, *Westermanns Monatshefte*, XCII, No. 8 (1951–1952), 85.

[10] Clara Menck, "Muster der Short Story," *Wort und Wahrheit*, VI (1951), 382–83.

[11] Engelbert Kirchner, "Short Story," *Frankfurter Hefte*, V (1950), 508.

[12] *Ibid.*, p. 509.

[13] Klaus Doderer, "Die angelsächsische Short Story und die deutsche Kurzgeschichte," *Die Neueren Sprachen*, II (1953), 417–49.

[14] *Ibid.*, pp. 419–23.

[15] Klaus Doderer, *Die Kurzgeschichte in Deutschland* (Wiesbaden, 1953), pp. 83–93.

[16] Johannes Klein, *Geschichte der deutschen Novelle von Goethe bis zur Gegenwart*, 4th ed. (Wiesbaden, 1960).

[17] Siegfried Unseld, "*An diesem Dienstag*: Unvorgreifliche Gedanken über die Kurzgeschichte," *Akzente*, II (1955), 139–44.

[18] Hermann Pongs, "Die Anekdote als Kunstform zwischen Kalendergeschichte und Kurzgeschichte," *Der Deutschunterricht*, IX, No. 1 (1957), 5–20; Helmut Motekat, "Gedanken zur Kurzgeschichte," *Der Deutschunterricht*, IX, No. 1 (1957), 20–35; Ruth Lorbe, "Die deutsche Kurzgeschichte der Jahrhundertmitte," *Der Deutschunterricht*, IX, No. 1 (1957), 36–54.

[19] Franz Link, "Tale," "sketch," "essay," and "short story," *Die Neueren Sprachen*, VI (1957), 351–52.

[20] Hanns Effelberger, "Probleme der modernen amerikanischen Literatur, *Die Neueren Sprachen*, VI (1957), 318–24.

[21] Schmidt, pp. 228 ff.

22 Lang, Hans–Joachim, "Kunst und Wirklichkeit in der Short Story," *Die Pädagogische Provinz*, XIII (1959), 398–404.

23 Theodor Wolpers, "Die amerikanische *short story* in der Schule: Gesichtspunkte und Vorschläge für eine representative Auswahl," *Die Neueren Sprachen*, V (1956), 300–1.

24 Karl Krebs, "Die amerikanische Kurzgeschichte in der Schule," *Die Neueren Sprachen*, V (1956), 306–7.

25 Young, pp. 1–27.

26 Cowley, "Hemingway at Midnight," pp. 190–95.

27 Dieter Wellershoff, *Der Gleichgültige: Versuche über Hemingway, Camus, Benn, und Beckett* (Berlin, 1963), p. 19.

28 Blöcker, *Die neuen Wirklichkeiten*, pp. 242–45.

29 Wellershoff, pp. 24–25.

30 Stresau, pp. 32–33.

31 *Ibid.*, pp. 40–42.

32 *Ibid.*, pp. 60–62.

33 Werner Hüllen, "Gespräche ohne Verstehen: Versuch einer Deutung von Ernest Hemingways Kurzgeschichten 'A Day's Wait' und 'Cat in the Rain,' " *Die Neueren Sprachen*, VI (1957), 432–35.

34 *Ibid.*, pp. 436–38.

35 *Ibid.*, p. 438.

36 *Ibid.*, pp. 438–39.

37 *Ibid.*, p. 439.

38 John V. Hagopian and Martin Dolch, eds., *Insight I: Analyses of American Literature*, 3rd ed. (Frankfurt am Main, 1967), p. 5.

39 Broder Carstensen, "Das Zeitmoment und einige charakteristische Motive in Ernest Hemingways Kurzgeschichte 'The Killers,' " *JAS*, IV (1959), 181.

40 *Ibid.*, pp. 182–85.

41 *Ibid.*, pp. 186–89.

42 Hans Galinsky, "Beharrende Strukturzüge im Wandel eines Jahrhunderts amerikanischer Kurzgeschichte (dargelegt an E. A. Poes 'The Masque of the Red Death' und Ernest Hemingways 'The Killers')," *Amerikanische Dichtung in der höheren Schule*, eds. Hans Galinsky, *et al.* (Berlin, 1961), p. 28.

43 *Ibid.*, pp. 32–42.

44 Horst Kruse, "Hinrich Kruses *Weg un Ümweg* und die Tradition der Short Story Ernest Hemingways," *GRM*, XLIII (1962), 287–88.

45 *Ibid.*, pp. 294–95.

46 W. Hüllen, W. Rossi, W. Christopeit, eds., *Zeitgenössische amerikanische Dichtung*, 2nd ed. (Frankfurt am Main, 1964), pp. 94–95.

47 Franz Schulz, "Der nordamerikanische Indianer und seine Welt in den Werken von Ernest Hemingway und Oliver La Farge," *Mainzer amerikanistische Beiträge*, VII (1964), 13–17.

48 *Ibid.*, p. 14.

49 *Ibid.*, pp. 15–16.

50 *Ibid.*, pp. 19–20.

51 *Ibid.*, pp. 19–21.

52 *Ibid.*, p. 28.

[53] Gerhard Hoffmann, "Kontrast und Parallelität in den Kurzgeschichten Ernest Hemingways," *Anglia*, LXXXIII (1965), 199.

[54] *Ibid.*, p. 201.

[55] Gerhard Hoffmann, " 'The Gambler, the Nun, and the Radio': Untersuchung zur Gestaltungsweise Hemingways," *GRM*, XLVI (1965), 423.

[56] *Ibid.*

[57] *Ibid.*, pp. 424–25.

[58] *Ibid.*, p. 425.

[59] *Ibid.*, pp. 426–28.

[60] *Ibid.*, pp. 428–29.

[61] Hoffmann, "Kontrast und Parallelität," pp. 210–12.

[62] *Ibid.*, pp. 214–15.

[63] *Ibid.*, pp. 220–23.

[64] *Ibid.*, pp. 223–24.

[65] Schirmer, pp. 804–05.

The Sun Also Rises (1926), the first of Hemingway's novels to be translated in Germany, was published by the Rowohlt Company as *Fiesta*[1] in 1928. Helmut Papajewski has observed that the novel's reception in the late 1920's and early 1930's was "very mixed":

> those critics who were very bourgeois and conservative in their attitude, together with strictly Catholic critics, rejected it in no uncertain fashion. Their main point of attack was centered on the characters in the novel whose useless and apparently amoral lives seemed, they thought, to make the translation of the novel unjustifiable.

But at the same time, Papajewski pointed out, another group of critics, although they often ignored critical problems of technique and style, were "interested in the affinity between Hemingway's characters and their own generation." Particularly fascinating to them was the idea of a lost generation, a concept first introduced by Clifton Fadiman, in an article which was translated into German and published in *Querschnitt* in 1933.[2]

During the first decade following World War II German critics paid relatively little attention to *The Sun Also Rises*, for they considered it an early work of lesser significance than the other major novels and assumed that German readers were already familiar with it. This explains in part why the two conflicting reactions to the novel, outlined by Papajewski, carried over into the postwar years. Critics were content with repeating the clichés that stemmed from pre-war criticism, and they were still greatly influenced by the Hemingway legend and the romantic concept of a lost generation. The influence of American criticism encouraged a more objective approach in the late 1950's, but it was not until the 1960's that Germans demonstrated originality in their reaction to Hemingway's first major novel.

Typical of the early response Papajewski described is Paul Wiegler's statement in his *Geschichte der fremdsprachigen Weltliteratur*, 1949, that the novel of American Bohemians in Paris and Spain "should be banned for its immorality."[3] Similarly Adolph

Volbracht, reviewing Rowohlt's edition of *Fiesta* (*The Sun Also Rises*) in the East German *Aufbau*, 1948, observed that it was astounding the way in which Hemingway could hold his readers' attention with the description of banalities and countless drinking situations. However, after considering the characters themselves, the way in which they face up to the meaningless world about them, and the determination they have in searching for their own scale of values, Volbracht became more sympathetic. Between drinking and carousing, they finally emerge "as decent, if ill-trained, boys and girls [*sic*] who detest all feeling, but who nevertheless follow their deepest impulses and end up by doing the right thing." Volbracht clearly identified with Hemingway's characters when he questioned, "Who will hold it against them if, as representatives of the twentieth century, they do not like carrying their hearts on their sleeves?" *Fiesta*, he concluded, "is an invaluable contribution to the literature of the last twenty years."[4]

Volbracht's superficial, subjective review was characteristic of the German reaction to *The Sun Also Rises* during the early 1950's. Roland Wiegenstern (*Hier und Heute*, 1951) wrote that this was a novel in which form and content were totally integrated, but he neglected to illustrate the integration in his review. He merely commented that reflections on the inhumanity and loneliness in the modern world stand behind every word, and that this extreme negativism leads to the society of the lost generation, the community of the lonely.[5]

The public image of Hemingway was still very much alive in Henry Lüdeke's brief evaluation of *The Sun Also Rises* in his *Geschichte der amerikanischen Literatur*, 1952. After summarizing Hemingway's adventuresome life and his participation in three wars, Lüdeke added, "even after his literary successes he continued his restless wandering in all parts of the world." Hemingway, Lüdeke explained, was regarded as the most gifted representative of "the lost generation" whose fullest expression came in *The Sun Also Rises*. Lüdeke offered no analysis of the novel, but added rather anticlimactically that it dealt with a group of former soldiers, sensitive to the moral break up of the old world and the meaninglessness of the new, who travel from Paris to Pamplona in order to seek meaning in the life among bullfighters.[6] Similarly Broder Carstensen in his article "Evelyn Waugh und Ernest Hemingway," (ASNS, 1954) wrote that Hemingway in *The Sun Also Rises* and Waugh in *Vile Bodies* served as spokesmen for the lost generation: both saw "modern man's rootlessness and lack of fixed standards . . . as the main sources of his suffering."[7] Gotthilf Dierlamm claimed that *The Sun Also Rises* contained "the most complete expression of certain basic moods of modern man."[8] And Adalbert Schmidt (*Literaturgeschichte: Wege und Wandlungen moderner Dichtung*, 1957) stated simply that the novel showed "the submergence of unstable American and French intellectuals in the frenzy of Paris night life and in the delirium of bullfighting in Pamplona." Hemingway is a modern rebel (Schmidt, like Clifton Fadiman, compared him to Lord Byron), yet in responding to his sense of isolation, he is not "romantisch-pathetisch" or "lyrisch-sentimental" but brutally realistic. Schmidt had little to say about Hemingway's realistic style except that it was not ornate and relied on objectivity and laconic understatement.[9]

Wilhelm Grenzmann in his discussion of *The Sun Also Rises* in *Weltdichtung der Gegenwart*, 1957, quoted Gertrude Stein's statement (a favorite with German critics), "You are all a lost generation," and pointed out that the chaotic events, the hurried activities of all the characters and the meaninglessness of their actions, illustrated the instability and rootlessness of those who after the war sought both a physical and a spiritual home. Grenzmann noted the settings—postwar Paris, Burguete, and Pamplona —but failed to consider the artistic significance of the change in setting or the link between the aesthetics of bullfighting and the lives of the characters. Pamplona, he wrote, is simply the place where all activities become chaotic. The characters, because of their hunger for adventure and their fear of death, flee from themselves to one new experience after the next and find diversion in alcohol and sex.[10]

Hermann Stresau in his monograph, *Ernest Hemingway* (1958), also stressed Hemingway's kinship with the "lost generation," but took an important step forward in praising his artistic use of dialogue and tightly disciplined form in *The Sun Also Rises*. Stresau explained the symbolic nature of Jake's wound and recognized the change of tone that occurs in the San Sebastian scene. Although it is generally uneventful, he wrote, the reader knows that Jake awaits news from Brett, and this increases tension in spite of the lack of action and Hemingway's deliberately flat style.[11] Similarly Leo Lania's *Bildbiographie* of Hemingway, 1960, although not a very scholarly work and dependent for the most part on American criticism, attempted to put Hemingway's early fiction and his expatriation in a proper perspective. Lania agreed that Hemingway became the chronicler of the "lost generation," but pointed out something unknown to many Germans—that Hemingway regarded Gertrude Stein's observation "You are all a lost generation," as "magnificent bombast."[12] *The Sun Also Rises*, he stated, first attracted attention for its shocking events, sexual intrigues and the colorful background of Montparnasse and Pamplona, but these are secondary to the theme of the novel. Lania saw Brett Ashley and Jake Barnes as symbolic representatives of a generation which had been afflicted by war, and the characters Mike Campbell and Robert Cohn as representative of those losing themselves in the confusion of the age.

"This was not typical of the whole generation," he explained, "but this hopelessness, this feeling of being lost, this tired cynicism were shared by millions of young people." Although the theme is not as timely as it once was and readers no longer recognize the original models for the fictional characters, the novel, Lania argued, has lost none of its power: "In language and in style, in the descriptions of nature and the characterization, Hemingway proved he was a master in his very first novel."[13]

The gradual emergence from the subjective approach to *The Sun Also Rises* which began with critics such as Stresau and Lania, reached a new level in Dieter Wellershoff's discussion of the novel in his book *Der Gleichgültige: Versuch über Hemingway, Camus, Benn, und Beckett*, 1963. Wellershoff was strongly influenced by the criticism of Philip Young, but he probed more deeply into the structural and stylistic subtleties of *The Sun Also Rises* than any German critic had done previously. In focusing on the San Sebastian episode near the end of the book, Wellershoff explained that it is a high point of the novel, although at first reading it appears full of inconsequential details. It is on the trivialities of the scene that the value rests, for we learn that Jake is an exhausted, sick man who seeks to be alone and to put his life in order with the aid of the regulated activities of the hotel. He searches for both relief and healing aid, Wellershoff explained, and his "swim in the ocean is a purifying act of liberation." [14]

In such scenes in which Hemingway has his hero resort to simple, non-problematic activities, Wellershoff observed the subtle way in which Hemingway alters his style to correspond to the hero's state of mind:

> the apparently primitive concreteness, the plain succession of short sentences, the detailed commentary, the objective tone—all are manifestations of a highly stylized language. And this style corresponds perfectly to a definite attitude. Hemingway's prose is an expression of controlled fright. [15]

Wellershoff also dealt with the theme and structure of the novel, which most previous criticism had ignored: "Not being able to live and yet living in spite of it, that is the theme of the book. Escaping complications and then being overcome by them again, that is the rhythm of the plot." Both structure and rhythm, he pointed out, depend upon the change in setting: Paris (chaos), Burguete (peace), Pamplona (chaos), San Sebastian (peace), Madrid (chaos). The final scene with Jake and Brett in the taxi is the most pathetic in the novel. Thus *The Sun Also Rises* is Hemingway's most pessimistic work, for all of the characters' weaknesses are revealed, and they end in the same state they have begun. [16]

Hemingway's style, Wellershoff indicated, was a direct result of his personal search for stability. After the traumatic shock of his wound in World War I and the suicide of his father, Hemingway could only cope with death through the strictest mental discipline. In learning to accept death, he was forced to seek it out and even to write of it:

> He could only achieve the desired concreteness and precision in his prose if he trained himself to endure the brutal realities of life. His writing was a part of this training. Learning how to write and courageously accepting the hardest fact, that of death, were two parts of the same process. [17]

The absurdity of death, claimed Wellershoff, forces into loneliness and isolation the individual with no cultural tradition to fall back on. It destroys all high-sounding generalities and illustrates that only the concrete is real. This is what Hemingway has Frederic Henry discover in *A Farewell to Arms*—the emptiness of honor, fame, and sacrifice over against the meaningful numbers, dates, and street names. All that remains are naked facts or senselessness. For Frederic the war has become senseless and life real; therefore he deserts. The same is true, according to Wellershoff, for the characters in *The Sun Also Rises*. Their horizon does not extend beyond the purely factual ("Die Dinge sind aus allen Sinnzusammenhängen entlassen und erscheinen in purer Faktizität").[18]

Already in 1926, Wellershoff claimed, Hemingway experienced the absurdity of existence that later became the themes of Camus and Sartre. Absurdity is not expressed directly in Hemingway's works, but it is recognizable in the penetration of the factual and in the banality in the lives of his characters in *The Sun Also Rises*. Hemingway did not go as far as the French existentialists:

> there is not the awareness of alienation from all that is real, the fear of the incomprehensibility of everything apart from ourselves. His characters have not yet awakened like Sartre's Roquentin in that strangely foreign place where all that exists appears to be a meaningless outgrowth of nothingness.[19]

However, Hemingway's "Konkretismus" does lead to the edge of this experience. When Hemingway names each of the streets his characters pass in a city and quotes the names and prices of drinks that they buy, one receives the impression, wrote Wellershoff, that to a great extent life is made up of meaningless activities and consists of meaningless things. In rejecting the principle that the artist is able to distinguish the essential from the non-essential, Hemingway offers a myriad of realistic details; everything appears as equal, and this results in the "penetration of the banal." Sartre, Wellershoff pointed out, carries this still farther in *Nausea*, 1938, in which the factual not only penetrates man's existence, but threatens to destroy it. With Hemingway the situation is not so grave, for in his fiction the growing presence of the concrete is a gain in immediacy. But already behind this is the fundamental experience that man is no longer capable of transcending his human predicament, and consequently the writer must give up his omniscient position and place himself before an overpowering realism. Thematically, Wellershoff claimed, this is reflected in the passivity and weakness of the fictional characters. *The Sun Also Rises,* a novel of "Lebensunfähigkeit" illustrated by Jake's impotence, presents characters who no longer find it possible to escape from the "pressure of the factual." Thinking or praying only leads to nihilism and an awareness of the loss of values: "Universally speaking, stability does not exist any longer; one must find strength within one's self. Hemingway's answer to this situation was stoicism."[20]

Another idea Wellershoff borrows from Philip Young is that of the code hero, a man capable of facing death and danger calmly, and of preserving his dignity even in defeat. Such men have an objective, practical attitude towards the world and already have anticipated death in their own consciousness. To them the world is as it must be and they see themselves as a part of it; consequently they do not attempt any kind of transcendence: "Most important is to accept misfortune gracefully, to control one's feelings and to develop one's competence." In this context the most rewarding activity for Hemingway and his romantic fictional heroes, according to Wellershoff, is "struggling passionately with concrete reality." Phases of this struggle in Hemingway's fiction as well as in his own life, Wellershoff pointed out, are marked by a dramatic acquiring of knowledge, growing out of brotherly love and respect between opponents. The hero needs the stimulation of danger to escape the existential predicament developed in *The Sun Also Rises.* In the absence of danger the stoic attitude can only be practiced in understatement. However understatement is not enough, for it only intensifies "the cold indifference of the world." Thus Wellershoff explained the need for special jargon and private rituals among Hemingway's characters, which they use to combat the emptiness that threatens to engulf them.[21]

Hemingway was well known in Germany after the publication and translation of his early short stories and *The Sun Also Rises* in the 1920's, but it was *A Farewell to Arms* (1929) that established his reputation as a prominent writer. Translated by Annemarie Horschitz as *In einem anderen Land,* Hemingway's second major novel was published by the Rowohlt Company in 1930. The reasons for the novel's early success in Germany have been outlined by Papajewski:

The pacifistic beliefs of many individuals—so very widespread in Germany after the First World War—were of course a fertile ground for the message of the novel. The moral of the story was readily accepted by the general reading public. Now for the first time, Hemingway's narrative skill was emphasized and praised by the critics. Even a periodical such as the *Gral* (a publication of strict denominational principles) now made a distinction between the artistic and the ethical elements of Hemingway's writing. Although a number of critics still complained of the disregard of the ethical norms in the novel, there was great recognition of Hemingway's remarkable narrative technique. The critics were a little disconcerted and at a loss to find a quite satisfactory interpretation of this new technique. Attempts were made to compare details in Hemingway with those in Hamsun and the apparent 'directness' of expression was emphasized. It was also pointed out that some elements of the technique were borrowed from the film, as e.g., the loose sequence of scenes.[22]

Indicative of the early reception of *A Farewell to Arms* is the laudatory statement of Thomas Mann in 1929: "It is one of the most beautiful, carefully restrained modern love stories. . . . [It is] a genuine, manly book, a masterpiece."[23] The opinions of other early reviewers, such as Klaus Mann, Max Dietrich, and Hans Fallada, support Papajewski's observation that Germans of the 1920's and early 1930's did not consider Hemingway primarily as an American, but praised him "as the champion of the protesting individual, as a writer whose realism and contempt for the bombastic and the high flown were signs that pointed to a new, humanistically oriented literature."[24]

Following World War II, *A Farewell to Arms* was the first Hemingway novel to be reissued. Published on newspaper print by the Rowohlt Verlag, it included an introduction by C. W. Ceram, author of the best-seller *Götter, Gräber und Gelehrte*. According to Papajewski, "the book was generally acclaimed by readers of all ages"; the aspects of the novel which contributed to its widespread success, he explained, were not only its political implications, but also its captivating love story and the powerfully tragic ending.[25] Although *A Farewell to Arms* was well received by the German public (the blurb on the Steinberg-Verlag's edition in 1948 proclaimed that over 100,000 copies in the German language had already been sold), the critical reaction to the novel was like the postwar critical response to *The Sun Also Rises* in that critics hesitated to review a work that was so familiar to the average reader.

The early postwar German criticism of *A Farewell to Arms* was not nearly as sophisticated or penetrating as that of Robert Penn Warren's article entitled simply "Hemingway," which first appeared in *Kenyon Review* (Winter, 1947) and was translated in the *Amerikanische Rundschau* during the same year.[26] The majority of German critics agreed that it was Hemingway's best novel to date, but instead of discussing the theme, structure, point of view, or character development, they spoke in very general terms of a moving love story or a realistic account of war. The East German critic A. Zahn in his article "Der fünfzigjährige Hemingway" (*HM*, 1948), referred to the novel as Hemingway's most mature and greatest work and reserved special praise for the movingly tender love story ("rührendzarte Liebesgeschichte"). But Zahn's critical naiveté became evident in his claim that Hemingway's early short stories and the first two novels were still under the strong influence of O. Henry, the American master of the short story. Like the characters of O. Henry, Zahn pointed out, Hemingway's heroes are the average figures of everyday America—gangsters and hard-drinking, reckless, successful men of the capitalistic system, men whose forefathers were the hard, durable pioneers of the colonial times. Zahn recognized a new technique at work in *A Farewell to Arms*, but he was extremely vague in attempting to explain it: *A Farewell to Arms* is the first work in which he probes more deeply; he seeks an inner coherence beneath the surface of that which he describes.[27]

In *Wort und Wahrheit*, 1949, Paul Viator wrote that *A Farewell to Arms* ("a love story with death hanging over it") was a "Paradestück" for the lost generation of America, of which Hemingway was a representative. Desertion and mutiny, he added, are the last flight of individuals before the menace of a world which war has made senseless. Viator did mention the hidden lyricism, the banality of the dialogue, the strong sense of realism, but concluded that all of these reveal the aesthetic nihilist.[28] On the same superficial level of the two previous articles is Henry Lüdeke's commentary on *A Farewell to Arms* in his *Geschichte der amerikanischen*

Literatur, 1952. Although the novel, he stated, suffers from the lack of a sustaining ethic,

> The remarkably life-like descriptions of conditions in the Italian army, the circumstances surrounding the desertion of the hero, [and] the adventuresome flight of the lovers . . . are among the outstanding achievements of the new art.[29]

The East German Karl-Heinz Schönfelder (*ZAA*, 1959), praised the novel for its description of the "fervent love" of Frederic and Catherine, and for its presentation of war as immoral, senseless, and disillusioning. Schönfelder disagreed with the Russian critic I. Kaschkin, who claimed Hemingway presented organized death as a natural social phenomenon of the capitalistic system. According to Schönfelder, Hemingway does not attempt to probe the causes of war, but shows the effect of war on the bodies and minds of individuals. The desertion of Frederic Henry is not typical or representative, but is one individual's escape. Frederic and Catherine attempt to find in love the counterbalance to a self-destructive world, but with the death of Catherine and the baby, all their courage and bravery are shown to have been in vain. Hemingway, Schönfelder wrote, leaves nothing positive remaining: "All that is left is a conception of the meanness of life, a picture of a world order characterized by the 'dirty tricks' it employs."[30]

The German critic most strongly influenced by Robert Penn Warren's study was Helmut Papajewski, whose article "Die Frage nach der Sinnhaftigkeit bei Hemingway" appeared in *Anglia* in 1951. Following Warren, Papajewski pointed out that Hemingway's works do not present a broad picture of society ("Es mangelt ihnen an gesellschaftlicher Dichte.") and many of his characters are people outside society, e.g., boxers, bullfighters and criminals. Like Warren, Papajewski drew attention to the prominence of alcohol in Hemingway's fiction, but he discussed it from the existentialists' point of view. The enjoyment of alcohol, he wrote, is for Hemingway's characters a kind of "Daseinslegitimation":

> It takes away the fear and dread man has when he faces the meaninglessness of the outer world and the emptiness of the inner. . . . It is a remedy for the threatening, negative feelings that play such a significant role in Hemingway's philosophy of life.[31]

Through alcohol, suffering is made milder and the fear of death can thereby be overcome. Closely related to this, as Warren had also observed, is the relief one seeks in love and sex. According to Papajewski the sexual relations in Hemingway's works are described with complete openness and at times shocking cynicism, but it would be useless, he added, to attempt a moralistic judgment or condemnation of Hemingway for his position.[32]

Like many German critics Papajewski was interested in Hemingway's portrayal of women:

> The women in Hemingway's fiction are characterized by their almost exclusive subjection to impulse. Their range of interests is sharply limited; it seldom extends beyond sports, alcohol and sex. As the result of their impulsive natures they are uninhibited, and they speak about sexuality with astonishing frankness.

Often, Papajewski pointed out, Hemingway's women suffer from some disillusioning experience in love, and consequently they seek forgetfulness in sexual encounters. Eros no longer has idealistic qualities for them and they seek in a man primarily physical power and courage. To such a man they completely subordinate themselves and wish only to please him sexually and to admire his accomplishments.[33]

However the contacts between men and women in Hemingway's fiction are not always limited to the physical. According to Papajewski, Hemingway emphasizes the physical because sex, like alcohol, strengthens "das Lebensgefühl." Hemingway's characters thus seek concrete things to which they can give themselves wholly without the necessity of thinking; it is this which allows them to obscure consciousness of their existence. But in his most mature works, such as *A Farewell to Arms* and *For Whom the Bell Tolls*, Hemingway, Papajewski stated, arrives at the conclusion "that the momentary release which the sexual act offers is not enough to defend one against the awareness of nothingness." After the sexual act his characters feel all the more strongly the isolation and emptiness that they sought to escape. To counteract this despair Hemingway develops a kind of mystical union between the lovers in these two novels: "Hemingway also sees finally that existential fear can only be overcome through a strong bond with the 'you' which transcends sexual union." Seen from this point of view, Hemingway's devoted women who serve their men in slave-like fashion take on metaphysical proportions. Women like Catherine and Maria, who illustrate a strong devotion to the "you," show Frederic Henry and Robert Jordan the way out of their existential predicament: "The 'I' which was linked with the tormenting knowledge of finiteness becomes so far submerged in the 'you,' that the immediate threat of death no longer exists."[34]

Later commentaries by Herman Stresau, Leo Lania, Walter Schirmer and Wilhelm Grenzmann did not go beyond the surface of the novel. Stresau remarked that *A Farewell to Arms* had more variety than *The Sun Also Rises*, and pointed out that it depended less on dialogue and more on narration with symbolic overtones. The tender love story, he stated, is an almost unromantic version of the old theme of Tristan and Isolde, and "Nothing can be more moving than the conclusion."[35] Lania praised the Italian defeat at Caporetto as "one of the best and most thrilling battle scenes in world literature";[36] Schirmer pointed out the deliberate contrast between the realistic war events and the simultaneous love affair, and commended the tension Hemingway was able to create during the flight of the lovers.[37]

The most important aspect of the novel, according to Wilhelm Grenzmann, is the love between Frederic and Catherine which develops in the midst of the accurately described war misery. Like most German critics, Grenzmann was deeply touched by the love story and read no undertones of irony in the lover's dialogue, as a number of American critics have: "For the most part the novel is a perpetually refreshing lover's dialogue developed with great tenderness." Unlike the Americans Warren and Trilling,[38] who were sharply critical of Hemingway's female characters, Grenzmann approved of the way Hemingway has Catherine Barkley give herself to Frederic with "unselfish, blissful devotion."[39]

NOTES

[1] *Fiesta* was also the British title of the novel.

[2] Helmut Papajewski, "The Critical Reception of Hemingway's Works in Germany Since 1920," *The Literary Reputation of Hemingway in Europe*, ed. Roger Asselineau (New York, 1965), pp. 74–75.

3 Paul Wiegler, *Geschichte der fremdsprachigen Weltliteratur* (Munich, 1949), p. 462.

4 Adolf Volbracht, "Wiederbegegnung mit amerikanischer Prosa," *Aufbau* (Ost), IV (1948), 713.

5 Roland Wiegenstein, "Film und Hemingway," *Hier und Heute*, I (1951), 20.

6 Heinrich Lüdeke, *Geschichte der amerikanischen Literatur* (Bern, 1952), p. 514.

7 Broder Carstensen, "Evelyn Waugh und Ernest Hemingway," *ASNS*, CXC (1954), 119.

8 Dierlamm, p. 119.

9 Adalbert Schmidt, *Literaturgeschichte: Wege und Wandlungen moderner Dichtung* (Stuttgart, 1957), p. 392.

10 Wilhelm Grenzmann, *Weltdichtung der Gegenwart*, 3rd ed. rev. (Bonn, 1961), p. 422.

11 Stresau, *Ernest Hemingway*, pp. 44–46.

12 Lania, *Bildbiographie*, p. 46.

13 *Ibid.*, pp. 77–81.

14 Wellershoff, pp. 15–17.

15 *Ibid.*, p. 18.

16 *Ibid.*, pp. 20–22.

17 *Ibid.*, p. 28.

18 *Ibid.*, pp. 30–32.

19 *Ibid.*, p. 32.

20 *Ibid.*, pp. 32–35.

21 *Ibid.*, pp. 36–37.

22 Papajewski, "The Critical Reception," pp. 74–75.

23 Thomas Mann as quoted by Ballenger, p. 95.

24 Papajewski, "The Critical Reception," p. 76.

25 *Ibid.*, p. 77.

26 Robert Penn Warren, "Hemingway," *Kenyon Review*, IX (1947), 1–3.

27 A. Zahn, "Der fünfzigjährige Hemingway," *Heute und Morgen* (Ost), I (1948), 455.

28 Paul Viator, "Perspektive zu Hemingway," *Wort und Wahrheit*, (1949), 144–45.

29 Lüdeke, *Geschichte*, p. 515.

30 Karl-Heinz Schönfelder, *ZAA* (Ost), VII (1959), 216–18.

31 Helmut Papajewski, "Die Frage nach der Sinnhaftigkeit bei Hemingway," *Anglia*, LXX (1951), 191–92.

32 *Ibid.*, p. 192.

33 *Ibid.*, pp. 192–93.

34 *Ibid.*, p. 194.

35 Stresau, *Ernest Hemingway*, pp. 49–52.

36 Lania, *Bildbiographie*, pp. 84–85.

37 Schirmer, p. 789.

38 Lionel Trilling, "Ein Amerikaner in Spanien," *Der Monat*, I, No. 5 (1949), 90–93.

39 Grenzmann, pp. 423–24.

Before the National Socialists came to power in Germany, all of
the translations of Hemingway's works into German were done
by Annemarie Horschitz for the Rowohlt Verlag. When Miss
Horschitz received an "Übersetzungsverbot" from the Nazi "Reich-
skulturkammer" and was forced to leave the country in 1933,
Hemingway refused to allow his books to appear in German. In
1941, however, the Bermann-Fischer Verlag in Stockholm was
granted permission by Hemingway to translate and publish *For
Whom the Bell Tolls*. Thinking Annemarie Horschitz had been
a war casualty, the Bermann-Fischer publishers appointed Paul
Baudisch to do the German translation, *Wem die Stunde schlägt.*[1]

According to Papajewski, one of the primary reasons for the
early publication of *For Whom the Bell Tolls* in Germany following World War II was to encourage political re-education.[2] This
may in part explain why so many of the first postwar critics of the
novel in Western Germany chose to emphasize Hemingway's objectivity in dealing with a complex political situation. The critic
R. H. stated in *Gegenwart*, 1949, that unlike the other novelists of
the Spanish Civil War (e.g., André Malraux, *L'Espoir*), Hemingway spent three years writing his novel in order to produce a
"truthful book":

> He gathered facts, listened carefully, and paid close attention
> to everything. He was able to distinguish between appear-
> ance and reality, and he learned that the truth is much more
> gratifying than all lies and legends.[3]

For Whom was valuable to German readers, R. H. claimed, both
for what it offered as a literary experience, and for what it added
to the German political or historical consciousness. The novel
itself is not propagandistic, for the characters are not embodiments
of political ideas, but individuals acting out their own fates. Yet
Hemingway is able to present the division of the world, a division
which forces each individual to make a definite choice, to declare
yes or no. With obvious reference to the German conscience, R. H.
added, "Jordan-Hemingway is neither a non-party member nor a

non-participant who can retreat from his conscience by pleading neutrality and claiming that it was duty, command, or instruction which forced him to act." It is possible to believe that Jordan's blowing of the bridge could be a turning point for humanity, R. H. concluded hopefully, for it happened in the moment Jordan decided to act, not for one party or the other, but for the new world to which man had directed himself: "It is the decision of our time, in which the bell tolls for each of us."[4]

Similar praise for Hemingway's objectivity in treating the political implications of *For Whom* came from critics, such as Bernt von Heiseler, G. Wolf, and Gerhard Lepiorz. According to Heiseler (*Zeitwende*, 1949–1950), readers of *For Whom*, even though they may not care for Hemingway, must admire his "astoundingly powerful description of characters and setting, of war and destiny . . . and also his determination to see things correctly." Fortunately, he added, Hemingway had keen insight into the political affairs of Spain and could write of them objectively: "Hemingway fought [in the civil war] as a party member, but he has not written propaganda; that fact has added the most to his credit."[5] According to Wolf (*SZ*, 1950), the reader sees in the novel the bad side of both opposing forces, and is exposed to desperadoes, murderers and gypsies as well as heroes. Hemingway, he added, describes events in a journalistic style "with the objectivity of a film camera": "There are facts . . . not interpretations."[6] Lepiorz (*NZ*, 1950), echoed Wolf's praise for Hemingway as an artist who stands above politics; not only does he portray brutality objectively, stated Lepiorz, but he also allows warm, human feelings to break through on both sides.[7]

In marked disagreement with the preceding reactions to *For Whom* were East German critics, who as a rule adhered closely to Marxist principles. Critics like A. Zahn, Wolfgang Joho, and Eberhard Brüning generally had praise for Hemingway's writing talents, but unlike West Germans they were often critical of Hemingway's attempted political objectivity.

The mildest of the reviews came from A. Zahn (*HM*, 1948), who stressed what he felt were favorable political implications in the novel. Zahn claimed that although Hemingway was encouraged by Franco supporters in America to align himself with fascism, he remained true to his objective social criticism: "Today Hemingway is among the most respected of the American writers who have placed themselves on the side of progress, against neo-fascism."[8]

In the East German journal *Ost und West*, 1949, Wolfgang Joho praised the German translation of *For Whom* and referred to the novel itself as one of the most noteworthy of recent books. Joho admitted that the fictional characters were brilliantly and fittingly drawn and that Hemingway understood how to present realistic situations and landscapes. "To dispute Hemingway's reputation as a superior writer and artist," he added, "would be ridiculous." However the primary concern of the reader and critic, claimed Joho, should be to examine what Hemingway as a writer brought from his experience as an actual participant in the Spanish Civil War. For the hero of this novel, unlike other Hemingway heroes, is not a member of a fringe group outside society, but is a representative of society itself. And unlike so many novels of Hemingway's colleagues, this novel does not deal with murder, sex, boredom, and alcohol, but with the cardinal questions of our time. Unfortunately, Joho pointed out, Hemingway's answer is "Jein," with a commitment to neither side. For Jordan, although he participates on the side of the communists, remains aloof from complete commitment to their cause, and Hemingway gives him a variety of other motives for fighting in addition to political ones. Paradoxically, Joho claimed, Hemingway thus gave additional propaganda material to the fascists.[9]

Another paradox Joho pointed out was that Hemingway, who in this novel appeared to demonstrate a new sense of political responsibility, was in reality the old Hemingway who looked upon the war as he would watch a bullfight—a spectator enjoying a spectacle, refusing to take sides. It is this lack of commitment that Joho found disturbing and even dangerous. For to the mass of less critical readers the novel appears to present some vague, yet objective "third power" which either aligns itself with fascists or anti-fascists. This is typical, Joho claimed, of the writers of the "lost generation" (Faulkner, Steinbeck, and Dos Passos are included) who cover up their fear of boredom, rootlessness, and lostness with powerful language, eminent literary skill, and fictional characters posing as free, independent pioneers. In *For Whom* Hemingway, he concluded, turned back to the "isolation of weary non-commitment."[10]

A third East German critic, Professor Eberhard Brüning of

Karl-Marx University in Leipzig, wrote in *ZAA*, 1963, that Hemingway was more qualified to write a novel about the Spanish Civil War than any other writer, for his personal contacts with the Spanish people, their land and culture, reached back to the 1920's, and already he had written about them in *In Our Time*, *The Sun Also Rises*, and *Death in the Afternoon*. Brüning expressed the typical East German attitude towards Hemingway's early heroes ("the uprooted, lean, intellectual and ironic 'he-man' with his liking for strong drinks and sexual debaucheries"), and in discussing *For Whom* his strongest criticism was directed at Jordan's uninvolvement. According to Brüning, Jordan leads an estranged, isolated life, sees no class struggle at stake, and fails to understand the real reasons why the Spanish people are at war. Brüning assumed the hero was based upon the American volunteers of the International Brigade, and therefore claimed Hemingway's presentation of him as an unpolitical soldier fighting on the Loyalist side was an obvious distortion and a misinterpretation. Not only did Hemingway fail to make Jordan convincing enough, but in trying to be objective (e.g., the account of the brutal punishment handed out by Pablo and the villagers), he did not do justice to his own personal attitude. At the same time, he provided propaganda for the enemies of the Loyalist cause. The only positive effect of *For Whom*, Brüning concluded, may have occurred when Fidel Castro and his troops took the novel into the mountains to learn about modern civil war.[11]

Aside from the political controversy *For Whom* aroused in Germany, West German critics were most impressed by the sense of realism they found in Hemingway's latest novel. Alfred Günther, writing in *WS*, 1946, expressed his admiration for the clarity, objectivity, simplicity and sparseness of Hemingway's style. Hemingway excels, he stated, in describing violence, such as an airplane or cavalry attack, and in creating dialogue which expresses the necessary information precisely and at the same time reveals the essential nature of the speaker, the immediate atmosphere, the growing suspense, and details of the senses.[12]

According to Gerhard Lepiorz (*NZ*, 1950), *For Whom*, more than any other novel based on the Spanish Civil War, probes deeply into the relations of the Spanish people. Most remarkable, stated Lepiorz, is Hemingway's authenticity in developing Spanish characters, such as Pablo, Pilar, and Anselmo and in creating "many brilliantly described scenes," e.g., the destruction of El Sordo's men and the slaughter of the fascists. Like Günter, Lepiorz pointed to the realism Hemingway strives for in his reproduction of dialogue by the use of (1) Spanish words and idioms; (2) literal translations of Spanish expressions into English; (3) philological explanations; and (4) Spanish obscenities in the dialogue of the bandits. Although the result may seem forced in English, Lepiorz claimed that to one who knows Spanish, the dialogue of *For Whom* is "uncommonly lively and realistic." The entire book "reads like a factual report; it is one of the most authentic novels on the civil war in Spain." [13]

In reviewing *For Whom* in his book *Der unbehauste Mensch: Motive und Probleme der modernen Literatur*, 1952, Hans Holthusen also pointed out that Hemingway was driven by a desire for the truth and a passion for the real:

> His aggressive, electrifying prose and the artistic integrity manifest in all his characters, events and situations . . . fill a metaphysical vacuum. The question of meaning is answered by the concrete reality he provides. [14]

Freely evoking the legendary figure of Hemingway, Holthusen explained that this massive man with whiskey glass and popular full beard was a leader in the American writers' revolt against a Puritan heritage. Although Hemingway might not offer solutions to man's predicament, "this 'down to facts,'" according to Holthusen, "is more convincing and more satisfying than the wary, nihilistic rationalism which one finds in the writings of certain modern Frenchmen." Holthusen received the impression from this novel and other recent American fiction that what man loses in the higher regions of his being, or in freedom, he has gained on the lower level of primitive feelings and outer senses. [15] Hermann Stresau and Leo Lania, both authors of short books on Hemingway in 1958 and 1960, respectively, agreed that what assured *For Whom* its place among the great works of literature was its concrete portrayal "of the subsidiary characters, the local colour, the bloody fighting at the front and the intrigues in the background." [16]

Another facet of Hemingway's realism in *For Whom* was explored by Willy Feyerabend in his book *Die Erotik im ameri-*

kanischen Roman, 1959. Feyerabend introduced his study, which was inspired by the Kinsey Report, with an explanation of the European fascination for American fiction:

> An explanation for the significance of the North American novel can be found in its terrifying, and at times shocking, concreteness. There is no place left for the human imagination to seek an escape from the horrors of reality. The smallest commonplace details are described with almost malicious regularity.[17]

According to Feyerabend, Hemingway (whom he refers to as one of the greatest "Kuszschriftsteller") excels in his realistic descriptions of the intimate physical contacts among his characters. In *For Whom,* he contended, eroticism "celebrates its real triumph." Especially impressive to Feyerabend was the scene in which Jordan teaches Maria how to kiss. The difference in the previous sexual experience of the two, he explained, makes the scene "especially tense" and contributes to the "urgent eroticism": "There is hardly a more moving description of kissing in all of fiction."[18] Feyerabend was also fascinated by the way in which Hemingway allows his female characters to speak openly of sex, especially in the case of Maria in the sleeping bag scene:

> The realism in this description of love making is without boundaries. Even the physical pains and their causes, those which almost prevent the tender Maria from becoming the lover of the North American volunteer, . . . are described.[19]

Hemingway's description of sexual intercourse, Feyerabend concluded, is characterized by a healthy sense of freedom and realism, which at the same time does not neglect spiritual overtones. It is this comprehensiveness which Feyerabend felt made Hemingway and his fellow American novelists masters of realistic eroticism: "One can say in good conscience that the fiction of other nations can hardly boast of similar achievements in this area."[20]

A more subtle kind of realism in *For Whom* was pointed out by Franz Schulz in his study of Hemingway's treatment of Indians. In this novel, according to Schulz, Indians are used to develop the secondary characters and to illuminate the mind of the hero Robert Jordan. El Sordo, he explained, has "a thin-bridged nose like an Indian"; Fernando looks like a "cigar store Indian," and Pilar has a "heavy brown face with the high Indian cheekbones." Hemingway has Robert Jordan use his remembrance of earlier contacts with Indians as a psychological means to overcome unpleasant impressions and fearful anxiety: (1) Pilar's description of the death smell he counteracts with the recollection of the scent of sweet grass Indians used for their baskets; (2) through the remembrance of his grandfather's Indian wars he is able to come to terms with the cruelty of the fascist troops who behead El Sordo's followers.[21]

Contrary to Lionel Trilling's review (first published in the *Partisan Review* in 1941 and later translated in *Der Monat* in 1949), which focuses on Hemingway's inadequacies in treating death, love, and war on a tragic scale in *For Whom*,[22] many German critics considered Hemingway's most recent novel to be a significant advancement over his previous fictional works. According to Alfred Günther (*WS*, 1946), the earlier Hemingway appeared as a man who did not expect much from life, who built up a defense not only against all big words, but also against strong feelings. However *For Whom*, Günther pointed out, is filled with a new respect for life, death, love and the sensations of the immediate present (a deepening of the "Lebensbewusstsein"). From the disillusionment and indifference of earlier characters we move to the manly decisiveness of Robert Jordan. Jordan's statement, "The world is a fine place and worth the fighting for," was understood by Günther to be a manifestation of Hemingway's own attitude. This awareness, he claimed, permeates the novel and turns all guilt, need, and doubt to something positive: "Out of the negation which was once in Hemingway's works has come the proud, bold Yes."[23]

According to Helmut Papajewski (*Anglia*, 1951), Hemingway stresses "causes," "values," and "moral obligations" for the first time in *For Whom*. In this novel, Papajewski claimed, "Hemingway discovered a purpose, a meaning; either that or history provided him with one." As Günther had done, Papajewski linked Hemingway himself with Jordan's expression of devotion to the revolutionary cause: "It gave you a part in something you could believe in wholly and completely and in which you felt an absolute brotherhood with the others who were engaged in it." This was seen as a major turning point for Hemingway, a move from isolation to the feeling of brotherhood.[24]

Henry Lüdeke wrote in his *Geschichte der amerikanischen Literatur*, 1952, that *For Whom* marked the high point of Hemingway's art. For by providing his hero with a sense of ethical behavior ("the simple ethic of human solidarity in his love for the republican girl"), he had finally overcome his earlier amorality.[25] Hermann Pongs (*Im Umbruch der Zeit*, 1956) also pointed to a new sense of vitality and optimism in *For Whom*, which he referred to as "an adventure novel characterized by the boundless energy and light-heartedness of America." Although Robert Jordan gives vent to nihilistic expressions, it is the typically American nihilism which explores all possibilities and ambivalences. More than this, Pongs added, the novel expresses an unconquerable optimism filled with "Lebenskraft." The greatness of the subject matter Pongs found not in the adventures of the hero, but in the bravery, the expression of noble sentiments, and in the feeling of togetherness that those struggling for the same political ideology have.[26]

Similarly Karl Heinrich Frahne (*Von Franklin bis Hemingway*, 1949), Hermann Stresau (*Hemingway*, 1958), and the Swiss critic Heinrich Straumann (*American Literature in the Twentieth Century*, 1965) agreed that *For Whom* was a general development of the new value of brotherhood Hemingway expressed through Harry Morgan in *To Have and Have Not*.[27] Straumann concluded that Jordan was the typical Hemingway hero, but in *For Whom* there emerged "a new balance between the meaning of the hero's death and the hope attached to his deed. Though the nature of the deed is still of the old order, namely one of destruction, it is born of a belief in the claims of duty and solidarity and done for a definite cause."[28]

One of the few dissenting opinions was expressed by Günter Blöcker in *Der Monat*, 1952. Blöcker accused critics of finding changes or developments in Hemingway's work which were not really there. In the case of *For Whom*, he stated, critics focused on Robert Jordan's last monologue and claimed that this showed Hemingway taking a step back from earlier nihilism. However in their eagerness to find weak points in Hemingway's position, wrote Blöcker, critics overlooked how little Robert Jordan actually differed from earlier Hemingway heroes who seek adventure for adventure's sake, or simply for diversion, not for some ethical purpose. And above all, according to Blöcker, these critics overlooked the fact that Hemingway had no need to change—that no matter how muffled they were, his humanistic concerns were always present in his fiction.[29]

Another group of German critics emphasized signs of spiritual elevation which they felt contributed to the new affirmation in *For Whom*. An example of criticism with a religious bias is an article in the *Frankfurter Hefte*, 1947, by Ida Görres, who compared Ernst Wiechert's *Die Jerominkinder* with Hemingway's *For Whom*. Wiechert's book, Görres stated, was written to justify his own rebellion against Christianity. Although the humanistic values it propounds are worthwhile, the book itself is dangerous because young readers lack the experience and knowledge necessary to contradict him, to recognize that the world he creates contains many reflections of a single mind, that all the characters are simply variations of Ernst Wiechert himself. Görres's major concern was that young readers brought up in the Third Reich, outside the church, would not be able to see through Wiechert's antagonism, to recognize that at the basis of his ethical message was a pure Christian inheritance. Unlike Wiechert, Hemingway, she felt, had no axe to grind; in *For Whom* savagery, horror, and cruelty are revealed on both sides: "The narrative is brutal and plain, shockingly exact, colorful and vital; it is no book for delicate readers."[30]

Although neither Robert Jordan nor the members of the guerrilla band are orthodox Christians, the novel, Görres claimed, illustrates the majesty of God and the dignity of man. It is in the critical situations during which the reality of war becomes most terrifying that Hemingway reveals the spiritual side of Jordan's rough band of followers. In support of her thesis Görres pointed to Anselmo, who thinks of praying before blowing up the bridge; Jacinto, who prays before bombing, and on the other side Lt. Berrendo, who performs a mercy killing, decapitates the dead, but then prays for them. In Wiechert's book faith and piety appear only when life is smooth flowing; during any tumult religious intentions soon fade. However in *For Whom* Görres found just the opposite taking place:

> When the masks of man are lifted, signs of Christianity emerge—the real man "miraculously created and more miraculously redeemed" in the midst of guilt, delusion, and

error; the christened man, who from generation to generation is influenced by Christianity whether he wants to be
or not.[31]

For Whom, according to Görres, has something in common with
the Bible, for it "bears witness to the creation, which in all its
variations carries the mark of the creator and especially that of the
redeemer." Stylistically the novel provided Görres and her fellow
religiously-oriented critics with the combination of the realistic
and the transcendent that they looked for, especially in the early
postwar years.[32]

G. Wolf (SZ, 1950) and Martha Glaser (Zeitwende, 1951–1952)
also focused on the religious strains in For Whom. Glaser pointed
to the religious sincerity of Maria and Anselmo;[33] Wolf in his review took issue with those critics who labeled Hemingway a pessimistic writer of the hopeless. Although Robert Jordan apparently
dies in vain, the respectability and purity among his followers
lives on. Citing the prayers of Anselmo and Jacinto, Wolf concluded, "If one still prays while hanging over an abyss, there is
always hope."[34]

Similarly Wilhelm Grenzmann in his book Weltdichtung der
Gegenwart, 1961, stated that Hemingway was concerned with the
total predicament of man in For Whom, rather than with the
causes of the Spanish Civil War. The microcosm he creates allows
him to concentrate on man's struggle for survival and search for
meaning in life. The first answer Hemingway supplies, according
to Grenzmann, comes from the voice of humanity which each man
has within himself. But as we see in the inhuman cruelty on both
sides during the Spanish Civil War, the voice is often heeded too
late. The second answer is love with its healing, conciliatory powers. In the love story of For Whom, Grenzmann pointed out that
the hard, realistic dialogue takes on a softness in tone, and Robert
and Maria are able to build a new existence in the middle of destruction. But also there is the shadow of mortality, which Robert
knows better than Maria: "human love does not lead one beyond
the finite world." The limiting of the love affair to a few days and
nights is, Grenzmann contended, a symbol for the time limitation
of love itself. The third and most encouraging answer is in the
call of the divine which stems from "the hearts of the tormented."

It is a faint voice (recollections of early teachings or a former faith), but this is enough to indicate that the novel did not grow out of a nihilistic attitude, but out of an attitude that was "half agnostic, half Christian."[35]

Another group of critics such as Curt Hohoff, Inge Meidinger-Geise, Alfred Günter, and Hans Holthusen found traces of the religious or the transcendent in the love story Hemingway develops between Robert and Maria. In the Catholic journal *Hochland,* 1949, Hohoff wrote that *For Whom,* like many contemporary novels, was "poorly constructed." There is no reason for the switch in setting from the battle front to the hotel in Madrid or for the death of the hero at the end. The religious background of the war is not integrated into the novel, Hohoff added, although Hemingway did describe skillfully "the death of Christian martyrs in the Catholic cause." However with the love scenes, Hohoff claimed that "new tones" emerge in the novel and a natural theology develops, which is a conscious break from the Puritan traditions and conventions of America. Although the hero has long since given up the "rigid doctrinairism of ideology," as Hemingway himself had, the sleeping bag conversations, according to Hohoff, are based on levels of existence which open the way to true transcendence.[36]

Similarly Alfred Günther stated in his review of *For Whom* in 1946 that the love story of Robert and Maria "radiates its miracle over all the dangers that continually threaten them, including the danger of death."[37] Inge Meidinger-Geise wrote enthusiastically of the new sense of harmony Hemingway achieved in his depiction of the lovers: "The saving redemption of the I and you, the passion of the union, moves continuously in the lovers' dialogue . . . towards a silent merging into oneness."[38] Hans Holthusen pointed out that Hemingway's conception of love in *For Whom* is permeated by an elementary "Seelenkraft" that adds depth and fullness to his view of the world.[39] According to Hermann Stresau it is the love story that gives charm and meaning to the novel and allows the hero to affirm life.[40] Only Wolfgang von Einsiedel (*Merkur,* 1950)[41] and Leo Lania (*Bildbiographie,* 1960),[42] both of whom were strongly influenced by American criticism, agreed with Trilling's appraisal of the love affair as dull and conventional.

A group of German critics who adopted the existential terminology of Jaspers and Heidegger also found added significance in

Hemingway's description of love. According to G. Prause (*Welt und Wort*, 1951), Hemingway places his characters in the middle of a world which has deprived them of their belief in traditional values. Although in moments of danger or isolation characters may have vague ideas of God, there is no lasting consolation: "the events in Hemingway's fiction remain entirely meaningless. Man appears lost, alone and powerless." Yet, Prause pointed out, Hemingway provides a means by which his characters can affirm life. Robert Jordan says that loving Maria has made his life as beautiful as it could be, and shortly before his death he admits: "The world is a fine place and worth the fighting for and I hate very much to leave it." Love, according to Prause, does not prevent death from haphazardly killing the good and the courageous, but it prevents existence from being totally meaningless.[43]

Hemingway also provides "the assertion of stoic conduct" ("die Behauptung der inneren Haltung"), with which his characters can defy the destructive meaninglessness of existence. Robert Jordan refuses to commit suicide when confronted with certain death; Anselmo holds on to his distaste for killing although it costs him his life. The best example of "stoic conduct" is that of Pedro Romero in *The Sun Also Rises*, who by his courage and flawless form in the bullring "is a contrast to the entire 'lost generation.'" Prause, like other critics relying on existentialists' terminology, explained that it is only in critical situations that men are able to prove their "Haltung," and therefore Hemingway often writes of war, bullfighting, and big game hunting. Stoic conduct and the power of love "build in Hemingway's fiction the only basis upon which men can live with one another in spite of the meaninglessness of the world around them. They [stoic conduct and the power of love] free man inwardly from the continual threat of nothingness."[44]

Helmut Papajewski also pointed out the role of love in overcoming "Existenzangst." Hemingway, he wrote, sees love as a gift of grace that destiny bestows, one which man should receive with humility. In *For Whom* it is linked with "a religious feeling" and acts as a changing force in the lives of Pilar, Maria, and Robert Jordan: "Robert Jordan's love for Maria changes his entire outlook, and enables him to see the value in other forms of association as well."[45] According to Hans Holthusen (*Der Unbehauste*

Mensch, 1952), the sudden love affair in *For Whom* belongs to the typical borderline situation ("Grenzsituation") in Hemingway's fiction:

> in a language reminiscent of religious ecstasy, Hemingway describes the predicament of man in the characteristic borderline situation of the century: between absolute nothingness and the immediate "now" of physical love. . . . It is man at the zero point of being; it is the absolute "now" of existence becoming conscious of itself.[46]

Adalbert Schmidt (*Literaturgeschichte*, 1957), like the previous critics, explained the significance of the "tender love idyl" in *For Whom* in existential terms. The theme of the novel, he argued, lies not in politics, but "it deals with the finiteness of existence and the probing questions of life's meaning." The way out of the existential predicament is through the love of one human being for another: "In the borderline situation of extreme danger, in the face of death, one's awareness of life is intensified; in the joy of love it reaches a high point."[47]

German critics were also fascinated by the way in which Hemingway's characters respond to death. Very few agreed with Lionel Trilling, who claimed that Hemingway's treatment of death was indirect, thwarted, and sentimental. According to Walter Schirmer, the ending of *For Whom* is "a gripping conclusion" in which the wounded hero sacrifices himself without bitterness and bravely faces his own certain death.[48] Death, claimed Hermann Stresau, permeates the novel and at the same time serves as an educator. Jordan's statement—"If we win here, we will win everywhere"—he pointed out, relates to death as well as to the Spanish revolution.[49] Engelbert Kirchner (*FH*, 1951) stated in his article on death in Hemingway's fiction, that it is his characters' intimate association with death that distinguishes them. Because Hemingway makes death a part of life in *For Whom*, Kirchner added, he can, like the Greek tragedians, omit describing the actual act of death; the waiting for death is "the decisive moment," the moment of truth.[50]

A slightly different opinion of Hemingway's treatment of death was offered by Eberhard Lämmert in *Bauformen des Erzählens*,

1955. In the ending of *For Whom*, he pointed out, Hemingway does not describe the actual moment of Robert Jordan's death, not because it is the waiting for death that is decisive, as Kirchner claimed, but because what actually will happen has already been made clear by what has gone before. The tone of the last scene (Jordan's separation from Maria and his own private reflections) forecasts the end, and even more important, according to Lämmert, is the statement in Chapter Thirteen, which is placed significantly between the central love encounter of Robert and Maria and the prophecy of Pilar: "I suppose it is possible to live as full a life in seventy hours as in seventy years." By the time of the ending, these seventy hours have run their course and there is no need for further description: "With this forewarning comes the perception of a fitting . . . conclusion—the tolling of a bell, not louder than the heart beat which it stops."[51]

Helmut Papajewski examined the subject of death from an existentialist's point of view. Hemingway is more concerned with violent death and thus with direct fear than are Kierkegaard and the "Existenzphilosophen," stated Papajewski, but nevertheless the uncertain type of fear of the existentialists appears in his fiction. At night Hemingway's characters see their lives in a different perspective, and they become especially aware of their loneliness and feeling of abandonment. Papajewski noted a preference for electric lights and fear of the "Urdunkel" in both Hemingway and Thomas Wolfe: "The artificial light is intended to protect them from the unknown, [and] from their own neurotic demons. . . . They are afraid of the dark, the unknown, of unprotected sleep and fearful dreams." Occasionally Hemingway's characters are overcome with feelings of hopelessness and meaninglessness even during the brightness of daytime. They find themselves in a position of "Geworfenseins," not exactly in the sense of Heidegger and other existentialists, according to Papajewski, but related to it.[52]

Yet Hemingway's characters, in spite of their feelings of alienation and guilt, do not commit suicide. According to Papajewski, this is because they love life, and with most of them their excesses are only part of a pose. As Jake explained in *The Sun Also Rises,* "I paid my way into enough things that I liked, so that I had a good time. Either you paid by learning about them, or by experience, or by taking chances, or by money. Enjoying living was learning to get your money's worth and knowing when you had it." A private scale of values, claimed Papajewski, is what provides Hemingway's characters with stability. At the same time the role of determinism encourages them not to take themselves too seriously, and Hemingway continually emphasizes individual courage in facing whatever fate subjects them to. Unlike many critics, Papajewski concluded that Robert Jordan's outcome was consistent with his character and occupation and could not be read as Hemingway's pronouncement on suicide.[53]

The most thorough study of Hemingway's treatment of death was that by Rudolf Haas, "Zum Todesmotiv im Werk Hemingways," which appeared in *NS*, 1959. Haas's study is penetrating and objective, taking both American and German Hemingway criticism into account, relating Hemingway to his American and European contemporaries, and separating the traditional from the original in Hemingway's fiction. According to Haas, Philip Young,[54] although he makes the chapter "Death and Transfiguration" a central part of his book, does not do justice to the title. Carlos Baker[55] is vague in his judgment and evaluation of the theme of death, and the thesis of M. F. Moloney[56] (concerning death in "The Snows of Kilimanjaro") is, stated Haas, a bold misjudgment. With obvious reference to the above critics, Haas added,

> If one surveys the many individual essays dealing with the problem of death in Hemingway's works, one discovers that attractive titles are not enough to answer the necessary questions.[57]

Other difficulties in Hemingway criticism, Haas pointed out, stem from (1) the legend of the author himself; (2) the fixed, conventional viewpoint critics have established, involving the use of favorite phrases, such as "lost generation," "violence and discipline," "valor and defeat," and "Hemingway's code." Too often, Haas claimed, critics deal with the function of death in the works of Hemingway, rather than the manner in which he presents it. Death is thus regarded as a test situation for the characters and not as a theme of the writer. Critics hesitate to make comparative studies of death, and seldom employ the proven methods of philology in their analyses.[58]

Haas first turned his attention to Hemingway's own contact with death which came as a boy when he accompanied his father on emergency medical calls. The unsympathetic attitude he formulated towards death became obvious in his early fiction: "For a long time Hemingway . . . remains fascinated by the clinical; therein lies his uniqueness and his limitation." Later Hemingway's wounds and near death in 1918 affected both the style and content of his writing: "From this time onward Hemingway stays incessantly on death's trail, driven by an urgent need to exorcise his own traumatic experience." Because death became a fixation for him, he was unable to achieve the breadth and totality of works such as *War and Peace* and *The Charterhouse of Parma*. Hemingway's third personal connection with death stems from his "kultisch-aesthetischens" interest in the phenomenon of death and the moment of its occurrence. This accounts for his fascination with the bullfight. Whereas Byron depicted it as an "ungentle sport," and Rilke observed it for its metaphorical possibilities, Hemingway saw the moment of giving and receiving death as "the highest self-realization of mortal life."[59]

Haas next turned to Hemingway's conception of writing, which influenced his treatment of death. Hemingway's "klinischer Realismus," which encourages him to describe death with scientific precision as in "A Natural History of the Dead," is effective, according to Haas, but at the same time has definite limitations. It discourages the use of metaphor which may add to the intensity of a description, and it deprives the writer of a sympathetic reaction towards the victims, such as Defoe expressed in his *Journal of the Plague Year*. However, the point at which Haas felt that clinical realism was particularly appropriate was in revealing the minds of characters just before their deaths. In his death scenes, Haas wrote, "the author [Hemingway] creates the most significant prototypes in world literature."[60]

To illustrate his claim, Haas chose Robert Jordan's monologue at the end of *For Whom*. Hemingway, Haas contended, succeeds artistically at this point by allowing Jordan's mind to follow a pattern of simple associations on the surface, and by interspersing these with strongly emphasized utterances from Jordan's subconscious:

> The conscious mind is involved in a final argument with the unconscious, and in this dialogue Hemingway is able to make the barely expressible, comprehensible—perhaps not so much with words as with the pauses between the two levels of [Jordan's] mind. Dialogue, which Hemingway prefers to employ in all of his works because it is the form of speech most true to life, proves itself in this case as an excellent means for the dramatization of death.

It is in this scene that Hemingway displays original talent; according to Haas, Robert Jordan's dying moments compare favorably with Chekov's handling of death in *Goussiev* and Tolstoy's description of death in the trenches at Sevastopol.[61]

In his use of symbols in death scenes Hemingway, Haas stated, comes closest to the traditional portrayal of death. Although there are no direct personifications of death in Hemingway's work, such as are found in Thomas Mann's "Death in Venice," there are figures on intimate terms with death, like Pilar, the bullfighters, and Santiago, the fisherman. Hemingway's fiction is also rich in symbols which accompany death or forecast it. And although Hemingway with his clinical realism was attempting to take death out of its mythical framework, his symbols, according to Haas, have led to a new mythologizing of death, e.g., (1) in "The Snows of Kilimanjaro" the "boat of death" is represented by an airplane and Compton is Charon; (2) in *Across the River and Into the Trees* the gondola carries Richard Cantwell over the river Lethe; (3) in *For Whom* Hemingway approaches the traditional dance of death motif in Pilar's story of the murder of the fascists in the small Spanish town. Pablo plays the role of Death himself, as he forces the men to run the gauntlet between armed farmers, who resemble the "laboreurs" in the late medieval French "danses Macabres"; (4) in numerous other works rain becomes an accompanying symbol of death and catastrophe. These of course are not new with Hemingway, but the technique of incorporating death symbols into a realistic landscape is, according to Haas, Hemingway's own discovery.[62]

Hemingway's preoccupation with death, Haas maintained, accounted for both his intensity and his narrowness. Even among Hemingway's lovers there is a longing and ripeness for death in the Elizabethan sense. For this reason, Haas concluded that "Hemingway, in spite of his emphasis on vitality and the increased intensity of life in the face of death, is not a writer of love, but a writer of death." And the assertion that Hemingway's work is more of a succession of scenes on the theme "Los Desastres de la Muerte" rather than a capturing of the passing time in great epic breadth, is perhaps true.[63]

For Whom the Bell Tolls (publication date 1940) was naturally more immediate to German postwar critics than either *The Sun Also Rises* or *A Farewell to Arms*; consequently their reaction depended less upon secondary criticism, either from pre-war Germany or the United States. Their reaction was overwhelmingly favorable and in marked contrast to the translated American criticism represented by Lionel Trilling and Robert Penn Warren. Reflecting the effects of political turmoil in their own country, they praised Hemingway for his objectivity in handling the political complexities in the background of the Spanish Civil War. They were particularly impressed by the powerful sense of realism they found in his depiction of the violent struggle of the Spanish people and in his tender love story of Robert and Maria. Contrary to Trilling, who contended that Robert Jordan was dull and inarticulate, Germans, as a rule, praised what they felt was a new feeling of affirmation in the Hemingway hero, a sense of brotherhood and a willingness to sacrifice for others.

Another distinctive characteristic of the German reaction is the search for the spiritual or the transcendent in Hemingway's writing. A number of critics were quick to point out the awareness of the Catholic faith among Hemingway's secondary characters; others focused on the metaphysical implications of love and death in the novel. The love story of Robert and Maria, highly praised by the majority of critics, was seen by some as mystically elevating, and by others as a solution to man's existential predicament. As they had done in reviewing *The Sun Also Rises* and *A Farewell to Arms*, a number of critics freely employed existentialists' terminology in assessing Hemingway's treatment of love, death, and war. A new sense of objectivity is evident in the article by Rudolph Haas, 1959. Attention is shifted from the abstract and philosophical to a detailed examination of specific passages from the novel. Hemingway's use of symbols is concretely analyzed, as is his portrayal of human consciousness at the moment preceding death.

NOTES

1 Hans-Günter Mucharowski, *Die Werke von Ernest Hemingway: Eine Bibliographie der deutschsprachigen Hemingway-Literatur und der Originalwerke. Von 1923 bis 1954* (Hamburg, 1955), p. 10.

2 Papajewski, "The Critical Reception, . . ." p. 84.

3 R. H., "Bücher von Heute," *Gegenwart*, IV, No. 8 (1949), 20.

4 *Ibid.*, p. 21.

5 Bernt von Heiseler, "Erzähler des Auslands," *Zeitwende*, XXI (1949–50), 51–52.

6 G. Wolf, *SZ*, CXLVI (1950), 315–16.

7 Gerhard Lepiorz, "Ernest Hemingway: *For Whom the Bell Tolls*," *NZ*, II (1950), 383–84.

8 Zahn, p. 456.

9 Wolfgang Joho, "Ernest Hemingway und der spanische Krieg," *Ost und West* (Ost), III (September, 1949), 91–92.

10 *Ibid.*, pp. 93–95.

11 Eberhard Brüning, "The Spanish Civil War (1936–1939) and the American Novel," *ZAA*, XI–XII (1963), 43–47.

12 Alfred Günther, *WS*, XVII (1946), 43.

13 Lepiorz, pp. 483–85.

14 Holthusen, *Der unbehauste Mensch*, p. 23.

15 *Ibid.*, pp. 23–25.

16 The quotation is from Lania, *Bildbiographie*, p. 106; see also Stresau, *Ernest Hemingway*, pp. 67–70.

17 Willy Feyerabend, *Die Erotik im amerikanischen Roman* (Stuttgart, 1959), p. 12.

18 *Ibid.*, pp. 36–37.

19 *Ibid.*, pp. 76–79.

20 *Ibid.*, p. 80.

21 Schulz, pp. 30–32.

22 Trilling, pp. 63–64.

23 Günther, pp. 40–43.

24 Papajewski, "Die Frage . . . ," pp. 207–08.

25 Lüdeke, *Geschichte*, p. 515.

26 Hermann Pongs, *Im Umbruch der Zeit*, 2nd ed. (Göttingen, 1956), pp. 166–69.

27 Stresau, *Ernest Hemingway*, p. 70. Karl Heinrich Frahne, *Von Franklin*

bis Hemingway (Hamburg, 1949), p. 230.

28 Heinrich Straumann, *American Literature in the Twentieth Century*, 3rd ed. rev. (New York, 1965), p. 107.

29 Blöcker, "Der Unbesiegte," *Monat*, V (1952–1953), 229.

30 Ida Görres, "Zwei Bücher: Ein Vergleich," *FH*, II (1947), 858–59.

31 *Ibid.*, pp. 859–62.

32 *Ibid.*, p. 863.

33 Martha Glaser, "Dichtung am Rande des Christentums," *Zeitwende*, XXIII (1951–1952), 529.

34 Wolf, pp. 315–16.

35 Grenzmann, pp. 425–29.

36 Curt Hohoff, "Das religiöse Problem in der erzählenden Literatur," *Hochland*, XLII (1949–1950), 187.

37 Günther, p. 43.

38 Inge Meidinger-Geise, "Stimmen am Ufer: Zum Werke von Ernest Hemingway und Thomas Wolfe," *Die Erlanger Universität*, IV, No. 2 (1950), 2.

39 Holthusen, *Der unbehauste Mensch*, pp. 22–23.

40 Stresau, *Ernest Hemingway*, pp. 67–68.

41 von Einsiedel, p. 1225.

42 Lania, *Bildbiographie*, p. 106.

43 Gerhard Prause, "Ernest Hemingway," *Welt und Wort*, VI (1951), 49–50.

44 *Ibid.*, p. 51.

45 Papajewski, "Die Frage," p. 195.

46 Holthusen, *Der unbehauste Mensch*, p. 24.

47 Schmidt, pp. 392–93.

48 Schirmer, p. 789.

49 Stresau, *Ernest Hemingway*, p. 71.

50 Engelbert Kirchner, "Der Tod des Soldaten," *FH*, VI (1951), 443.

51 Eberhart Lämmert, *Bauformen des Erzählens* (Stuttgart, 1955), p. 155.

52 Papajewski, "Die Frage," pp. 196–98.

53 *Ibid.*, pp. 199–205.

54 Philip Young, *Ernest Hemingway* (London, 1952), pp. 51–105.

55 Carlos Baker, *Hemingway: The Writer as Artist*, 2nd ed. (Princeton, 1956), p. 287.

56 M. F. Moloney, "Ernest Hemingway: The Missing Third Dimension," *Fifty Years of the American Novel*, ed. H. C. Gardiner (New York, 1951), p. 186.

57 Rudolph Haas, "Zum Todesmotiv im Werk Hemingways," NS, VIII (1959), 456.

58 *Ibid.*

59 *Ibid.*, p. 458.

60 *Ibid.*, pp. 459–61.

61 *Ibid.*

62 *Ibid.*, pp. 462–63.

63 *Ibid.*, pp. 464–65.

Across the River and Into the Trees (1950) was translated as
Über den Fluss and in die Wälder and published in Germany by
the Rowohlt Company in 1951. No other novel illustrates as convincingly the uniqueness of the German critical reaction to Hemingway. Overwhelmingly scorned in England and America, *Across
the River* received high praise from the foremost of German critics.
Hemingway's treatment of the theme of love and death, which
Germans had found fascinating in *A Farewell to Arms* and *For
Whom the Bell Tolls*, reached in their estimation a new level of
intensity and poetic beauty in this novel. Earlier they had praised
Hemingway's development of the devoted female figure and the
tenderness with which he described the love affairs of Catherine
and Frederic, Robert and Maria. In Renata of *Across the River*
they found not only a devoted mistress, but a benefactress who provided the means for the hero to purge himself of bitterness, to
escape his existential isolation, and to face his death courageously.
Overtones of Gretchen-Faust, Beatrice-Dante, and Tristan-Isolde
are present in their criticism, and Germans continued to focus on
passages in which Hemingway suggests that love allows man to
approach the spiritual and the transcendent.

In creating the atmosphere of death, Hemingway, they claimed,
came close to the artistry of Thomas Mann in "Death in Venice."
As Rudolph Haas explained,

> If one does not approach the controversial work *Across the
> River and Into the Trees* (1950) as a study of death ("Thana-
> tosprosa"), as fiction which attempts to dramatize the last
> stages of Colonel Cantwell's life in a style similar to that of
> "Death in Venice," one will all too easily align oneself with
> the majority opinion, which has overlooked the value . . . of
> the novel.[1]

Critical focus should not be on the admittedly slight plot, German
critics frequently maintained, but on the symbolic structure of the
novel (the cold, gray morning scenes at the beginning and the end)

and the mythic overtones existent in Cantwell's passing from life to death.

Another significant difference is in the German reaction to Colonel Cantwell. Whereas American critics, familiar with the details of Hemingway's life, were sharply critical of his lack of detachment in creating Cantwell as a fictional spokesman for himself, Germans concentrated on Cantwell's development within the novel. Through the aid of Renata, they claimed, the embittered old army officer gradually reaches the level of the archetype or "Urbild," representing all those who have endured the catastrophes of two world wars. As a rule, German critics did not resent Hemingway's lack of taste when he chose to express his own opinions of recent historical events and personages in the novel. An explanation for this may be in his hero's notably sympathetic attitude towards the German people, and in the critics' fascination with Hemingway himself.

The most positive, comprehensive, and at the same time influential discussion of *Across the River* was by Horst Oppel, whose review appeared in *Die Neueren Sprachen* in 1952. Oppel placed all of Hemingway's works in the mainstream of American literature which, he pointed out, gives expression to an inherent conservatism. This development in literature stems from a preoccupation with "social solidarity," and a turning to the "democratic beginnings of the nation" and to a "collective humanism." According to Oppel, Hemingway, Thornton Wilder, Thomas Wolfe, and John Dos Passos all write skeptical, nihilistic fiction, but it is of the typically American kind. Not only negative, "it plays with all possibilities . . . and ambivalences." Thus Oppel could find something positive emerging from a dramatization of death in *Across the River.*[2]

After summarizing the most frequent objections to the novel, Oppel first came to the defense of the plot. Many critics had gone astray in their appraisals, he stated, for they failed to separate *Across the River* from Hemingway's earlier fiction. This novel is not concerned with a series of adventures which produce suspense, but instead it presents a type of argument that we might look for in Renaissance drama or the novels of the baroque period. Accordingly the novel consists of a series of juxtaposed scenes which supply an appropriate background for the type of analytical dialectic that Hemingway creates. The design of the novel also explains the lack of individual character development; the characters are intended to be types. Richard Cantwell represents all those whose entire life has been determined by participation in two world wars. The other main character, Contessa Renata, is also confined to a type, that of the completely devoted mistress. In the fiction of both Dos Passos and Hemingway, Oppel stated, the individual destinies of personages are representative of the collective experience. To support his thesis, Oppel turned to Hemingway's non-fiction publications which contain smatterings of his theory of writing. From *Death in the Afternoon* Oppel quoted Hemingway's statement, "A writer should create living people; people not characters." This he found consistent with Hemingway's objection to the abstract and artificial order with which novelists must approach their character creations.[3]

While noting many stylistic and thematic similarities between this novel and earlier Hemingway fiction, especially the concern with facing death, Oppel stated that this does not mean that Hemingway returned to his earlier sarcasm and skepticism, as several critics had maintained. And this is the key to Oppel's reading of the novel, for he claimed that Cantwell's preoccupation with death is of a different kind than that of the bullfighters or big-game hunters Hemingway readers had become familiar with. The aging colonel has already faced thirty years of "living every day with death"; thus the threat of extinction here is from within rather than from without. And the former reliance on bravery, skill, and luck no longer suffices. In spite of Cantwell's attempts to spend his last days free from the torment of introspection, he is plagued by a deep uncertainty. For this reason he devotes himself to an intense love affair which he hopes will allow him to escape reality.[4]

At this point, Oppel observed that Hemingway, in developing the beneficial role of Renata, introduces something entirely new to his writing. She comes to Cantwell with a naive security stemming from her elevated family tradition and with a submissive belief in the order of the Catholic faith. The certainty of her existence is set in direct contrast to the bitter cynicism of Cantwell, and she is the one who prompts him to speak of his war experiences. What results, according to Oppel, is a type of confession or purgation. Renata knows that Cantwell, by sharing his last few days with her, and by articulating his previous experiences, can deprive those experiences of their horror and purge himself of bitterness.[5]

Oppel claimed that in developing this purgation experience, Hemingway was giving dramatic expression to the "fundamental paradox of our existence," defined by Karl Jaspers as "being able to live in the world only by living above it." Only in so far as he is able to live his world to the end can Cantwell escape it and gain the inner freedom which can change a violent death to a "happy death." Through the power of castigation Cantwell is able to see his life in a new perspective. He speaks of the horror of war, but no longer does it concern his own joys and sufferings, successes and failures; instead, at the basis is the sorrow of the world. Only through the help of Renata can he do this: "this bond enables him to break through the terror of the ego, and leads his consciousness to a higher plane where it is touched and at the same time moved by the eternal mysteries of existence."[6] Oppel was careful to point out that Hemingway remains on a deterministic level that has little in common with the religious overtones of a Graham Greene or Evelyn Waugh, or the mysticism of Aldous Huxley or W. Somerset Maugham. But a type of optimism emerges from the "Lebenskraft" and unconquerable vitality running through the novel. It is this element which places Hemingway in a different category from war novelists Norman Mailer or James Jones. While they stress the hopelessness of the human condition, Hemingway, stated Oppel, presents the disheartening experience of two world wars, and yet preserves the hope and dignity of mankind.[7]

Oppel was not alone in finding the love affair of Renata and Cantwell healing, elevating, and at times transcendent. Günter Blöcker (*Monat*, 1952) also saw something new and positive in *Across the River* and Wolfdietrich Kandler (*Weltstimmen*, 1953), labeled those who considered it a return to earlier cynicism or nihilism "wesensfremde oder instinktlose Kritiker."[8] Robert Fritzsch in a convincing, well-balanced article, "Der Hemingway'sche Held und die Frau" (*W und W*, 1958), used the relationship of Renata and Cantwell to refute a charge leveled against the "Sexualfrivolität" in Hemingway's novels. In recounting the few idyllic days Cantwell and Renata have together, he wrote, "This juxtaposition of love and death, of brief togetherness and painful separation, is the most characteristic element in Hemingway's dramatization of love."[9] Similar situations he found facing Robert Jordan and Maria in *For Whom the Bell Tolls*, Frederic Henry and Catherine in *A Farewell to Arms*, and Jake Barnes and Brett in *The Sun Also Rises*. Death is the extreme expression of the world's injustice continually confronting man. But love between a man and a woman at least brings momentary brightness and joy, forgetfulness and sympathy; though it does not give the world meaning, it does make life bearable. Therefore, Fritzsch contended, Hemingway often develops his female characters as ideal partners for the male figure, rather than as real persons in their own right: "The arms of each of these loving women form an enclosure in which man finds reconciliation, peace and security; his spirits are revived and he receives a new sense of power."[10]

Although few of the love affairs in Hemingway's fiction would be sanctioned by society's conventions, moral applications, Fritzsch stated, are not relevant to them. Developing on a very elemental level, they sooth, offer release from loneliness, and supply a bond against death. It is Hemingway's clear, direct treatment of sex which often shocks his German readers and leads to misunderstanding. Readers, explained Fritzsch, must understand what sexual relations mean for Hemingway's characters, who attempt to experience fully the immediate moment: "The act of love is for them an ecstatic celebration, which offers one of life's greatest joys." Hemingway excels in describing the sensual side of love, Fritzsch claimed, and at the same time he creates a tenderness of feeling between his characters, a spiritual exchange which fits the name of marriage better than many officially approved attachments.[11]

Like Oppel, Fritzsch considered one of the most beautiful scenes in Hemingway's works to be the subtle presentation of the exchange between Cantwell and Renata, the way in which she gradually succeeds in drawing out his repressed emotions, his feelings of tenderness and protectiveness. Fritzsch also has high praise for the much-criticized sexual encounter during the gondola ride. Here, he wrote, and in the sleeping bag scenes of *For Whom the Bell Tolls*, Hemingway presents physical intimacy with unequalled boldness and at the same time with tenderness and restraint, a combination that only he can master so well. A powerful mystery affects both male and female, and through this experience Hemingway's characters find themselves becoming deeply attached to each other and reconciled to an affirmation of life. This transformation, Fritzsch concluded emphatically, "is far removed from a superficial, purely biological conception of physical togetherness!"[12]

Hermann Stresau (*Ernest Hemingway*, 1958) stated that *Across the River* appeared weak when placed alongside Hemingway's earlier works or when compared to the fullness of *For Whom the Bell Tolls*. Nevertheless, he considered it a significant novel "for it contains Hemingway's strongest, and perhaps final, treatment of death." At no time do death and life come so near each other, according to Stresau, as in the "Tristan-Motiv."[13] During the ecstacy of physical intimacy, love appears almost to lead to death "in der winddurchwehten Dünsternis des acherontischen Todesnachtens." The sexual encounters in the novel succeed artistically and thematically, Stresau maintained, for through them Hemingway allows his characters to forget themselves, to come closest to the secret of life and death, to transcend the sensual, and proceed to a complete fulfillment of the human.[14]

The Swiss critic Heinrich Straumann (*American Literature in the Twentieth Century*, 1965) was likewise attracted by Hemingway's treatment of love and death in *Across the River*. Hemingway, he pointed out, achieved a delicate balance between Cantwell's bitter resignation and the tender love relationship. It is this relationship, according to Straumann, that replaces the one accepted value (human solidarity) in Hemingway's previous two novels, and "causes the disillusioned colonel to try and make sense of the events of his life." Straumann added that "Contrary to the numerous critical objections raised, the novel has not failed to appeal to the postwar reading public as the twentieth-century version of the eternal subject of love and soldiering."[15]

Expressing a similar view to that of the preceding critics was Heinz Politzer, writing in *Neue Rundschau* in 1951. He, too, was moved by Hemingway's development of the love affair between Renata and Cantwell, although he placed the main emphasis of his review on the universal aspects of the hero. Politzer recognized that Colonel Cantwell had many similarities with Hemingway himself—his speech habits, his age, his wounds, and his manners. In fact, he stated, *Across the River* "is a sick, neurotic book, and it has the egocentric preoccupation with self and the persuasive power of a genuinely disturbed mind." However Politzer's assessment of the novel did not end here, for he saw qualities beyond the main character's loud-mouthed crudity; his childish invective, and aggressiveness. Cantwell, he claimed, can also be tender, imaginative, and refined; though his fate has already been decided, he faces death with heroic helplessness and expresses no trace of self-pity. According to Politzer, Cantwell is in the same class as the conquistadors and the pioneers, who belong to American mythology. Cantwell, like Don Quixote, runs up against reality and then bemoans his fate at the hands of death, himself unaware that as the conqueror who desires fame on the battlefield, in love, in the hunt, and also in death, he has been seeking a flight into immortality all along.[16]

Politzer did not deny that Renata was at times lifeless and illusory, but like the preceding German critics who expressed admiration for Hemingway's handling of the love affair, he maintained that the description of Cantwell's conduct with her during their short time together was written with an almost "tragic delicacy." The usual detachment, character development, and plot movement are lacking, for the main objective of the novel is to present a character in the act of purging himself by pouring out past experiences in spontaneous declarations. Almost against his will, the reader is forced to listen to Cantwell and in the process to discover for himself the sincerity and beauty in his confession. By the end of the novel Cantwell has become the "Urbild" for men who have remained on the century's battle fields as victors and vanquished. Politzer found universal appeal in Cantwell's desire for fame and his fear of death, and "pathological beauty" in the symbolic implications of his final struggle. It is not an accident, he added, that the word "Götterdämmerung" appears in the novel and is linked with the lines from Bach, "Komm süsser Tod." For the time of the conquistadors, the Cantwells, the Rommels, and the Udets is at an end. The mythological has been destroyed by our rationality, and it is fitting that Cantwell should seek refuge in death.[17]

Other less penetrating, but notably positive reactions to *Across the River* came from Hermann Boekhoff, Wilhelm Grenzmann and the English novelist Evelyn Waugh, whose translated review appeared in *Universitas* in 1951. Boekhoff (*WM*, 1951) drew attention to the cold that permeates the Venice setting and connected it with the basic skepticism that stems from Hemingway's pursuit of truth. Love glows and shivers at the same time, he pointed out, and death hangs over the story from beginning to end. Boekhoff saw reflected in *Across the River* a new period in Hemingway's life, one leading to a dark, somewhat bitter maturity: "We know no other books of Hemingway's that love the dark, warm sound of the cello as this one does."[18]

Wilhelm Grenzmann (*Weltdichtung der Gegenwart*, 1961) also pointed out that after *For Whom* Hemingway's fiction becomes more meditative and melancholic. Even the lovers' dialogue is more reserved and in a lower key than in the earlier novels when passion held sway. Dark tones are more prominent and the nearness of death, always a factor in Hemingway's writing, becomes in *Across the River* a leitmotiv. It is the juxtaposition of life and death, according to Grenzmann, which encourages the use of symbols in both Hemingway's novel and Thomas Mann's *Novelle* "Death in Venice." As other critics had done, Grenzmann praised Cantwell's bearing in the face of death; nevertheless, he maintained, the book is full of sadness over the incomprehensible in life. Man goes unhesitatingly to his death with no answer, no light beyond the dark. Perhaps, he concluded, the isolated state of man at death is symbolically the final solution for the tension between Cantwell's active, carefree nature and the doubts that he expresses in his monologue with the picture of Renata.[19]

A final positive reaction came from Helmut Jaesrich (*Der Monat*, 1950), who judged the novel according to more orthodox criteria: plot structure, character development, and dialogue. Jaesrich drew attention to the mood Hemingway creates by putting the hunting chapter at the beginning, thereby allowing the icy, gray morning atmosphere to permeate the entire book. He, too, pointed out the similarities between Cantwell and other Hemingway heroes—"lebenshungrig, todesnah, und ausweglos"—and found nothing weak in Hemingway's portrayal of the American officer: "He is a rounded and consistent personality, a crude but devoted officer in his army." The language the lovers speak to each other, Jaesrich claimed, is somewhere between the uneven, one-syllable dialogue of early Hemingway novels and the level of children's speech, but rather than finding a weak point here, as do many

American critics, Jaesrich considered the dialogue ("meisterlich lautechte Wiedergabe einer erfundenen Wirklichkeit") the most significant element in the book. He added that the extremely negative reaction to the novel in England and America could in part result from Hemingway's unfavorable treatment of the English and Americans in *Across the River*; it is actually the Germans who come off best.[20]

In the light of the clear-cut differences in response to *Across the River*, Jaesrich's point is well worth considering. Cantwell, for example, dismisses Eisenhower as a "Political General," and Montgomery, he says, "was a character who needed fifteen to one to move, and then move tardily."[21] "Our British cousins," Hemingway has Cantwell say, "could not fight their way out of a wet tissue towel" (p. 223). The French fare no better in Cantwell's estimate: General Leclerc is "another jerk of the third or fourth water" (p. 134). To Renata he explains "the great clarté of the French military thinking": "*Vive la France et les pommes de terre frites. Liberté, Vénalité, et Stupidité.*" "They haven't had a military thinker," he added, "since du Picq" (pp. 26–27). German leaders, however, Cantwell holds in high esteem. Erwin Rommel, he explains, was an old friend and one of the few who would understand the campaigns of World War II in detail (p. 231). When Renata asks, "Did you like many Germans?" Cantwell replies, "Very many. Ernst Udet I liked the best." And when she objects, "But they were in the wrong," Cantwell's answer is "Of course. But who had not been?" (p. 122).

Similar statements expressing Cantwell's love, sympathy and admiration for the Germans appear in the following passages:

> "It certainly would be odd if instead of going to hell, as we always counted on, we should go to one of those Kraut joints like Valhalla and not be able to get along with the people. But maybe we could get a corner table with Rommel and Udet and it would be just like any winter-sports hotel." (p. 250)
>
> "What I know best I learned from the Krauts, studying them and opposing them. They are the best soldiers. But they always over-reach." (p. 272)
>
> "If ever you fight, then you must win it. That's all that counts. All the rest is cabbage, as my old friend Dr. Rommel put it."

"Did you really like Rommel?"
"Very much."
"But he was your enemy."
"I love my enemies sometimes more than my friends." (p. 286)

Cantwell can be critical of the German past, for example when he remarks that they "bought themselves a nice big piece of Süsser Tod at the end" (p. 88). But as the above passages suggest, he is more interested in tolerance and understanding. Cantwell's reply to the Venice boatman, who protested self-righteously that he had not believed in the Italian Regime during World War II, could as easily have been addressed to the Germans: "You don't have to give me that stuff. . . . It would have been quite natural for you to *have* believed in it. Do you think I hold that against a man after we've won?" (p. 44). Still more direct is a passage from his monologue with Renata's portrait: "I can't hate Fascists, he thought. Nor Krauts either, since unfortunately I am a soldier." " 'Listen, Portrait,' he said. 'Do I have to hate the Krauts because we kill them? Do I have to hate them as soldiers and as human beings? It seems too easy a solution for me' " (p. 176) . Cantwell's preference for those who had fought and suffered in war would naturally call forth a favorable response from the German reader: "Other people were fine and you liked them and were good friends; but you only felt true tenderness and love for those who had been there and had received the castigation that everyone receives who goes there long enough" (p. 71). Hemingway's harsh treatment of Americans and Englishmen in *Across the River* may have influenced the reaction to the novel in the United States and England, as Jaesrich suggested. At the same time, the favoritism for the German people that Hemingway has Cantwell express, is likely to have influenced the German critical reaction, especially in the early postwar period.

Even the German critics who saw evidence of a decline in Hemingway's talents did not consider *Across the River* a total failure. In an article entitled "Tod in Venedig" (again a reference to Mann's *Novelle*) which appeared in *Gegenwart* in 1952, Friedrich Sieburg claimed that in *Across the River* Hemingway did not follow his iceberg theory as closely as before, and consequently his prose expresses less between the lines. There comes a time, Sieburg added, when the reader cannot bear with the famous Hemingway conversations between waiters and bartenders, for he discovers that the frequent and monotonous drinking bouts no longer have anything of deeper significance behind them. Hemingway begins to repeat himself and fails to preserve the tension between apparent banality and poignant undertone. Nevertheless, had he limited himself to the very effective, though unorthodox dialogue between Cantwell and Renata in the parting scene, he would have created a "Meisterwerk":

> It is a moment of heart-rending sadness. Hemingway has never written anything more beautiful than the last shadowy dialogue in which a tired man courageously dissolves the bond of love and sets out alone on his way to death.[22]

Another critic, Ursula Brumm (*WS*, 1950), considered *Across the River* to be inferior to Hemingway's major works. One of her main objections was directed against Hemingway's continual references to tactical failures and inept leadership on the part of Montgomery, Leclerc, Eisenhower, and Patton during World War II. She criticized Hemingway's lack of detachment, but, strangely enough, she had no objection to his frequent use of autobiographical material in developing the main character. Cantwell, she stated, is "a rounded character, vital and original." Renata becomes the projection of the ideal lover—beautiful, loving, understanding and devoted. Her ability to teach the self-centered Cantwell the art of giving overshadows her lack of individuality. However, it is only the beginning of the novel that reaches the epic stature of *A Farewell to Arms*: "here Hemingway directs his keenly perceptive eye to the boat moving through the morning dimness; the scene is an illustration of his remarkable descriptive powers."[23]

Helmut Heissenbüttel (*DR*, 1963), like Brumm, praised the development of the hero Cantwell and found nothing amiss in the strong resemblance he bears to Hemingway himself. In fact, it is when Hemingway's own cynical attitude emerges from his spokesman-hero that the novel is closest to the truth: "It is just these accidental openings in the facade which permit the events and characters . . . to appear most real." Heissenbüttel contended that with the love affair Hemingway returned to the pattern of his earlier works, but he made the outcome distinctly different in this novel. In the lovers' dialogue, for example, there are passages similar to those in *A Farewell to Arms* and *For Whom the Bell Tolls*, which suggest a transcendent or mystical elevation during the act of love. But Cantwell's response while making love to Renata (She: " 'Oh please not talk. Please' "; He: "Yes, he thought. Please and please again.") Heissenbüttel found suspicious. It contradicts, he pointed out, the assertion of transcendence and erotic mysticism, and emphasizes that one is not able to transcend time or space.[24]

Two German critics who reflect the influence of the general American reaction to *Across the River* are Englebert Kirchner and Wolfgang von Einsiedel. According to Kirchner (*FH*, 1951) the novel is an involuntary "Selbstparodie" and was written at the expense of Hemingway's reputation. Even the classic Hemingway situation, that of the hero preparing himself for death, is treated as parody; the colonel does not contemplate the finality of death, but is instead angry at his heart muscle which has suddenly weakened, while the rest of his body, though battered, continues to function. Thus Kirchner felt Hemingway was reducing death to only its physical aspects, thereby robbing it of any transcendental significance. The colonel answers the threat of death by attempting to channel the deeds and thoughts of his entire life into his last three days, but, according to Kirchner, his knowledge of death is a senseless "self-deception," as is his knowledge of life.[25]

What destroys the character of Cantwell and therefore the novel is the disparity between the colonel's outward experience and inner immaturity. One may present a character as pathetic as Cantwell, said Kirchner, but he must not be accompanied by the fanfare Hemingway gives his modern "legendary hero." Although both main characters are minutely described as never before by Hemingway, this does not make them come alive. According to Kirchner, they remain "marionettes, carefully formed and manipulated," and Cantwell becomes Hemingway's "fairy tale prince." The self-parody turns Hemingway's "unqualified sincerity" against himself, and consequently his style suffers in this novel: "In these irrelevancies he exhausts his own dialogue, until the usual precise 'understatement' degenerates into meaningless chatter."[26]

Kirchner claimed that Hemingway lacked the artistic means to write about average men in a normal life, and his downfall began when he started to write about an average man in uniform. Although it is a shame, Kirchner stated, that such a travesty as *Across the River* was necessary to show what a great writer cannot do, the novel does display qualities which are above criticism: (1) Hemingway's ability to incorporate past events into his fiction and to make them live; (2) the anticipation of a great love story he effects in the first dialogue concerning the jewels; (3) and the atmosphere he creates in the beginning and concluding description of the hunt.[27]

In his negative review, "Ein Komet verblasst" (*Merkur*, 1950), Wolfgang von Einsiedel referred to *Across the River* as "a weak, flat, and at times, painful book," a late variation of Mann's "Death in Venice." According to von Einsiedel the novel offers no plot, but a notably inconclusive dialogue between an elderly American officer and a young Italian girl, who ironically represents the happiness and fulfillment that the officer can never find. Although Hemingway succeeds in capturing some of the charm of his short stories in his descriptions of the winter setting in Venice, stated von Einsiedel, he falls far short of the artistic level of *A Farewell to Arms*. It may be that Hemingway has become garrulous, he wrote, or our ears may have become more attuned to his style, or we are disappointed because we overestimated his powers in the first place; in any event, according to von Einsiedel, Hemingway in this novel not only seems to copy his early style, but even to parody it. In criticizing the lovers' dialogue, von Einsiedel wrote that Hemingway no longer excludes clichés from his writings, and he has the lovers reassure each other so often and in such a trivial way that the reader begins to doubt their sincerity. Like Sieburg and Kirchner, von Einsiedel felt that Hemingway had become a prisoner of his own style. His language, so suitable for expressing fear and melancholy, could not fit positive perceptions. And dialogues, formerly a symbol of man's inability to communicate, become sonorous, conventional opera duets. Von Einsiedel concluded his article with the hope that the failure of *Across the River* would bring Hemingway out of his lethargy and inspire him to experiment with new techniques.[28]

East German critics, never very favorable towards Hemingway, also saw evidence of his regression manifested in *Across the River*. Karl-Heinz Schönfelder, writing in *ZAA*, 1959, is a representative example. Schönfelder claimed the novel was astonishingly weak in dialogue, characterization, and intellectual content, but more disturbing, he felt, was Hemingway's retreat from the "ethic of human solidarity" that he developed with Robert Jordan in *For Whom the Bell Tolls*. Cantwell, unlike Jordan, never finds the way from the isolated "I" to "We." Cantwell needs Renata, the understanding "you," but only to confess to her and thereby to free the "I" from the burdensome shadow of the past. With the hotels, ordered meals, and costly wines, Schönfelder saw a return to the world of *The Sun Also Rises* and "the renewed glorification of egotism and sensuality." Reflecting the East German bias, he added that glorification of the only remaining abstract values—courage, bravery, and manliness—leads to a dangerous position, as when Cantwell-Hemingway praises former commanders in Hitler's army.[33]

NOTES

[1] Haas, p. 455.

[2] Horst Oppel, "Hemingway's *Across the River and Into the Trees*," NS, I (1952), 485.

[3] *Ibid.*, pp. 473–77.

[4] *Ibid.*, p. 480.

[5] *Ibid.*, pp. 481–82.

[6] *Ibid.*, p. 483.

[7] *Ibid.*, pp. 484–85.

[8] The quotation is from Wolfdietrich Kandler, *WS*, XXII (1953), 1. See also Günter Blöcker, "Der Unbesiegte," *Der Monat*, V (1952–1953), 229.

[9] Robert Fritzsch, "Der Hemingway'sche Held und die Frau," *W und W*, XIII (1958), 197.

[10] *Ibid.*, p. 198.

[11] *Ibid.*, pp. 199–200.

[12] *Ibid.*, p. 201.

[13] Stresau, *Ernest Hemingway*, pp. 73–74.

[14] *Ibid.*, pp. 86–87.

[15] Straumann, p. 109.

[16] Heinz Politzer, "Der neue Hemingway," *NR*, LXII, No. 1 (1951), 136–39.

[17] *Ibid.*

[18] Hermann Boekhoff, "Ein neuer Hemingway," *WM*, XCII, No. 12 (1951–1952), 82.

[19] Grenzmann, pp. 433–34.

[20] Helmut Jaesrich, "Tod in Venedig," *Der Monat*, III (1950), 93–95.

21 Ernest Hemingway, *Across the River and Into the Trees* (New York, 1950), p. 125. Future references to this source are indicated in the text.

22 Friedrich Sieburg, "Tod in Venedig," *Gegenwart*, VII, No. 1 (1952), 24.

23 Ursula Brumm, "Hemingways neuer Roman," *WS*, XX (1950), 49–55.

24 Helmut Heissenbüttel, "Versuch über den Ruhm Hemingways," *DR*, LXXXIX, No. 1 (1963), 53–54.

25 Englebert Kirchner, "Der Tod des Soldaten," *FH*, VI (1951), 443.

26 *Ibid.*, p. 444.

27 *Ibid.*, pp. 444–45.

28 Wolfgang von Einsiedel, "Ein Komet verblasst," *Merkur*, IV (1950), 1221–25.

29 Karl-Heinz Schönfelder, *ZAA* (Ost), VII (1959), 218–19.

PART VI: THE OLD MAN AND THE SEA

Of all Hemingway's works *The Old Man and the Sea* (1952), translated as *Der alte Mann und das Meer,* received the highest worldwide critical acclaim. Its subject matter was especially timely in postwar Germany, and almost all German critics praised its sparse language, its compactness, and its simple but powerful theme. As they had done with *Across the River and Into the Trees,* many critics sought out parallels and contrasts between Hemingway's fiction and other literary works employing similar themes and settings, and Melville's *Moby Dick* offered them the best starting point for this approach. For the most part their criticism focused either on Santiago, whom they felt was the new Hemingway hero representative of the modern age, or on the metaphysical implications of the man vs. nature conflict. Attention was drawn to various symbols Hemingway employed, but few German critics did more than mention them in passing, and none of the examined critics offered detailed explications.

Engelbert Kirchner, writing in the *Frankfurter Hefte* in 1953, first drew attention to the significant variations in Hemingway's fiction dealing with his favorite theme, man confronted with imminent death or defeat. In the early works Hemingway's hero usually remains alive at the end. It would be superfluous to have him killed, wrote Kirchner, for in the case of Frederic in *A Farewell to Arms* he has nothing left after his wife and child die, or in the case of Jake Barnes in *The Sun Also Rises,* his impotency has been stressed from the beginning. In the later fiction the Hemingway hero dies at the end and with good reason. The matador in "The Undefeated" and the colonel in *Across the River and Into the Trees* have lost contact with their surroundings, and they aspire to nothing more; the others, Robert Jordan, Harry Morgan, or Francis Macomber have grasped the last insight they were capable of and could not exceed this in a future life. But Kirchner found in Santiago of *The Old Man* a hero of a different mold. He suffers defeat as completely as the above-mentioned characters, but he continues to live in a way that no other Hemingway hero has

133

done. He is capable of the statement, "A man can be destroyed but not defeated," or in a very atypical way he is concerned with the possible sin of killing the fish so far out at sea. According to Kirchner, the old man can do this because he combines humility with honest pride. Unlike previous heroes he has not only learned of the cruelties of life, but he also knows how to adjust to them and continue living. He sees neither the highest victory nor the most disillusioning defeat in the outcome of his struggle; for him it is only a part of life. In his wise monologues, clear reminiscences, and complete isolation, Santiago is no longer a simple Cuban fisherman. He becomes a legendary figure, one of the greatest out of Hemingway's own "mythical world of hunters and soldiers, of individualists who remain outside our civilization."[1]

Santiago's one weak point, according to Kirchner, is that as an archetype he is not especially "life-like," but nevertheless he is the "embodiment of the Hemingway hero" and is much more realistically developed than Cantwell, the hero of *Across the River and Into the Trees*. Although he criticized Hemingway for still hanging on to the mysticism which began with the sentimental "Liebesgeplapper" in *For Whom the Bell Tolls*, Kirchner stated that the best of Hemingway's talents were displayed in *The Old Man*, e.g., his gripping account of the struggle with the fish and his gradual unfolding of the catastrophe. Especially effective, Kirchner concluded, was Hemingway's treatment of the sea: "the subtle way in which he allows the sea to become the feminine principle in the novel."[2]

The East German critic Erich Gronke (*ZAA*, 1954) was another who found a new type of affirmative hero emerging from *The Old Man*. Although he saw many similarities between Santiago and earlier Hemingway heroes, Gronke pointed out important differences in degrees of freedom and responsibility. On one level Santiago is more limited, for while Robert Jordan and Frederic Henry freely choose their own adventures, the action of Santiago is part of his necessary struggle for daily bread, thus making the outcome seem inevitable. Ethically, however, Gronke claimed Santiago has more freedom; Henry flees more *from* something than *to* something else, while for Jordan no means of escape exist. On the other hand Santiago could give up without hurting anyone and without incurring moral guilt, yet he is faced with a necessary and meaningful struggle of life and death.[3]

Santiago is not a deep thinker, Gronke admitted, but the reader does not expect the perceptions of an intellectual hero to be found in a simple fisherman. Nor can it be said that Santiago lacks heroic stature because his struggle is a private one. Although the subject matter has sharp limitations and the moral of endurance ("die Moral des Durchhaltens") can be dangerously incomplete, Gronke contended that within the narrow boundaries of *The Old Man* Hemingway showed that honorable human worth is still possible. Santiago's defeat is not a return to nihilism, for victory does occur within the mind of the old man, and it is this that is decisive. Gronke concluded that "The powerful style and the many beautiful passages affirming human will power and unwavering courage, earn for *The Old Man and the Sea* a favorable evaluation."[4]

Hans Daiber (*DR*, 1953) also noted a special significance in Hemingway's conception of the hero in *The Old Man*. Santiago represents individual man pitted against an unpredictable enemy, the symbolic situation for a modern tragedy. According to Daiber, the old man is a victor without victory, a hero without cause for triumph, a protagonist who fights back for only one reason—to be able to be with the boy again. The boy himself is only significant in that he understands and loves the old one, and remains faithful when fate selects Santiago out of the mass of fishermen to undergo the test of life and death.[5]

The title of Daiber's review, "Der alte Mann und Kapitän Ahab," is the key to his reading of the novel; his interpretation of Santiago rests on the differences he pointed out between *The Old Man* and *Moby Dick*, published some hundred years earlier. After briefly contrasting the fullness and variety of the latter with the sparse simplicity of *The Old Man*, Daiber moved on to the more important contrast between Ahab and Santiago, which he felt would illustrate significant differences in the intellectual climate of the nineteenth and twentieth centuries. Ahab is the adventurer attempting to explore the unexplorable, and it is daring hate that drives him to hunt Moby Dick. Santiago, on the other hand, is not an adventurer, and while admiring the beauty and nobility of the fish, he maintains a benevolent attitude towards it. This difference illustrates the transformation that has taken place in the hero of the twentieth century. Political, geographical, and economic complexities have contributed to the dying out of the classic adventurer. Contemporary man seeks protection from danger through treaties and large-scale armaments; and a new type of hero is called forth from the ranks of soldiers, scientists, and politicians. Thus Daiber considered man's struggle with the environment to have changed from an offensive to a defensive problem in the last hundred years. Santiago in his more passive, benevolent role became for him the embodiment of the modern hero.[6]

Like Daiber, Werner Richter in his article "Hemingway und die Helden," 1955, saw in Santiago a new Hemingway hero and at the same time a representative hero for the twentieth century. But whereas Daiber described the new hero as defensive, passive, and benevolent, Richter saw embodied in Santiago the adventuresome spirit of the American pioneer. From the beginning of his life Hemingway, according to Richter, has been in active protest against the comforts of a technological age which provides man with protective security from the cradle to the grave. The protest, as Richter saw it, was in the form of a quest to determine if it is still possible for a man who embodies the hardihood of America's first pioneers, Achilles of the Greeks, Mucius Scaevola of the Romans, or the dragon killers of the middle-Europeans, to exist in the twentieth century. The quest, Richter contended, was a part of Hemingway's life as well as his writing. This explains his early interest in boxing, his participation in World War I, his preference for the active life of skiing, mountain climbing, and bullfighting over that of the postwar cafe society of Paris.[7]

All of the protagonists in Hemingway's fiction were variations on the heroic theme, but all had left their author dissatisfied (here Richter claimed that to compensate Hemingway was forced to lead his own heroic life in the Spanish Civil War, the African expeditions, and World War II). But in his novel *The Old Man* Hemingway finally discovered the hero he had sought for so long. Embodied in Santiago's simple story is the experience that every man must face:

> To take countless troubles and dangers upon oneself, to finally have the victory in one's hands and in the last moment

watch it disappear, to know that the opportunity will never return, and in spite of this, to continue one's life with self-possession.

It is this realization, according to Richter, that allows Santiago to see the struggling fish as his brother; both are forced to submit to "the course of things." Santiago is not a hero in the classic sense—he lacks the magnificence and fury of an Achilles or a Hector—but in his capacity to suffer disappointment without complaint, in his readiness to make another attempt the following day, he embodies the spirit of the pioneers who were responsible for settling the United States. Richter concluded that the committee which awarded Hemingway the Nobel prize in 1954 realized that the old type of heroic courage was no longer valid for the contemporary hero. What was needed was the type of courage that allows Santiago to experience the injustice of the world, and in spite of this to affirm it and to struggle for its causes.[8]

In his article published in *Hochland*, 1955, Hans Blumenberg attempted to establish the kinship of all Hemingway's heroes. The hero, he stated, "is only a hardened residue of man, no doubt; but only in this reduced state can he withstand defeat. He is limited to one task, 'to endure.'" This is the position, Blumenberg explained, that Hemingway starts from; his characters are reduced to an elemental state with their backs against the wall. The brutal animosity of reality as it opposes humanity is thus Hemingway's ontological assumption, but simple survival is not his only concern:

> One who endures an antagonistic, intolerable world dominated by circumstance, who takes the blows without protest, who keeps his composure and abides by the rules of the game —this man, despite the overwhelming odds, wrests his freedom from blind fate.[9]

Blumenberg, obviously taking the idea of the heroic code from American critics like Baker and Young, pointed out that although a Hemingway hero loses his life by following his own prescribed "code" (e.g., Harry Morgan in *To Have and Have Not*), he is nevertheless the actual winner. The significance of the "game rules," Blumenberg wrote, lies in Hemingway's rejection of the fatalistic lack of discipline displayed by many of the characters in *The Sun Also Rises*. Thus the Hemingway hero knows exactly what man may and may not do, and once he has chosen to abide by these rules there is no turning back:

> They have something like a Cartesian *morale provisoire*— without discernable expectations, to be sure, that it would ever be redeemed by a *morale définitive*—, and they appear to follow the second maxim which Descarte has proscribed for this provisional moral: that one should follow stead-fastly and resolutely a chosen course of action, without re-peated self-examination and deliberation.[10]

Blumenberg also followed Philip Young in pointing out that Hemingway's protagonists are not the only positively accentuated figures in his novels. The figure of the old man begins in Hemingway's fiction in 1938 with the story "Old Man at the Bridge," and, according to Blumenberg, includes Anselmo of *For Whom the Bell Tolls* and Santiago of *The Old Man and the Sea*, both pathetic figures apparently out of step with their time. Anselmo, Blumenberg stated, was the intended opposite of Jordan; in his stronger feelings for fellow human beings and his hatred for death and killing, he actively changes the thought and code of the hero. The old man figure becomes increasingly important for Hemingway's later fiction and for his conception of the hero:

> The discovery of the figure of the "old man" marked the most significant thematic change in Hemingway's fiction since his experience in the Spanish Civil War—not only as a psychological achievement which added an entire dimension to his narrow scale of characterizations, but also as a correc-tive to the fixed presentation of the hero which usually domi-nated his early work.[11]

After brief comment on the old man figure in "The Undefeated" and *Across the River and Into the Trees*, Blumenberg moved on to what he called Hemingway's most mature work, *The Old Man and the Sea*. Santiago appears in the familiar Hemingway pattern (the protagonist, while following certain rules, faces a momentous trial alone), but, according to Blumenberg, he is different from previous Hemingway heroes. He does not engage in a struggle in order to follow game rules; rather the goal is set by him as a necessity of his life. The forces against which he battles do not come out of a blind brutality, nor is his defeat a meaningless one. True, he must face the fish alone, but it is not the solipsistic loneliness of earlier Hemingway heroes. The humanity that streams out from Santiago inspires love in the boy and even seems to reach the animal plane. Although other Hemingway figures could find no real partner in dialogue, the old man succeeds with the dumb fish, which he speaks to as a human. Santiago does not see the world around him as antagonistic, but brotherly, and his attitude upon losing is different from any of Hemingway's previous protagonists. Instead of resigning himself bitterly to defeat, he realizes he has exceeded his own limitations in going too far out. He actually apologizes to the fish for causing both of them to suffer, and takes consolation in his friends at sea (e.g., the wind) and thoughts of rest when he reaches shore. Blumenberg, too, marveled at the surprising phenomenon that out of the literature of one country two such great sea novels as *Moby Dick* and *The Old Man and the Sea* should be produced. But Santiago, he concluded, utters a sentence that neither Ahab nor any of Hemingway's previous characters could: "I am glad that we do not have to try to kill the stars." [12]

Hermann Stresau is another German critic who claimed Hemingway's conception of the hero reached its high point in *The Old Man*. Apart from Santiago, he explained, Hemingway's heroes lack the proper orientation to live happily in a society which no longer offers either consolation or protection. Experiences they have undergone make their return to the old world of order impossible, and consequently they are often cast in the role of the passive outsider. However a new spirit of affirmation permeates *The Old Man*, and for the first time Hemingway is able to overcome the "Todesmotiv" that has dominated his work. [13] Stresau added that Hemingway offers no specific ideology for his change in attitude, and the reader must be satisfied to see his picture of the old man as a symbol of human existence: "It is enough . . . to see the bitter, lonely suffering and the hope of the old man, and to be happy with him when he is able to dream of the lions on the African coast, and to understand the love of the boy." [14]

A second group of critics placed their emphasis on the epic, the transcendent, or the orthodox religious elements in *The Old Man and the Sea*. This approach had much in common with the German existential criticism of *Across the River and Into the Trees* and differed considerably from American reactions to the novel. One reason for this may be that Germans, especially in the early 1950's, sought out literature that was relevant to their postwar situation, and consequently their criticism was more subjective than it otherwise would have been. According to Hermann Pongs, the postwar time was one of ambivalence, double standards, and changing values in Germany. The answer, he claimed, was a return to the simple, the archetypal:

> Let us consider, therefore, the catastrophic time as something sent by God in order to force the German people back to their origins, from which God has spoken to them for a thousand years through the frequent archetypal voices ("Einfalt-Stimmen") of his world literature.[15]

The uniqueness of *The Old Man* for Pongs was in the paradoxical combination Hemingway developed in the simple old fisherman: humility and pride. Examples of Santiago's humility are to be seen in his speech to the boy, in his "awareness of destiny," his great wonderment and sense of awe in the world around him, his feeling of brotherhood with all creatures and his belief in a world order. Combined with this humility is something just as powerful and unchangeable, the distinctiveness of Santiago's pride ("this pride of a fisherman who is always prompted to go the farthest distance from the shore, who always dares to battle against the most difficult obstacles"). This combination explains the unity behind a number of the paradoxes in *The Old Man*. Because Santiago realizes he is battling against another of God's creatures, he is able to say, "I do not care who kills who"; during the struggle he remains calm and detached even in the most threatening moments. The only wrong for Santiago is not to hope, or to have doubts in himself and the creation. He is the complete, individual man, motivated by archetypes (e.g., Dimaggio), free and at the same time bound to them. Thus, Pongs claimed, Santiago himself becomes an archetype and the unity of humility and pride within him corresponds to the parable-like plot, which subjects him to the most severe of tests, but has him emerge victorious in spite of defeat.[16]

Hemingway's style also supports this paradoxical unity of humility and pride. At one point the language is humble, as with the great realistic writers, but balancing this is the pride that stems "from the monadic power of the soul." The result, according to Pongs, is a symbolic realism, permeated with a sense of depth. Instances of what Pongs called the symbolic "Stil der Einfalt" are (1) the simple fishing trip which reflects a world trip with universal implications; (2) and the healing power of undividedness which allows the fisherman to speak, not in soul-searching interior monologue, but to the bird, the fish, or the absent boy. In this way Santiago knows that he is never alone on the sea.[17]

In order to explain the paradoxical "Einfalt" more fully, Pongs drew upon Leibnitz's theory of monadology. As the monads are at the center of Leibnitz's philosophy, so at the center of Santiago's world picture is the fundamental simplicity made up of humility and pride. Both express the self reliance of the monad, while at the same time illustrating its paradoxical accord with the whole. Goethe's statement in his well-known speech with Falk in 1813 also belongs to the world picture of *The Old Man*, according to Pongs. Goethe saw in the monad a central power, the "simplicity of the most simple essence" and was convinced that strong monads carried on after an individual's death and thus removed the fear of dying. Pongs saw similarities between Goethe's idea of the monad and the case of Santiago, who is calm, brave and completely lacking in fear of death: "the most striking characteristic of the simple is thereby manifested for the first time in Hemingway's world view: victory over the fear of death."[18]

Pongs accepted the verdict of John Atkins (*The Art of Ernest Hemingway*, 1952) that the "Grundimpuls" of all Hemingway's works, stemming from the "Urerlebnis" of World War I is the fear of death. But Pongs pointed out that Hemingway gradually came to terms with this fear in his previous novels. In *For Whom the Bell Tolls* it is Anselmo who is dutifully brave, simple, proud of the idea of freedom and willing to sacrifice his life for it, and yet humble. In *Across the River and Into the Trees*, Cantwell is dying, but the brutal cynic is able to purge himself through the love of Renata, who sympathetically encourages him to speak. With Santiago and *The Old Man* Pongs stated that Hemingway reaches the third and final step: "the disgrace of man, his fear, is overcome through simplicity in which humility and pride are united." A return to simplicity, a delight in the common man and common pleasures, could be a remedy for contemporary Germany, and in this sense Pongs felt Hemingway's novel was instructive. Simplicity appears as man's greatest defense against fear, and once again returning to Leibnitz, simplicity "allows the monads of the ego to link themselves with the powers of the world."[19] Thus the novel was for Pongs a "contribution to the world's recovery."[20] Santiago becomes "the rebirth of the whole man out of the archetype"[21] and offers a means of escape from the phantoms of existentialism, "Geworfenheit und Angst." The return to simplicity that Hemingway achieved in *The Old Man* can be seen as part of a new trend in contemporary literature:

> Totality and unity of spirit are the ideal prerequisites. The same totality and unity join the symbolic realism in contemporary literature in calling for simplicity. This is clearly an archetypal value, beyond idealism and realism. The encompassing vision of the writer includes both the totality of being and the totality of individual powers which contribute to being. Adequate models are supplied by figures who lead simple lives: the fisherman, the mountain climber, and the shepherd. These are men who do not reflect, but act directly from the center of their being, from archetypes which teach them to fulfill their duties in life.[22]

A number of Pongs's opinions were shared by Wilhelm Grenzmann (*Weltdichtung der Gegenwart*, 1961), who referred to *The Old Man* as a parable "filled with allegorical meanings."[23] Another representative of this group is Joseph Baur, who wrote in his article in *Welt und Wort*, 1953, that *The Old Man* was neither a novel nor a *Novelle*, but "Ein Stück Epos." The title itself, he claimed, gives the reader the key to the archetypal approach: "sea," "man," and "old." Here also is indicated the basic tension around which the book revolves: the man, with emphasis upon his age, vs. the timelessness of the sea. Epic characteristics of the work come from its reducing life to its elementary form and placing it in the "unified wholeness" of the world. Transcendent elements ("Ausblicke ins Unermessliche"), Baur claimed, are continually present in spite of the compactness of the narrative, and although there is no direct feminine influence, "The principle of the eternal feminine remains in the background, hidden in the symbol of the sea."[24]

Hemingway, according to Baur, never presents only the biological or the material side of life: "He always includes the other side, the spiritual, in his portrayal of life. Alongside human cruelty he always depicts human nobility." As an example Baur mentioned the dream picture of the lions playing in the sun, which appears at the beginning and end of the novel. Here, he stated, Hemingway touches symbolically on the deepest region of the soul; this dimension of man can never be completely defeated because it is linked "mysteriously to the supernatural." Only critics who do not understand Hemingway's contrapuntal method of composition label him a nihilist, a pseudo-romantic, or a typical writer of the "lost generation." Paradoxical as it may sound, stated Baur, Hemingway is in a sense a religious writer. He goes beyond a one-sided view of nature, but yet follows the tradition established by Kipling, Hamsun, and Jack London, and thus preserves his native epic powers. Hemingway's simple language, which Baur claimed was based on the vital spoken English of contemporary America, is especially appropriate for the modern epic: "The stylistic simplicity permits the different levels of meaning to have that much stronger an effect."[25]

Another representative of the group of critics who emphasized a second or third level of meaning in the novel is Günter Blöcker (*Der Monat*, 1952). Blöcker mentioned the difficulty German critics had in labeling *The Old Man*, calling it a "Legende," a "poème en prose" or "Novelle," and then, like Baur, he suggested that it belongs to a genre all its own. In its elevated classic simplicity, its Homeric calmness, its fated struggle, Blöcker felt it was similar to Greek tragedy. The fish, he explained, is a symbol of fate directly affecting Santiago's life: "He loves the fish even though he must kill him—for only in killing him can he prove that this is the fish of his destiny." Santiago's battle with the fish Blöcker saw as a fair struggle between power and intelligence, but, he stated, the fate of the old man takes a grandiose turn to the tragic when the hungry sharks approach his dead trophy. The tragedy is not watered-down sadness, but true tragedy as Gerhart Hauptmann defined it, "bloody irony": the noble that destroys itself because it is noble; the high striving that by necessity must fail because it attempted too much. Blöcker found the paradoxical, always present in tragedy, here also. The reader admires the old man for his endurance, courage, and victory, yet he is aware of the impracticality of the attempt from the beginning.[26]

A significant accomplishment of contemporary literature, according to Blöcker, is that it has moved the tragic hero from the drama to fiction. Santiago, like the heroes of antique tragedy, is an elevated man who attempts to go beyond the limitations of human nature and can face the results of his inevitable failure. His battle with the fish is a "mystical struggle," one that inspires feelings of greatness in others. And the final scene in which the small boy goes to awaken the old man is "classical, an heroic idyl of calm serenity." According to Blöcker, *The Old Man* is consistent with the trend of individualistic, highly introspective contemporary literature; however, he did not feel, like Oppel or Papajewski, that this was a trend leading to a "Sackgasse" or dead end. Rather he saw the novel, as it moves farther away from the simple narrative and more towards the general or imagistic, returning to its mythological origins.[27]

Part of the attraction of *The Old Man* for Blöcker was in what he felt it revealed about Hemingway himself. The author, like the old man, he stated, remains undefeated. Critics who have attempted to trace his "regression" or his "development" from nihilism to social criticism to humanism, have too narrow a conception of the man and his works. For Hemingway, a cosmic writer like Goethe or Tolstoy, embodies the good and evil, high and low, and the tender and coarse. According to Blöcker *The Old Man* contains more of the versatile Hemingway than any of his previous works: "seldom does the whole man come to meet us so directly, in such a clear, straightforward manner . . . as does Hemingway in this new work."[28]

Wolfdietrich Kandler in a brief review published in *Weltstimmen*, 1953, quoted from Robert P. Warren's article (translated in *Amerikanische Rundschau*, 1947) which stated that Hemingway's works had created a symbol for the age. Kandler added that with *The Old Man* a symbol was not only created for an age, but for human existence itself. Hemingway, he stated, (1) presents the entire setting authentically; (2) gives the impression of depth and forward movement on different levels simultaneously (a characteristic that the majority of German critics praise in Hemingway);

(3) and includes as part of his "Metaphysik" traces of the pre-Christian mythological.[29]

Hermann Boekhoff stated that *The Old Man* belongs to the best narratives of world literature and he, too, saw its choice of subject and its "Weltgefühl" as representative of the modern age. Especially appropriate, according to Boekhoff, are: (1) the "Lebensgefühl" symbolized in the loneliness of the old man; (2) the "Menschenbild" that offers the simple moral, "A man can be destroyed but not defeated," and shows Santiago continuing his pursuit even though it remains hopeless; (3) the timeless subject matter that is handled with elevated simplicity. Like Kandler, Boekhoff drew attention to Hemingway's discreet use of symbols and praised the organic unity of the work despite its movement on at least two different levels: "This novel is one of the few modern works of art in which foreground and background flow together in a single grand surface." The novel, Boekhoff added, illustrates two lessons: "The art of narration is epic, and greatness is simplicity."[30]

Similarly, Hans Jürgen Baden (*Zeitwende*, 1953) pointed to Santiago's trial as a "battle against destiny," one that represents the struggle of every man who must undergo inevitable defeat. All that is left for Santiago is to endure his fate bravely, but nevertheless, Baden stated, the warmth and high spiritedness of the novel "are more deeply moving than one can express." Baden saw no lasting consolation in the story of Santiago, but he did find the novel instructive for the ultimate questions that it raised. Every man, Baden pointed out, must struggle with his "Schicksalsfisch" with only a thin plank between himself and destruction. Hemingway does not tell us that we will have more than this to depend on, or if we will have more than a skeleton when we return, but he does pose the question, Baden emphasized, and forces the reader to consider his final outcome.[31]

In *Die Kommenden* (1963), the German critic A. A. contended that the immediate reality of *The Old Man and the Sea* is so captivating that many readers remain unaware that behind the polished style and simply-constructed plot stands an imagination which reflects the destiny of our epoch. Santiago, A. A. claimed, is a representative of the "Ur-Imagination" which appears in many myths and fairy tales. It is the story of a man who leaves the shoreline, releases the powers of his soul from their connection to the body, and with them dives into the sea of the ethereal, the transcendental world of the imagination. This is the first step of a higher awareness during which spiritual powers allow symbolic pictures to become visible to man.[32]

The fisherman is, then, an "uralte Mysterien-Gestalt" who attempts to transfer the workings of the imagination into consciousness. The fish A. A. saw as the old catacomb symbol of the Christ-essence, the picture of the indestructable counterpart of the earthly "I." But in *The Old Man and the Sea*, the fisherman cannot bring the catch home; he cannot bring the great imagination into the area of conscious experience. He has gone out too far, and his powers are not developed enough. According to A. A., Hemingway is thereby illustrating that new powers must be awakened and patiently developed if man is to retrieve more than a skeleton from his imaginative endeavors. Only then will he succeed in defeating the sharks, those countless impressions from our external world which destroy the spiritual images from the world of the imagination.[33]

The following three critics focused on the religious implications of *The Old Man* and saw in Santiago's struggle a valuable lesson for contemporary man. Friedrich Hansen-Löve (*W und W*, 1952) wrote that although at first glance Hemingway seemed to be back again with his tough-guy sentimentality, and the grim struggle of Santiago with the huge fish appeared to be a repetition of Ahab and the white whale, *The Old Man* depicts the transformation of the old romantic into the "neue Klassik." Most important for Hansen-Löve was the religious attitude that he found in Santiago. Unlike Ahab he calls upon heaven for aid, and during his moving dialogue with the fish (not a huge symbol, exceeding natural limitations, but a simple creature of God) Santiago expresses an orthodox Catholic view of creation. Hansen-Löve saw the turning point of the novel coming when Santiago, back in the harbor, asks himself if anything has bested him in the struggle and answers, "Nothing . . . I went out too far." Here, Hansen-Löve claimed, one could almost speak of a natural awareness of sin, and one could believe that the entire struggle and the trials of all previous years were there only to teach the old man this lesson. Hemingway, according to Hansen-Löve, may be learning this lesson himself, for the prayer and conversation of Santiago with the fish sound like a turning away from the nihilism, the *nada* of "A Clean, Well-Lighted Place"; and his awareness "I went out too far" stresses the need for humility, which T. S. Eliot repeatedly recommended for our time. By renouncing the romantic-superhuman, Hemingway was able to concentrate on the concrete in his language, thus allowing the reader himself to see beyond the worldly to the divine: "The result was a masterpiece of realistic prose; the language is so *real*, that one can look beyond it to that which really exists."[34]

Ursula Brumm (*NDH*, 1958) in one of the few studies of symbols in *The Old Man* pointed out that the endured suffering of the old fisherman is crowned with the symbol of passion. As the luckless Santiago returns from his battle with the sharks, he carries the mast of the boat over his shoulder as Christ carried the cross; also like Christ, he stumbles under the burden. Finally, in his shack he lies on the bed, arms outstretched, and his bleeding palms facing upward.[35]

A third critic, H. B. Kranz, wrote of the powerful impact of this "simple, at times realistic, at other times poetical, fable of a struggle of man with nature and with himself." Kranz implied there was a pantheistic attitude permeating the book when he spoke of Santiago's relation to the fish as "strange love," but this led him to a questionable statement: "Hemingway, who has always stood in close relationship to God and nature, has written about it with deep feeling in this book." Kranz predicted there would be widely-diversified interpretations of Hemingway's symbols, but like most German critics, he offered none himself. Whether read as allegory or as poetic realism, the novel, he stated, remains "a small masterpiece."[36]

Interesting for its Marxist approach to Hemingway, which contrasts markedly with the mainstream of West German Hemingway criticism, was a review of *The Old Man* by B. U., published in the East German *Aufbau* in 1956. Here there was little emphasis on the mystic or the archetypal, and reaction to the novel depended on the presence or lack of Marxist implications. In spite of its limited perspective the book was praised for its classical compactness and simplicity, and for its dramatic presentation of the struggle for human existence. Important for this critic was not the inner victory of Santiago (in his exhausted, empty-handed condition he was compared to the exploited workers of the capitalistic world), but the overcoming of his own isolation. The absence of the boy during Santiago's battle with the fish was seen as a positive factor, for Santiago realizes that the hopeless struggle he carries on alone would have been different with the help of the boy. Seen in this light, the novel was still an acknowledgement of brotherhood and humanitarianism in spite of its tragic ending, and this critic felt Hemingway had turned his back on the anti-humanistic, pessimistic tendencies which stemmed from the romanticism of the "lost generation." For each reference in *The Old Man* about the insignificance of man, B. U. claimed there was a similar statement which counteracted it, e.g., Santiago first says that man does not count for much when compared with great birds or other wild animals, but later he refutes this with his statement about man's enduring spirit. As a rule, East German critics, once they approved Hemingway's subject matter, had high praise for his writing technique. The critic B. U. wrote that the experience on the sea and the actual battle with the fish were comprised of "masterful, stirring, and deeply moving descriptions"; added to this, he stated, is the depth in atmosphere Hemingway achieves through (1) artistically precise observations of nature; (2) intense character development; (3) the integration of both with the presentation of a socially relevant theme.[37]

Wolfgang Grözinger, writing in the Catholic magazine *Hochland*, 1953, expressed a strikingly similar view of *The Old Man*. He, too, stated that the theme of the novel traces the solicitous, reverential love of a young boy who enters the lonely, poverty-stricken world of Santiago and provides him with a link to humanity. In dogmatic fashion Grözinger disagreed with his fellow Germans who compared the book with Greek tragedy, for, he wrote, the fisherman is portrayed on the same elemental level of nature as the fish. Spiritual tragedy is beyond Hemingway's range, he claimed, and therefore the novel calls forth feelings of sadness rather than loftier feelings of fear and pity. In spite of this, Grözinger concluded that the story was narrated with "sovereign mastery" and with the skill that maturity lends.[38]

Common to both the German and the American reaction to *The Old Man and the Sea* was the search for an ideological background for the novel. Attention was directed not so much to Hemingway's technical achievements, but to the mythological, archetypal, and legendary overtones in Santiago's struggle with the fish. Germans were united in their belief that Hemingway had created a masterpiece which had special relevance for postwar Germany. They, like Santiago, had suffered overwhelming defeat, and critics found in him not only a new Hemingway hero, but also an instructive model for contemporary man. True, he was less adventuresome outwardly than Hemingway's previous heroes, but he compensated for this with his growing faith in humanity, his humility, and his indomitable spirit. Critics found the uncomplicated language of the new hero consistent with the simple but powerful theme of the novel, and perfectly suited to an uneducated fisherman. Santiago's struggle with death and defeat was considered more meaningful than that of other Hemingway heroes, because it was not a sought-after adventure, but a part of his daily life and necessary struggle for survival.

NOTES

[1] Engelbert Kirchner, "Die überwundene Niederlage," *FH*, VIII (1953), 74–75.

[2] *Ibid.*, p. 75.

[3] Erich Gronke, "Das jüngste Buch Hemingways," *ZAA*, II (1954), 74–75.

[4] *Ibid.*, p. 123.

[5] Hans Daiber, "Der alte Mann und Kapitän Ahab," *DR*, LXXIX (1953), 618.

[6] *Ibid.*, pp. 618–20.

[7] Werner Richter, "Hemingway und die Helden," *DR*, LXXXI (1955), 54–55.

[8] *Ibid.*, pp. 55–56.

[9] Hans Blumenberg, "Die Peripetie des Mannes. Über das Werk Ernest Hemingways," *Hochland*, XLVII (1955–1956), 221–22.

[10] *Ibid.*, p. 223.

[11] *Ibid.*, p. 229.

[12] *Ibid.*, pp. 230–33.

[13] Stresau, *Ernest Hemingway*, p. 77.

[14] *Ibid.*, pp. 25–26.

[15] Pongs, *Im Umbruch der Zeit*, p. 37.

[16] *Ibid.*, pp. 337–41.

[17] *Ibid.*, pp. 708–09.

[18] *Ibid.*

[19] *Ibid.*, pp. 709–10.

[20] *Ibid.*, p. 344.

[21] *Ibid.*, p. 363.

22 *Ibid.*, p. 382.

23 Grenzmann, p. 434.

24 Joseph Baur, "Ein Stück Epos," *Welt und Wort*, VIII (1953), 81.

25 *Ibid.*, p. 82.

26 Blöcker, "Der Unbesiegte," pp. 229–30.

27 *Ibid.*, p. 230.

28 *Ibid.*

29 Wolfdietrich Kandler, "Der alte Mann und das Meer," *Weltstimmen*, XXII (1953), 4.

30 Hermann Boekhoff, *WM*, XCIII (1952–1953), 85.

31 Hans Jürgen Baden, "Der alte Mann und die See," *Zeitwende*, XXIV (1952–1953), 556–57.

32 A. A., "Dichtung als Imagination," *Die Kommenden*, XVII, No. 9 (1963), 12–13.

33 *Ibid.*

34 Friedrich Hansen-Löve, "Ein Fazit Hemingways?" *W und W*, VII (1952), 947–48.

35 Ursula Brumm, "Christus in der amerikanischen Literatur," *NDH* (December, 1958), 792.

36 H. B. Kranz, "Literatur und die Literaturwissenschaft," *Universitas*, VIII (1953), 70–71.

37 B. U., "Umschau," *Aufbau* (Ost), XII (1956), 738–39.

38 Wolfgang Grözinger, "Erzähler, Denker, Träumer," *Hochland*, XLVI (1953–1954), 187.

CHAPTER FOUR
CONCLUSION

It is often the case that an artist's reception among foreign critics is considerably different from his reception among the critics of his own country. The preceding study has illustrated that this was true for Hemingway in Germany. Germans themselves have attempted to explain the reasons behind Hemingway's popularity in their country. Horst Oppel, for example, has pointed out that the belief that American writers could contribute to the reorientation of man in postwar Germany directly affected the critics' response to Hemingway. Earlier, German critics spoke of *The Sun Also Rises* and *A Farewell to Arms* as models of style— exactitude, compactness, preciseness—now, he stated, they more frequently turn to Hemingway's later work "with its symbolic realism, through which he creates parables of human existence and, in spite of the force of destiny, maintains the dignity of man." Germans reacted more favorably to *Across the River and Into the Trees*, Oppel explained, because German critics accepted the external events of war and saw the main value of the novel in the transformation of Cantwell and in his attitude towards death achieved through inner purgation. *The Old Man and the Sea* was the most highly praised of all Hemingway's works, for "In spite of complete defeat, the old man succeeds in maintaining his inner equilibrium, and his lonely struggle with the elements becomes a symbol of human fate; here we find a surprising return to the same timeless question which gives the American classics their permanent value."[1]

Other values that Germans found relevant to their situation Hemingway demonstrated in his own life. According to Gustav Blanke, Germans admired him because he was able to affirm life at a time when old values, including the belief in American democracy, were crumbling. Whereas Harry Crosby and Hart Crane were driven to suicide or Ezra Pound turned to fascism, Hemingway was able to preserve his integrity during a period of extreme isolation:

> Ernest Hemingway overcame his memories of the horrors
> and bloodshed of war . . . with the help of a strictly dis-
> ciplined prose style and a code of conduct which called for
> bravery in the face of death and meaninglessness.[2]

Heinrich Straumann concluded, "This is part of the reason why
Hemingway has probably had a greater following amongst the
postwar generation . . . than any other American writer. One might
say that the principle of absolute honesty is the one and only value
that emerges from the collapse of all other values."[3]

Helmut Papajewski pointed out that "Hemingway's great success in Germany, both with the reading public and the critics,"
was aided by the tradition of violence in German literature during
the Twenties and Thirties; after Germany's defeat in World War
I conservative writers had elevated violence to almost mythological
proportions. Another reason for Hemingway's popularity, Papajewski added, was the kinship of his works with existential philosophy. Earlier, Germans were interested primarily in social and
documentary material in American literature, but after 1954 their
attention shifted to literature which explored the individual soul.
Critics saw in Hemingway's simple style a deliberate artistic technique "resulting from the impact of great catastrophes upon the
human mind." Man was directed away from chaotic outside forces
"back to a realization of the great elemental forces at work in life
and thus to a true understanding of his own real existence." Drawing upon the existential thought of Kierkegaard, critics used familiar phrases such as "Nullpunktsexistenz" and "life at zero" in
their commentaries on Hemingway's fiction. After Karl Jaspers
coined the word "Geworfensein," meaning the helpless state in
which man finds himself in a hostile world, "readers immediately
connected the people in Hemingway's stories with the state of
'Geworfensein.' " Other existential qualities that Germans found
in Hemingway's works were (1) the isolation of the individual, and
the stress on "the terrors of existence," and (2) the boredom and
the sense of banality which seems to illustrate the type of boredom
discussed by Kierkegaard, "for it is through the experience of boredom that many of Hemingway's heroes become aware of their own
existence in an extremely painful way."[4]

Representing the East German point of view, Waldemar Damp
explained that Hemingway has become a phenomenon in world

literature because his works "reflect the modern class struggle and develop in accordance with the changing needs of the struggling masses." *A Farewell to Arms*, Damp contended, is the first of Hemingway's works to exceed national boundaries in describing a situation common to all people. Although it lacks a social dimension, the novel expresses opposition to the control of the "Monopolbourgeoise" and their military strength. Such works, according to Damp, point the way to a world literature which educates the masses of all countries in the spirit of international solidarity. In the class-conscious *To Have and Have Not* Hemingway reached a new level in the development of his art, and in *For Whom the Bell Tolls* he "came to the realization that literature is not only the arena, but primarily the weapon, for the progress of mankind." This book, Damp contended, grew out of a struggle for freedom; thus history itself formed these new heroic personages, which in Hemingway's novel embody the formative power of the struggling masses. *Across the River and Into the Trees*, although it is preoccupied with the past, expresses clear opposition to the politics of the cold war and also serves as a contrast to adventuresome, reactionary war novels. *The Old Man and the Sea* presents the unembittered struggle and the unconquerable will of the workingman. According to Damp, "the majority of readers in the world see in the parable the unresolved conflict of the proletariat with the social conditions of bourgeois society." The fable is filled not only with the tragic strivings of the individual, but also with the awareness that "the working man is the measure of all things." It is for these reasons, Damp contended, that Hemingway's novels, written in opposition to fascism and war, have already become lasting treasures of world literature.[5]

Peter Heller has explained in his article "Unterschiede in der Denkart amerikanischer und deutscher Intellektueller" (*NDH*, 1958), that the cultural tradition in Germany has fostered a fascination with the isolated hero. Emphasis on the perceptions of the individual, beginning with Kant and Leibnitz, was extended by Goethe, whose works, according to Heller, served for more than a century "as a preliminary step leading towards the canonical, all-inclusive ego." Stress on the individual was continued in the philosophy of Hegel, Schopenhauer, and Nietzsche, and more recently in the works of Hesse and Heidegger. The result, according to

Heller, is that "The German intellectual has come to focus on the singularity of the first person."[6]

Heller's thesis may in part explain why German critics found Hemingway's isolated heroes to their liking, and why they tended to judge them, not according to how convincing they were as fictional creations, but according to their ability, as isolated human beings, to find their own private values. They praised Robert Jordan for his love of Maria and his devotion to the cause of the Spanish rebels; they sympathized with Cantwell as an isolated man struggling with his past and finding purgation and release in the face of death. In Santiago they found Hemingway's most complete portrayal of the hero; one strangely modern in his isolation and defeat, but yet a hero offering them what they needed to hear. Santiago's courage, endurance, and undying spirit allowed him to achieve an inner victory in spite of defeat. His statement "A man can be destroyed but not defeated," critics applied unabashedly to their own situation.

Another factor in the German cultural tradition that would attract the German critic to Hemingway is a longstanding preoccupation and sympathy with death. It includes, according to Heller,

> Werther's suicide, the death wish of a Novalis, Tristan's self-fulfillment in *Liebestod*, the tendency towards self-destruction and ruin which we associate with the idea of *Götterdämmerung*; also Schopenhauer's chapter on death in the *Welt als Wille und Vorstellung*, Freud's conception of a death instinct, [and] Heidegger's definition of life as a first step towards the finality of death.[7]

Hemingway's fascination with death and its effect on characters who witness it is obvious in his earliest short stories, e.g., "Indian Camp" and "In Another Country"; in his works of the 1930's, *Death in the Afternoon*, *Green Hills of Africa*, "The Snows of Kilimanjaro," and in all his major novels. One of the reasons German critics found *Across the River and Into the Trees* more engrossing than did Americans was that the novel's primary concern was a man's confrontation with imminent death. Similarly, existentialist critics naturally felt immediate kinship with a writer who recognized death as the only absolute, as "Grenzsituation" which forced characters such as Cantwell and Jordan back upon themselves.

Hemingway's descriptions of love relationships also attracted the interest of German critics. One of the reasons was the frankness with which he described physical intimacy, but also important to them was the mystical or transcendent side of love expressed in *For Whom the Bell Tolls* and *Across the River and Into the Trees.* Hemingway seemed to say there was at least hope for a momentary escape from existential isolation, whether it be in identifying with another human being or, with the aid of love, in perceiving spiritual insights otherwise impossible. In addition, Germans have always been attracted to the submissive, devoted female character who lives to please the male. This explains why German critics in the 1920's had praised Dreiser's Jennie Gerhart as "the loving, yielding woman who gives her all to the man, . . . a type fundamentally and exclusively German,"[8] and why they favored the same type recreated in Hemingway's Catherine, Maria, and Renata. In certain of Hemingway's women they also found overtones of Dante's Beatrice and Goethe's Gretchen. Renata, for example, they saw as more than a confidante or lover for Cantwell in *Across the River and Into the Trees*; it was she who provided the means for the hero's purgation before his death.

Because they tended to read Hemingway primarily as a spokesman-philosopher for modern times, and secondarily as a literary artist, West German critics would rank Hemingway's major novels in a different order than do Americans. Leslie Fiedler,[9] Ray B. West,[10] and Philip Young,[11] for example, consider *The Sun Also Rises* and *A Farewell to Arms* to be Hemingway's greatest achievements. Germans would likely place *The Old Man and the Sea* first for its classic simplicity, its portrayal of the modern hero, and its moral of endurance. *For Whom the Bell Tolls*, with its objectivity, epic breadth, and closely linked themes of love and death would rank second. Third, mainly for its lyric qualities and tender, elevated love story would likely be *Across the River and Into the Trees.* These novels explored themes that naturally found favor among Germans, and they expressed the affirmation and hope that the critics felt were relevant to their own situation.

Although literary criticism in general did not recover from the effects of the Nazi regime until after 1955, Germans have made valuable contributions to Hemingway criticism, especially in recent years. Foremost among them are (1) Nikolaus Happel's articles on Hemingway's style; (2) explications of individual short stories by Hans Galinsky and Broder Carstensen; (3) an investigation of Hemingway's use of Indians by Franz Schulz; (4) Rudolph Haas's study of Hemingway's portrayal of death; and (5) the existential interpretations of Werner Hüllen, Dieter Wellershoff, Helmut Papajewski, and Horst Oppel.

The public reaction to Hemingway in postwar Germany is more elusive and can only be speculated upon in a study of this scope. We do know, however, that from the time of the first translations in the early nineteenth century, Germans have been avid readers of American literature. Their preferences have been for realistic social criticism (Upton Sinclair and Sinclair Lewis) and for adventure stories featuring a primitive setting and a strong, independent hero (J. F. Cooper and Jack London). In providing exciting adventure, realistic love scenes, and an atmosphere of war and destruction, Hemingway's fiction corresponded to these tastes. At first Hemingway's conception of the hero presented a problem to Germans, for they had become used to the propagandistic hero of Nazi times. But eventually, as Papajewski pointed out, they came to admire the strength and dignity of the Hemingway characters who were able to regulate their own behavior by strict adherence to a code. Bullfighting, Papajewski added, provides "the extreme form of the heroic code," and this explains the popularity of Hemingway's stories on bullfighters immediately after the war." [12]

The last three novels published before Hemingway's death could not have come at a more propitious time in Germany. By 1945 many of their own writers had emigrated, and German readers and critics longed for renewed contact with foreign literatures. The United States, as an occupational power, was overwhelmingly present, and the market for American books was at its peak. In the first postwar years, Germans were in desperate need of a spokesman. Hemingway, they felt, was qualified because as a writer, newspaper reporter, and soldier he had been closely associated with European affairs for nearly thirty years. Like the German people he, too, had suffered the disillusionment of two world wars. And unlike the Nazi propagandists who had led Germany to destruction, Hemingway pledged himself to truth and objectivity. His sincerity as an artist, critics felt, was reflected in his style.

The German reading public shared with their critics a fascination for the Hemingway legend. Hemingway's popularity did not depend solely on the artistic quality of his work, for it was his life that stirred the imagination of his readers. Germans often identified more with Hemingway's own life than that of his fictional heroes, and they remained fascinated by the man who could live his life as skillfully as he wrote his books. Consequently Hemingway's influence was not limited to literary circles or to the intellectually elite, but reached the common man as well. As Lania stated, "No writers of our time—and few writers of earlier times—have had such a large and loyal following. Readers of all levels and classes." [13]

Finally, Hemingway was well known in Germany as a biographer of the "lost generation" and as a revolutionary stylist before the Nazi's take-over in 1933. Although he was an American, his settings were usually foreign and therefore had a more universal appeal. Hemingway's style was easy to read in translation, and he had an excellent translator in Annemarie Horschitz-Horst, who won frequent praise from the German critics. Ernst Rowohlt, Hemingway's German publisher, was one of the foremost publishers in the country. By accurately judging the tastes and needs of the German reading public and issuing Hemingway's works accordingly, he assured for them a large public sale.

It becomes evident from this brief survey that the reasons behind Hemingway's popularity in postwar Germany, as a man and as a writer, are numerous and complex. A comprehensive explanation would necessarily include investigations in sociology, cultural history, and national psychology as well as literature and literary criticism. The present study, however, while limited for the most part to the opinions of German literary critics and newspaper reviewers, has suggested a number of significant conclusions relating to the Hemingway vogue in Germany. It was Hemingway's honesty, his expressed concern for truth, and his unconditional striving for his own artistic goals that won the admiration of the German public and the critics. The favorable reaction to Hemingway the man, even when he projected his public image into his own literary works, explains the overwhelmingly positive tone of German criticism during the two decades following World War II.

NOTES

[1] Horst Oppel, "American Literature in Postwar Germany: Impact or Alienation?" *NS*, V (1962), 2–4.

[2] Blanke, p. 159.

[3] Straumann, p. 101.

[4] Papajewski, "The Critical Reception of Hemingway's Works in Germany since 1920," pp. 78–82.

[5] Waldemar Damp, "Zu Ernest Hemingway als weltliterarischen Phänomen," *Wissenschaftliche Zeitschrift der Ernst-Moritz-Arndt-Universität Greifswald*, XIV, No. 4 (1965), 445–50.

[6] Peter Heller, "Unterschiede in der Denkart amerikanischer und deutscher Intellektueller," *NDH*, V (October, 1958), 620–22.

[7] *Ibid.*, p. 627.

[8] Schoenberner as quoted by Springer, p. 66.

[9] Leslie Fiedler, *Waiting for the End* (New York, 1964), p. 13.

[10] Ray B. West, "The Sham Battle over Ernest Hemingway," *Western Review*, XVII (Spring, 1953), 234–36.

[11] *Ibid.*, p. 237.

[12] Papajewski, "The Critical Reception of Hemingway's Works in Germany since 1920," pp. 80–81.

[13] Lania, "Hemingway," p. 240.

EPILOGUE

HEMINGWAY IN GERMANY, 1965–1971

One of the major factors in the German criticism of Hemingway during the past six years has been a reassessment of the Hemingway legend. Among the first to attack Hemingway's public image was a Frenchman, George Albert Astre, whose critical biography *Hemingway par lui-même* was translated into German and published in the Rowohlt Monograph Series as *Ernest Hemingway in Selbstzeugnissen und Bilddokumenten* in 1961. Astre's book, like the earlier German studies of Stresau and Lania, was replete with Hemingway's heroic poses, but it also included a number of photographs in which Hemingway appeared as a wistful, beaten old man. Astre contended that Hemingway inherited many of his father's weaknesses (e.g., his nervousness and sentimentality), and spent the greater part of his lifetime struggling to overcome them: "He is conscious of a great weakness and fear, and he struggles to overcome the ominous threats and the confusion which he finds in his secret loneliness, if it be only through the projection of a kind of superior self."[1] What he succeeded in creating, stated Astre, was a gigantic, silent, clumsy figure, one who wore open shirts and allowed his hairy breast to show.[2]

The first extended German reassessment of Hemingway's personality and the legend that grew up around it is Hans Jürgen Baden's *Literatur und Selbstmord* (1965), a didactic, thesis-ridden study developed from Baden's lectures at the University of Münster. Using Klaus Mann, a German, Cesare Pavese, an Italian, and Hemingway as the American representative, Baden sought to illustrate through the use of negative examples, that man requires the redemptive grace of Jesus Christ in order to find justification for his life. All attempts to find self-justification ("Rechtfertigung") through finite means, such as political engagement, love, or literary endeavors, are doomed to failure, he claimed, and in the case of these three writers, suicide was the inevitable consequence.[3]

Although Baden's approach was misleading and his biographical information, especially in the case of Hemingway, was unreliable, he did offer a new, critical look at the Hemingway myth. The key words to understanding Hemingway's life, his works and also his tragic death, Baden claimed, are to be found in the title of his early volume of short stories *Winner Take Nothing*.[4] Baden, as Astre had done, contended that Hemingway inherited many of his father's weaknesses and attempted throughout his life to compensate for them with exaggerated robustness. Journalists and photographers aided him in creating a strong-man myth, but very early, according to Baden, it becomes evident that behind the pose of bravado stands anxiety and despair.[5] As he grew older, the credo of endurance Hemingway created in *The Old Man and the Sea* no longer served him, and "He was deserted by his courage, his bravery in facing destiny." In the light of Hemingway's suicide, Baden claimed, we are justified in reading the novel as "a document of overwhelming resignation."[6] One knows that Santiago will never recover from his defeat even though he dreams of going out to sea again. Like Hemingway himself, "He has experienced the terrible senselessness that destroys all human endeavor and thwarts all human bravery."[7]

Since 1965 *Der Spiegel*, the news magazine which contributed to the making of the Hemingway legend in Germany during the 1950's, has published several articles emphasizing Hemingway's personal weaknesses. An example is "Hemingway-Manuskripte: Keine Widerrede," which appeared in *Der Spiegel* in 1967. The article described the recent sale of an unpublished story and several letters of Hemingway's, put up for auction by a former friend living in Spain. The *Spiegel* journalist quoted excerpts from Hemingway's letters, making the legendary warrior-hunter sound like a henpecked husband: "Day and night, with unfailing regularity, I am told what a heartless, thankless, selfish, stupid, spoiled, indifferent, egotistical, publicity-hungry son of a bitch I am." And in a more submissive vein: "Mary is very dear, but she has positively decided to be neither a slave nor a cook. She also does not want my writing to come into conflict with her life, her plans or her writing —so I give in and do not dare to object."[8]

Another unflattering picture of Hemingway appeared in the article " 'Häng dich auf, tapferer Hemingstein!' " (*Der Spiegel*, August 23, 1971), which summarized Irvin and Marilyn Yalom's recent psychoanalytic study published in *Archives of General Psy-*

chiatry (June, 1971). Basing their analysis on Hemingway's novels, stories, and his letters to former U.S. Army officer Charles Lanham, the Yaloms contended that "Hemingway suffered almost his entire life from severe depression, and finally, in the years immediately preceding his suicide, from paranoia." During World War II, Hemingway, according to the Yaloms, sought to identify with Lanham, and often looked up to the American officer with a child's admiration for the professional soldier. Shortly after the war had ended, Hemingway, they claimed, was languishing in inactivity and secretly envying Lanham's military reputation. It was at this time that he began to transfer his feelings of inadequacy to other people. In 1960, reported *Der Spiegel*, Hemingway felt the overwhelming destructive force of age; the concern for his failing body led to hypochondria, accompanied by weight loss, insomnia, and loss of appetite. Electroconvulsive treatment failed to restore his psychic balance, and Hemingway was in a state of total despair before he took his own life.[9]

Similar reassessments of the Hemingway legend have become an integral part of the Germans' critical response to the books by and about Hemingway which have appeared in Germany since 1965. Helping to keep the German interest in Hemingway alive have been the translations of three posthumous publications: *A Moveable Feast (Paris—Ein Fest fürs Leben*, 1965), *By-Line: Ernest Hemingway (49 Depeschen*, 1969), and *Islands in the Stream (Insel im Strom*, 1971). A translation of A. E. Hotchner's *Papa Hemingway* appeared in 1966; Audre Hanneman's *Ernest Hemingway: A Comprehensive Bibliography* in 1967, and Carlos Baker's *Hemingway: A Life Story* in 1969.

The reaction of British and American critics to *A Moveable Feast*, Hemingway's first posthumous publication, was generally favorable. Frank Kermode, for example, drew attention to the "sharpness and suggestiveness" of the style, and added that in some ways *A Moveable Feast* was Hemingway's best work since the 1920's. Although the subject is a familiar one, Kermode stated, "no other book [of Hemingway's] is of this authority and distinction, and no other so strongly conveys (largely by omission, of course) the sense of time regained."[10] Alfred Kazin pointed out that *A Moveable Feast* was not necessarily non-fiction, for it "is too splendidly, too artfully written; the chapters are sketches and anecdotes often as fine in their texture as Hemingway's famous stories."[11]

Among German critics, however, *A Moveable Feast* did not fare nearly as well. As Helmut Braem stated in his review "Blick zurück in Rührung," written for the *Stuttgarter Zeitung* in September, 1965: "One man's meat, another man's poison: thus the reception of Ernest Hemingway's posthumous book *A Moveable Feat* [*sic*] is divided." According to Braem the difference in critical judgment could be attributed in part to the generation gap among critics. The most favorable reactions came from critics who belong to Hemingway's generation and thus associate Paris of the early 1920's with their own youthful experiences. Younger critics, Braem explained, discovered Paris and Hemingway for the first time after 1945 and consequently they are in a position to be more objective. Among them "the voices of the dissatisfied and disappointed dominate—those who criticize the monotony of sound and the labored sentence constructions, and occasionally, the exaggerated pathos."[12]

An illustration of the divided reaction to *A Moveable Feast* in Germany, which Braem outlined in the *Stuttgarter Zeitung*, can be found in his own review, printed in *Die Zeit* in October, 1965. Braem, as did a number of German critics, questioned the role of Mary Hemingway in tampering with her late husband's manuscripts: "It belongs to the fine art of widowhood to emphasize enthusiastically that she, the survivor, has 'scrupulously' edited the work of her deceased husband. Why is this defensiveness necessary? Is it, by chance, justified?" Mary Hemingway's shortening of the original text is a matter of ethical concern: " 'Papa' controlled the literary art of omission magnificently. And now his widow is practicing it. That is not at all magnificent; it is only irritating." Although Braem praised several of the portraits in *A Moveable Feast*, reflection, he contended, was never Hemingway's strong point. Only "when the remembered moments are reduced to their timeless essence and attention is directed to concrete details, does the familiar Hemingway style emerge." The descriptions of early morning Paris contain some of Hemingway's best sentences, but "There are notably few of them in this book," Braem concluded.[13]

Similar to Braem's review of *A Moveable Feast* is Hans Sahl's "Hemingways Spätwerk," *Universitas*, 1965. According to Sahl, the time has come for readers to take a more objective look at Hemingway and his works. Seldom, he stated, has an American writer been able to write about Paris with as much understanding for the French way of life, but at the same time, seldom has a writer of Hemingway's calibre been so unreceptive to the spiritual dimensions of the city, to its language, culture, and literature. Sahl contended that Hemingway had little understanding and sympathy for the friends of his Paris days, such as Joyce, Ford, Stein and Fitzgerald. In *A Moveable Feast* he places more emphasis on drinking, fishing, and racing than on his meetings with the great writers of his time.[14]

Hemingway's hesitation to talk about art and the anti-intellectualism which he cultivated were, Sahl claimed, part of the myth which he created for himself. After his suicide, one must ask, "Had he noticed, and was he aware that others had noticed, that the parable of his masculinity had been only a mask, a facade behind which an inner danger was hidden? And was this violent closing act not an attempt to bring about a last meaningful gesture, something which he was no longer able to do in his writing?" Sahl then posed the question which so many German critics began to ask: "Could it be that the great writer who played the strong man so enthusiastically, who loved boxers and bullfighters, was not at all as strong and manly as he pretended to be?"[15]

According to Barbara Bondy in "Auf der Suche nach dem verlorenen Hunger" in *Süddeutsche Zeitung*, 1965, readers approached *A Moveable Feast* eagerly, looking forward to the re-encounter with Hemingway. Instead they experienced "irritation over the declining skills, the short breath, the failing pen, the indiscretions without wit and subtlety." Bondy, too, questioned the right of Mary Hemingway to tamper with her husband's manuscripts, and she denied the claim of some that Hemingway in this book embodied the spirit of Paris in all its complexity: "here speaks the boy from Oak Park near Chicago, a barbarian obsessed with writing, born to eat, not to think; one who occasionally succeeds in creating wonderful pictures." Bondy contended that the famed Hemingway style was mannered, his portraits sketchy and at times in poor taste, and the structure "distressingly fragmented." *A Moveable Feast*, she concluded, is "a book of exhaustion, not expansion."[16]

An example of a more favorable German response to *A Move-*

able Feast came from Günter Blöcker, whose critical evaluations of Hemingway have often been closer to those of American critics than to German. Great literature, like great painting, Blöcker stated, teaches us to see. "Hemingway is one of those whose art has changed the world. There are places and things which we will always see with his eyes." The pictures of Paris in *A Moveable Feast*, each one complete in itself, belong to these places and things. The reminiscences are as carefully constructed as paintings: "Words are blended together like colors; a character or an event is not only described, but carefully developed out of simple declarative sentences." Hemingway's stylistic artistry is still very much in evidence, according to Blöcker, and aids the reader in actively participating in this earlier period of Hemingway's life.[17]

Another critic expressing a favorable response to *A Moveable Feast* was Werner Helwig, writing in *Merkur*, 1967. The sketches, he claimed, are characterized by the powerful energy that pulses through most of Hemingway's work. The description of Vorarlberg is among the most beautiful ever written about this area: "That is Hemingway, entirely himself, because he is alone." Helwig was not as skeptical of Mary Hemingway's editing as were many German critics: "The Paris memoirs, which were gathered from Hemingway's unfinished works, are fascinating enough to interest us in additional publications from his literary estate."[18]

In 1966, one year after the publication of *A Moveable Feast*, Hemingway was again a newsmaker in Germany with the appearance of Paul Baudisch's translation of A. E. Hotchner's *Papa Hemingway*, and Rowohlt's *Sämtliche Erzählungen* (containing translations of *The Fifth Column and the First Forty-nine* in addition to *The Old Man and the Sea*). From the biographical studies of Leicester Hemingway and George Astre, German readers had learned of Hemingway's mental and physical illnesses during his later years, but never in such explicit detail from a man who claimed to be among Hemingway's closest friends. Consequently Hotchner's book aroused considerable interest. *Der Spiegel*, in an article entitled "Hemingway-Biographie: Vertrauen verletzt," announced the publication of *Papa Hemingway*, and gave the book added publicity by mentioning Mary Hemingway's attempts to have it suppressed. *Der Spiegel* also repeated Hotchner's disclosure that Hemingway had made other suicide attempts before the one which finally succeeded.[19]

In her review of *Papa Hemingway* in the *Süddeutsche Zeitung*, Barbara Bondy defended both A. E. Hotchner's methods and motives: "In reality it is a sympathetic book—no stroke of genius, no betrayal; it is a record which gives a modest and fond account of a friendship lasting over thirteen years. It is an account without ulterior motives."[20]

However, more thoughtful German reviewers openly questioned Hotchner's writing skills and the validity of his sources. Reviewing *Papa Hemingway* for *Die Zeit*, Hanspeter Dörfel stated that the book had become "big business" in Germany as well as in the United States, and although some enthusiastic reviewers praised Hotchner highly, he was by no means an Eckermann or a Boswell. Dörfel criticized Hotchner's lack of documentation, the triviality of much of his material and the clumsy arrangement of observations, anecdotes, and conversations. Hotchner was seldom in Hemingway's company, Dörfel stated, although he poses as a close friend in his attempt to give the impression that there was little of importance in Hemingway's last fourteen years that escaped his notice. Dörfel warned that those looking for new insights into Hemingway's creative writing process would be disappointed, for Hotchner did not go below the surface of Hemingway's art.[21]

In spite of these strong objections, Dörfel felt that Hotchner's book could not be ignored. By providing valuable information on the aging Hemingway, it added support to the claim of recent scholarship that Hemingway's artistry did not parallel the development of his legend:

> It has become common knowledge among Hemingway critics —except here in Germany—that Hemingway reached his artistic high point very early; and that all his attempts to break out of his narrowly confined thematic concerns failed, just as his attempts to broaden his narrative techniques failed. . . . Also it is no secret that the older Hemingway began to copy himself with greater frequency.

In *Papa Hemingway* we see a Hemingway who becomes less and less critical of his own work, and slowly loses his self-confidence.

We also see how in his mannerisms he copies and parodies himself, how, artistically, he attempts to uphold the image of the he-man. Hotchner's book, Dörfel stated, exposed Hemingway's weaknesses, but it will not damage "the real Hemingway." After one has read *Papa Hemingway*, he concluded, one should reread several of Hemingway's short stories.[22]

An opinion similar to Dörfel's was expressed in an anonymous review in *Die Welt der Literatur*, 1966. According to the reviewer, Leicester Hemingway's book, *My Brother, Ernest Hemingway*, if less sensational, was more reliable than Hotchner's *Papa Hemingway*. This reviewer, too, criticized Hotchner's prose style, his loose organization, and his reliance on triviality to cover up for his lack of understanding Hemingway himself. Hotchner, he concluded, "covers the life and works of Ernest Hemingway with banalities, and the result is sticky sensationalism."[23] According to Werner Helwig (*Merkur*, 1967), Hotchner's book of recollections was written in an attempt to preserve the Hemingway myth. Like many other German critics, Helwig no longer believed that Hemingway's public image was a true expression of his personality: "For his entire life Hemingway forcefully opposed his natural characteristics." We can conclude, Helwig added, that this was the disguise of a lonely, desperate man.[24]

The following year, 1967, Audre Hanneman's *Ernest Hemingway: A Comprehensive Bibliography* appeared, and although its listings of German secondary literature were not comprehensive, it was well received by German scholars. Peter Nicolaisen noted that literary critics' interest in the works of Hemingway had declined markedly in recent years, and expressed the hope that the new bibliography would serve to keep interest in Hemingway alive. Additional research was necessary, Nicolaisen felt, especially investigations into Hemingway's political outlook, his aesthetic statements, and the artistry in his short stories.[25]

Hans-Joachim Kann, reviewing Hanneman's bibliography in *Die Neueren Sprachen*, saw its main value in the inclusion of letters, reports, poems, introductions, and commentaries. However, the incomplete listings of foreign newspapers, literary journals and dissertations, he stated, would be bothersome to the German reader.[26] In *Anglia* Dieter Meindl also questioned the comprehensiveness of Hanneman's work, but concluded that "The new

Hemingway bibliography . . . can serve as a model for future comprehensive bibliographies of other prominent American writers of our century."[27]

William White's edition of Hemingway's journalism, *By-Line: Ernest Hemingway*, published by Scribners in 1967, first appeared in German translation as *49 Depeschen* in 1969. A brief review in *Der Spiegel*, accompanied by pictures of Hemingway and Ilja Ehrenburg during the Spanish Civil War, and of Hemingway in 1947 receiving a military medal in Cuba, informed the German public of the book's existence shortly after its appearance in English.[28] The response of German literary critics to *By-Line: Ernest Hemingway* was generally more favorable than their response to *A Moveable Feast* had been. Assured that the original material had not been tampered with, they did not question the authenticity of the articles as they had questioned the Paris sketches. Critics were impressed by the accuracy of Hemingway's military and political prognostications, and they praised the succinctness of his journalistic style. Many still appeared eager to read Hemingway's first-hand accounts of fishing, soldiering and bullfighting, but now that the truth behind his legend had been made public, they were quick to point out signs of Hemingway's waning talent and his tendency to project the he-man image into his later news dispatches.

Helmut Braem contended that the distinctive Hemingway style is already evident in the earliest pieces: "There are fewer adverbs, and the adjectives are used with such concise expressions that they appear to take on a new significance." The later dispatches written in the 1950's Braem saw more as the public gestures of a famous man: "No doubt the descriptions are realistic and it is exciting to be in the company of 'Papa,' but the reader is left with an uncomfortable feeling." It is the reliable Hemingway reporting, "But he appears to be wearing a mask, one that resembles his face exactly. It is uncanny."[29]

Braem was most impressed by Hemingway's versatility as a journalist, for as *By-Line* illustrated, Hemingway could write as confidently about political events as he could about boxing and horse racing. In his journalism he was able to capture the intensity of the moment and his technique of omission, later perfected in his fiction, served to heighten the significance of the observed: "Little is stated; very much is said. This is news which even after more than thirty years still remains news." As did other German critics, Braem spoke highly of the translation by Ernst Schnabel and Elizabeth Plessen: it is more rhythmic, "richer in detail and distinguished by a much greater accuracy than the translations of Annemarie Horschitz-Horst, which have given many Germans a false impression of Hemingway."[30]

Reviewing *By-Line* in the *Süddeutsche Zeitung*, Hellmuth Karasek stated that although one could consider Hemingway's journalism simply as source material for his fiction, it is deserving of greater recognition than this: "These dispatches themselves are so important, so moving, that one need not connect them with the famous Hemingway in order to appreciate their significance. They clearly illustrate that Hemingway's reputation as a journalist should equal his reputation as a writer of fiction." At his best, Karasek claimed, Hemingway was a keen and sympathetic observer whose descriptions relied solely on concrete facts. During the late 1940's and early 1950's, however, Hemingway became more self-conscious, and his reports from World War II no longer have the "uncorruptible fullness" of those coming out of the Spanish Civil War.[31]

In her review in *Die Welt der Literatur*, Monika Mösslang praised the "simplicity," "precision," and "authenticity" of the dispatches in *By-Line* and pointed out that they trace Hemingway's development chronologically, his travels, his interests, and major events in his life. As did Braem and Karasek, Mösslang claimed that the later pieces lose the precision, balance, and objectivity of Hemingway's earlier efforts. Consequently, she added, the reader who does not like Hemingway will find confirmation for his opinions: "The man Hemingway, who appears more frequently in the foreground of his writing, especially in his later years, is often vain, naive and snobbish. His witty or satirical tone often sounds unnatural."[32] Similar to Mösslang's review was that of Hans-Jürgen Heise (*Christ und Welt*, 1969), which stated that *By-Line* was especially valuable for its perceptive analysis of historical events. It is true, Heise observed, that Hemingway pushes himself too much into the foreground in the later pieces, but it is because Hemingway's dispatches are so personal that "They clearly reveal the character of the author."[33]

In the same year that the Rowohlt Company published *By-Line* in translation, Carlos Baker's *Hemingway: A Life Story* appeared in German bookstores and libraries. The German translation, however, still had not appeared by the summer of 1971, and consequently the influence of Baker's biography of Hemingway has been kept at a minimum. Considerable information about the man behind the Hemingway myth has already been revealed by many lesser works, e.g., those by L. Hemingway, Astre, Baden, and Hotchner. Baker's study, simply by exposing further weaknesses in Hemingway's personality, will likely give added impetus to the re-evaluation process currently under way in Germany.

According to *Der Spiegel*, the most interesting section of "Super-Rechercheur" Baker's biography is the last chapter entitled "Journey Down." *Der Spiegel* listed Hemingway's failings which Baker documented: his insomnia, chronic headaches, diabetes, liver ailment, high blood pressure, depression and paranoia. Hemingway tried, unsuccessfully, *Der Spiegel* concluded, to write an homage to President Kennedy in February of 1961. In tears he turned to his doctor and said he could not write anymore.[34]

In another review of Baker's biography (*Universitas*, 1969), Herbert von Borch informed his readers that the book, whose copyright Mrs. Hemingway shared, would finally settle the matter of the Hemingway legend and his controversial suicide. Rather than review Baker's biographical methods, von Borch discussed Hemingway's accidents, his illnesses, and the loss of confidence in his writing ability which led to his suicide. "For Hemingway," he concluded, "the fear that he could no longer write was fatal. Perhaps it is the noblest form of despair; it is certainly the most incurable."[35]

The third of Hemingway's posthumous publications, *Islands in the Stream* (1970), was scheduled to appear in German translation in the Fall of 1971. Judging from the recent trends of German criticism and the reassessment of Hemingway which has been under way since the mid-1960's, one can conclude that *Islands in the Stream*, prepared for publication by Mary Hemingway and Charles Scribner, Jr., will not meet with great success in Germany. As their reaction to *A Moveable Feast* illustrated, many German critics are skeptical of Mary Hemingway's editorial skills, and they have called into question her right to tamper with the original manuscripts. Now that the truth behind the Hemingway legend has been revealed, Germans have expressed more freely their negative responses to Hemingway's writing. Perhaps a preview of the reception of *Islands in the Stream* can be found in the following remarks of an anonymous reviewer in the *Mainzer Anzeiger*, August 6, 1971. After announcing the experimental trend in the new book releases for the fall season, among them Erich Maria Remarque's *Schatten im Paradies*, Stefan Andres's *Die Versachung des Synesios*, Uwe Johnson's second *Jahrestage* volume, and Andy Warhol's *a*, the reviewer observed: "How little excitement Hemingway's new book *Islands in the Stream* has generated. This is especially noticeable if one recalls that only a short time ago the entire literary public looked forward impatiently to a new Hemingway publication."[36]

In 1968, Peter Nicolaisen stated that "the interest of literary critics in the works of Hemingway has markedly declined in recent years."[37] This observation is especially true if one applies it to recent German interest in Hemingway's major novels. Only the following studies, published since 1965, are worthy of mention: Helmut Liedloff's comparison of *A Farewell to Arms* and *All Quiet on the Western Front*,[38] Paul G. Buchloh's "Bedeutungsschichten in Ernest Hemingways *The Old Man and the Sea*," Wolfgang Wittkowski's "Gekreuzigt im Ring: Zu Hemingways *The Old Man and the Sea*," and two shorter articles on *For Whom the Bell Tolls* by Barbara Bondy and Robert Leicht.

Paul Buchloh's study appeared in *Amerikanische Erzählungen von Hawthorne bis Salinger* (1968), a collection of critical interpretations which originated in the American division of the English Seminar at the University of Kiel. The Kiel critics (Buchloh, Horst Kruse, Peter Nicolaisen, and Dietrich Jäger), who appear to share an enthusiasm for *explication de texte* and the theories associated with new criticism, have contributed several excellent studies of Hemingway's short fiction. However, the dangers of the new critical approach are perhaps best illustrated by Buchloh's unreliable interpretation of *The Old Man and the Sea*.

Reminding readers of Hemingway's iceberg theory and the deeper meanings beneath the simple surface of his prose, Buchloh attempted to elucidate four levels of meaning in the novel. In discussing the level of social criticism, Buchloh interpreted Santiago's advice to Manolin, "The Yankees cannot lose. . . . Have faith in the

Yankees my son," as an expression of Hemingway's belief in the American Dream. The references to other professional baseball teams, he speculated, also contain hidden significance: "The word play with the names of baseball teams perhaps becomes more understandable when Santiago warns the boy not to fear the Tigers of Detroit (perhaps the captains of industry), the Indians of Cleveland (perhaps the new immigrant groups), and the Reds of Cincinnati—the leftists in the intellectual stronghold of Cincinnati." As if to give credence to the final speculation, Buchloh added that Hemingway's attitude towards the communist scare in the early 1950's is well known.[39]

On the religious level, Buchloh pointed to the hidden significance of the names Hemingway chose for his characters. In Central and South America Santiago de Compostela is revered as a patron saint. The name brings to mind the disciple who left fishing in order to follow Christ and eventually became a martyr, and the author of the letter of Jacob who uses Job as a model and praises patient endurance of suffering. The name Manolin also has religious significance: "Manolin is a nickname for Immanuel, that Immanuel in Isaiah 7.14, who, according to prophecy, is to be the Savior of the future. According to Isaiah 9.6 the child will become the 'Everlasting Father,' and Matthew 1.22-23 links this prophecy to the birth of Jesus." Buchloh contended that the permanent defeat of Santiago is thus absolved by his true partnership with Manolin, who has been prophesied to be the Eternal Father. "The other names," he added, "that of the trustworthy Pedro (Peter) and the good-hearted Martin, are unequivocal and do not require an explanation."[40]

Although Hemingway may explore Christian values, Buchloh pointed out, this is not to say that he is a Christian writer. Santiago and Manolin can bind themselves in a positive partnership which gives cause for hope, but whether such a move by humanity is possible remains an open question. Man's self-destruction is always possible, and the new weapon Santiago hopes to grind from a spring leaf of an old Ford (a symbol of modern technology, according to Buchloh) could destroy a large fish, but also the sun and the moon if destiny drives man too far out and he can no longer control the consequences. In writing of individuality and the close sharing of mutual interest, Hemingway, Buchloh claimed, is still affirmative. However in discussing man and his relation to the cosmos he remains nihilistic.[41]

Wolfgang Wittkowski's more reliable study of *The Old Man and the Sea*[42] is similar in many ways to Richard Kopp's excellent monograph *Der Alte Mann und das Meer: Versuch einer Analyse*, 1964. Kopp had pointed out that in the character of Santiago two separate models are combined: "The figures of the matador and the crucified Christ are so closely paralleled that one could refer to Santiago as 'the crucified bullfighter.' " Through the fate of his hero, Hemingway expresses his existential truth. One does not sit back and enjoy security, but one provokes danger in order to determine one's self worth: "Clearly this attitude creates a new ethic. It is a bold ethic, the ethic of a man who has only himself and this life. . . . He is alone with the tormenting freedom to determine his own fate; his success is determined by his conduct."[43]

Similarly, Wittkowski argued that recent criticism of the novel has stressed the parallels of Santiago and Christ at the expense of the hero's "battle ethic." Santiago's pride, his gentlemanly conduct, the love he expresses for his opponent, his disciplined training for the ordeal, his concern for performing well, are all part of the "fighter's code." Thus, the struggle in *The Old Man and the Sea* does not revolve around guilt and sin, but around victory and defeat.[44] How can Hemingway link his hero with Christ and at the same time allow him to follow the code of a competitive athlete? Often, Wittkowski explained, Hemingway set his own scale of values up against those specifically associated with Christianity. To do this "he frequently secularized religious ideas in order to link them with the characters and events of his profane world, thereby elevating and justifying the latter." Wittkowski's conclusion is similar to Kopp's: "all of the allusions to the crucified Christ, especially the last, most obvious ones, are at the same time allusions to the fighter in the ring. The synthesis never provides for the dominance of the specifically Christian meaning; rather, it elevates the non-Christian fighter's code."[45]

On April 17/18, 1971, the *Süddeutsche Zeitung* printed under the heading "Hemingway: *Wem die Stunde schlägt*" two revealing responses to *For Whom the Bell Tolls*, "Schlafsack-Gespräche" by Barbara Bondy, a critic of the older generation, and "Von den Schönheiten eines Bürgerkriegs" by Robert Leicht, representing younger readers in Germany today.[46] Bondy's reactions to *For Whom the Bell Tolls* are significant, for they parallel the general response of Germans to Hemingway's works during the last twenty-five years: the early postwar enthusiasm, and following Hemingway's suicide, the more objective reassessment.

Bondy's generation read *For Whom the Bell Tolls* for the first time in English during 1946 and 1947. She and her fellow students were greatly moved by the novel, she wrote, especially by the love story of Robert and Maria: "we were fascinated by the dialogue in the sleeping bag scenes . . . again and again we read the talk of love and death, of the exchange of 'I' and 'you,' which reminded us of the second act of *Tristan*." Students at that time, she stated, regardless of nationality, saw in the destroyed lives and love, in the senselessness of Robert Jordan's entire endeavor, an echo of their own experience during the last years of the war.[47]

In 1971, however, twenty-five years after her first encounter with *For Whom the Bell Tolls*, Bondy no longer felt the same sense of identification with Hemingway's lovers, and their dialogue appeared to her like something out of a fairy tale. In her re-evaluation of the novel, she expressed the opinion of the most recent of Hemingway's critics in Germany—that Hemingway's best work was done in the earlier part of his career (the 1920's), when he relied most heavily on implicit rather than explicit narration. In *For Whom the Bell Tolls*, Hemingway, Bondy contended, is too explicit; his prose no longer carries with it an undercurrent of horror, and his artistic sensibility disperses itself in the description of minor events.[48]

Another reason that the novel no longer seems as powerful as it once did, Bondy explained, is that "The use of war as a means of intensifying life is an old motif which we no longer value." Robert Leicht, who represented the younger generation of readers in Germany, agreed. In the mass executions which Pilar describes, for example, Leicht pointed out that the novel offers "a description of malevolent precision." Robert Jordan is not saddened or shocked by this information; instead he admires Pilar's masterful description. Hemingway himself, although he neither encourages slaughter nor describes such events for propagandistic purposes, seems to take pleasure in writing about violence. According to Leicht, Hemingway's choice of subject and his means of treating it lead to the question whether, indeed, there can be good war literature, or whether one can turn to war as subject matter for only aesthetic reasons. Leicht answered negatively: "If literature distinguishes itself by maintaining aesthetic distance (and by considering the ability to achieve distance a virtue), then it appears impossible to create war literature. In war there is no distance and no problem of aesthetics—one either glorifies it or abhors it." Hemingway, Leicht contended, expends his efforts in describing the events of war, rather than reflecting upon Jordan's role in it. War and love, aggression and sexual drive, death and luck are all woven together without a sufficient sense of conflict. The best example appears when Maria wishes to hold the legs of Jordan's machine gun while it fires, and to make love to him at the same time. In *For Whom the Bell Tolls* the soldier's relation to his weapon is a sensual one, and most distressing to Leicht is that the sensual pleasures of a civil war appear to please Hemingway.[49]

The most encouraging development in recent German criticism of Hemingway has been a shift in interest from the novels to the short stories. The ground work of Klaus Doderer and Johannes Klein paved the way for university dissertations on Hemingway's short stories, and earlier discussions of the short story as an independent genre, such as those of Unseld, Lorbe and Motekat, have been expanded upon in the period following 1965.

Doderer, who had contended in his book *Die Kurzgeschichte in Deutschland* (1953) that Hemingway served as a model for German short story writers, recently came under attack in Ruth J. Kilchenmann's *Die Kurzgeschichte: Formen und Entwicklung* (1967). Kilchenmann argued that the *Kurzgeschichte* is German in origin and development, and that it has distinct characteristics which set it apart from American short stories, especially those of Hemingway.[50] Most of Hemingway's stories, she claimed, depict the exploits of heroic individuals in extreme situations; consequently they lack necessary breadth, and at times the dialogue exists of and for itself rather than being carefully integrated into the story. "Hemingway," she concluded, "provided the impetus for the development of the modern German *Kurzgeschichte*, but not the actual model."[51]

Unlike Kilchenmann, however, most of Hemingway's critics among the younger generation in Germany feel that it is in the short story form that he excels. Hillebrand-Stadie, for example, wrote that the short story was more suited to Hemingway's talents; with it he achieved the unity of form and content lacking in his longer narratives.[52] According to Hanspeter Dörfel, "The reason Hemingway's artistic achievements were greater in the short stories than in the novels is . . . that the shorter form forced him to limit interior monologue while, on the other hand, it provided him with a perfect medium for his objective-behavioristic method of narration."[53] In their brief introductory history of the American short story in *Amerikanische Erzählungen von Hawthorne bis Salinger*, Freese, Jäger, Kruse, and Nicolaisen stated:

> Indeed he [Hemingway] achieved the greatest success with his novels, but since they do not possess the complexity or thematic richness that this genre requires, it is unlikely that they will last. On the other hand, Hemingway's short stories, distinguished by their uniqueness and originality, are among the most significant contributions to American literature of the twentieth century.[54]

In their analyses of Hemingway's short stories German critics in the years since 1965 have continued to rely on the methods of new criticism.[55] Less emphasis, however, has been placed on the existential qualities of Hemingway's fiction. And with increasing frequency critics, following the guidelines established by theorists such as Emil Staiger, Günter Müller, Wolfgang Kayser, Franz Stanzel, and Eberhart Lämmert, have focused their attention on possible variations in point of view and the use of time as a structuring device.[56] In Dietrich Jäger's "Die Darstellung des Kampfes bei Stephen Crane, Hemingway, Faulkner and Britting," for example, the major emphasis is on the distinguishing characteristics of Hemingway's method of narration in "Fifty Grand" and "The Undefeated," as opposed to the narrative patterns in selected examples from the other three writers.[57]

In comparing 121 lines of "Fifty Grand" with selected passages from Crane's *Maggie* and "The Blue Hotel," Jäger observed that in Crane's fiction the narration consists of divisions which occasionally overlap: exact descriptions of events, summary reports, and general descriptive commentary. In "Fifty Grand," however, the narration is sharply divided between the narrator's subjective summary reports and his detailed description of external events. In the second part of "Fifty Grand" the control of the narrator is no longer apparent in his general comments on the technique of the boxers, but rather in the language he uses to describe the fight. The number of minute factual details which Hemingway has his narrator reproduce distinguishes his fiction from Crane's. According to Jäger, "this joy in the specialist's knowledge of details is an expression of Hemingway's desire to keep reality under control." This desire is behind both methods of narration in the story: "In the first case one immediately recognizes the detailed reproduction of the thought process; in the second, it is the action which is described with concrete accuracy."[58]

In "The Undefeated," Jäger noted a similar pattern in the narrator's alternating back and forth between inner monologue, objective description and the reproduction of physical sensations. Characteristically, he provides few overall descriptions of either the arena or the spectators. Manuel and Zurito, for example, hear the sounds of the arena when they are relatively inactive, but once the bullfight has begun, these details are omitted and only those of pragmatic importance are included. The sharp control required on the part of the narrator, Jäger contended, corresponds to the control which the characters must exert upon their own conduct. Through this correspondence Hemingway achieves unity of form and content in "Fifty Grand" and "The Undefeated": "The astounding parallel between the way Hemingway reduces physical reality to specific dates, basic contrasts, and simple outlines, and the way many of his characters restrict their actions by committing themselves to endurance or perseverence . . . is one of the main reasons for the great (if also one-sided) impact of his fiction."[59]

A similar investigation into the problems of point of view and the unity of form and content is offered by Peter Nicolaisen's "Hemingways 'My Old Man' und Faulkners 'Barn Burning': Ein Vergleich," which also appeared in *Amerikanische Erzählungen von Hawthorne bis Salinger*. In focusing first on Joe Butler as Hemingway's narrator, Nicolaisen noted that considerable time has elapsed between the actual events and the telling of them in the story. Since Joe is recollecting these events rather than describing them directly, his narration does not follow a linear development or a rigid time schedule. His casual method of narration suggests that he perceives no logical connections between the separate events in the story, and at the same time illustrates that this is the boy's limited way of perceiving reality. Unlike Sarty in "Barn Burning," he is not aided by an omniscient consciousness, and readers of "My Old Man" are not permitted to know any more than he does.[60]

Paralleling the three divisions of the story which are marked by the stay in Italy, the shift to Maisons and Paris, and the purchase of a horse, are three specific events sharply limited by time: the difficulties in Milan, the race in St. Cloud, and the final race in Auteuil. Following each of these events, Nicolaisen pointed out, the boy becomes aware of something new which is in contrast to what he has experienced previously. Joe's picture of his father and in part his picture of the world are corrected three times; placed together, these reactions constitute the subject of the story.[61]

However, at the end of "My Old Man," after Joe has lost both his father and his illusions, he is incapable of drawing the logical conclusions concerning his father's guilt. Instead he speaks of an anonymous "they" who have not left him much and thus absolves himself from the necessity of abstract reasoning. According to Nicolaisen, this failure on the part of the protagonist-narrator corresponds to the distinguishing stylistic and structural characteristics of the story. The sparse description, the uncomplicated syntax, and the emphasis on concrete details suggest that the narrator's outlook is sharply limited. His failure to link the three structural units of the story is paralleled by his failure to perceive the reality of his own situation.[62]

Horst Kruse, another member of the Kiel group,[63] has recently published two studies involving Hemingway short stories. In the second, "Hemingway's 'Cat in the Rain' and Joyce's *Ulysses*," which appeared in *Literatur in Wissenschaft und Unterricht*, 1970, Kruse argued unconvincingly that Hemingway likely borrowed Joyce's man in the raincoat from *Ulysses* to use symbolically as a "harbinger of death, of sterility, and of the death of love" in his short story.[64] A thorough, more convincing study is Kruse's "Ernest Hemingway's 'The End of Something': Its Independence as a Short Story and Its Place in the Education of Nick Adams," which appeared in *Studies in Short Fiction*, 1967. The article illustrates both the strong emphasis on *explication de texte* and the new spirit of independence which has characterized recent German criticism of Hemingway. In contrast to Philip Young, who maintained that one must read "The Three Day Blow" to fully understand "The End of Something," Kruse stated, "I feel that Young's eagerness to prove his overall thesis has led him to misinterpret 'The End of Something' and that the general validity of his thesis has apparently precluded an exhaustive evaluation of one of Hemingway's finest stories." [65]

Focusing first on the structure of the story, Kruse contended that the cyclical history of Horton's Bay in the introduction "is meant to be an analogue for the subsequent plot . . . which also deals with the completion of a cycle, that of Nick's love for Marjorie." The introduction "also elucidates and interprets the story, a necessary function, as the story itself does not detail the whole course of Nick's love affair." Thus the fate of Horton's Bay explains "the lesson that the story has for the protagonist: all things run their natural course, and submission and acceptance are the only sensible responses." Once one has perceived the independence of "The End of Something," Kruse argued, one must also re-evaluate Young's reading of "The Three Day Blow." Although the stories complement each other, he concluded, they are mutually independent. [66]

In addition to their continued emphasis on *explication de texte* and their more recent concentration on the problems of point of view in Hemingway's fiction, German critics have begun to examine the translations of Hemingway's works more closely. Annemarie Horschitz-Horst, who was responsible for the German translations of all but one of Hemingway's first seven novels and nearly all the short stories, was frequently praised by critics during the twenty-year period following World War II. In 1946, Hemingway himself wrote to Ernst Rowohlt: "Please let Annemarie Horschitz-Horst know that I am counting on her to do the translating. Of all my translators, she was the best." [67] In recent years, however, Hemingway's German critics have placed a greater emphasis on textual analysis, and in doing so they have become more critical of Horschitz-Horst's translations.

Indicative of this new attitude is the observation of Marcel Reich-Ranicki: "Hemingway exerted an influence on the prose style of a generation of German writers. But who really exerted the influence—Hemingway or his German translator Annemarie

Horschitz-Horst?"[68] Hanspeter Dörfel stated that "Mrs. Horschitz-Horst's authorized translations appear too erratic in their attempt to transform Hemingway's colloquial diction into a slovenly German prose interwoven with dialect and slang expressions."[69] A more outspoken critic of Horschitz-Horst's translations has been Helmut Braem, who stated in his review of *A Moveable Feast* in *Die Zeit*, 1965, that one becomes weary of hearing that Horschitz-Horst's translated versions of Hemingway are "exact reproductions of the original text." "We are certain," Braem stated, "that the respectable Rowohlt Company can do little to correct such an exaggerated claim, but this does not alter the disagreeable impression it gives, that either Hemingway writes like Annemarie Horschitz-Horst, or that she imitates him."[70] In his review of *By-Line: Ernest Hemingway* in *Die Zeit*, 1969, Braem contended that the translation by Ernst Schnabel and Elizabeth Plessen was much more accurate than those of Horschitz-Horst had been.[71]

Dealing directly with many of the difficulties involved in translating Hemingway's fiction into German is Hans-Joachim Kann's dissertation, "Übersetzungen von drei anglo-amerikanischen Kurzgeschichten: Aldous Huxleys 'Green Tunnels,' Ernest Hemingways 'The Killers' und 'A Clean, Well-Lighted Place,'" written under the direction of Hans Galinsky at the University of Mainz in 1968. Kann explicated the two Hemingway stories carefully and explained the ways in which the German translation affects the original dialogue, time, place, character, plot, motive, and style. His analysis included an examination of the changes in rhythm, alliteration and echo effects and an assessment of the total impact of the translation on German readers. In a similar study of the German translation of "The Snows of Kilimanjaro," Christopher Longyear had illustrated that the story's "literary impact on the reader is markedly not the same as in the original."[72] According to Kann, the same might be said for the translations of "The Killers" and "A Clean, Well-Lighted Place." Both Hemingway and Horschitz-Horst have influenced German writers, he concluded.[73]

Kann's shorter study "Ernest Hemingway's Knowledge of German," which appeared in the *Jahrbuch für Amerikastudien* in 1970, offers few insights into Hemingway's fiction, but nevertheless it attests to the continuing interest Germans have in Hemingway. Kann agreed with Charles Fenton's statement that Hemingway "never responded to Germany, either in its terrain or its people, as he did to France or Italy," but he stressed Hemingway's use of German for atmospheric purposes and character development and pointed out that "All of Hemingway's novels contain references to German, Germans, and Germany."[74]

Speaking of the reassessment to which a new generation of readers will subject Hemingway and Faulkner, the American critic Hyatt Waggoner recently reminded us that "Re-appraisals of extremely eminent writers after their deaths are seldom upward at any time." "Nearly everyone," he added, "seems to want to scale down Hemingway's reputation."[75] An example of such an attempt is Alan Lebowitz's "Hemingway In Our Time," which appeared in the *Yale Review*, 1969:

> To a nation that has always been suspicious of its writers, he gave public proof that literature was a glamorous and manly calling to which any normal, sissy-hating, over-mothered American boy could honorably respond. Yet it is hard today, to do him more than skimpy justice. For a working novelist who published fiction for nearly thirty years, he wrote few novels, and those are repetitious and obsessed, dealing with the same themes through the same stereotyped characters and situations. Nor does the often repeated judgment that, if not a novelist, he was at least a great story-writer, carry real weight. He wrote no more stories, proportionally, than he did novels, and the same essential weaknesses show clearly in these as well.[76]

In Germany during the past six years there has been a gradual reassessment of Hemingway in progress, but it seems unlikely that German critics will ever reach a point of dealing with Hemingway in the overwhelmingly negative, cursory manner of Lebowitz. Even though the dismantling of the Hemingway legend will likely continue and the current critical interest in Hemingway's short stories may fade, Germans will not soon forget the inspiration and hope Hemingway's works offered them during the most critical years of their country's history. Perhaps Helmut Braem explains it best:

> It may be that many of us have admired Hemingway without sufficient reserve. For us he was more than a writer who could construct "true sentences." He was a man who was able to show us how to endure the chaos of the world through a self-

created order, through strict discipline and a firm code of behavior, through fine craftsmanship . . . and fairness. Therefore his death was very painful to us.[77]

NOTES

[1] *Ernest Hemingway in Selbstzeugnissen und Bilddokumenten*, Rowohlt Monographien, No. 73 (Reinbek bei Hamburg, 1961), pp. 5–17.

[2] *Ibid.*, pp. 43–44.

[3] *Literatur und Selbstmord* (Stuttgart, 1965), pp. 9–10.

[4] *Ibid.*, pp. 163–64.

[5] *Ibid.*, pp. 32–33.

[6] *Ibid.*, p. 29.

[7] *Ibid.*, p. 181.

[8] "Hemingway-Manuskripte: Keine Widerrede," *Der Spiegel*, XXI (May 29, 1967), 144.

[9] " 'Häng dich auf, tapferer Hemingstein!' " *Der Spiegel*, XXV (August 23, 1971), 96–97.

[10] *Continuities* (London, 1968), pp. 161–67.

[11] "Hemingway as His Own Fable," *Atlantic*, CCXIII (June, 1964), 54–57.

[12] "Blick zurück in Rührung," *Stuttgarter Zeitung*, September 11, 1965, p. 20.

[13] "Die nicht mehr gefüllte Leere: Hemingway kopiert eigene 'wahre Sätze,' " *Die Zeit*, October 15, 1965, p. 17.

[14] "Hemingways Spätwerk," *Universitas*, XX (1965), 1151–53.

[15] *Ibid.*, pp. 1153–54.

[16] "Auf der Suche nach dem verlorenen Hunger," *Süddeutsche Zeitung*, June 26–27, 1965, p. 88.

[17] *Literatur als Teilhabe: Kritische Orientierungen zur literarischen Gegenwart* (Berlin, 1966), pp. 248–50.

[18] "Als ihm die Stunde schlug," *Merkur*, XXI (1967), 596–98.

[19] "Hemingway-Biographie: Vertrauen verletzt," *Der Spiegel*, XX (January 24, 1966), 93–94.

[20] "Hemingway ante portas," *Süddeutsche Zeitung*, November 19–20, 1966, p. 78.

[21] "Der alternde Hemingway: A. E. Hotchners zweifelhafter Freundschaftsdienst," *Die Zeit*, December 2, 1966, p. VI.

[22] *Ibid.*

[23] "Privatissima Hotchneriana," *Die Welt der Literatur*, December 22, 1966, p. 9.

[24] "Als ihm die Stunde schlug," pp. 597–98.

[25] "Buchbesprechungen," *Literatur in Wissenschaft und Unterricht*, I, No. 1 (1968), 154–55.

[26] "Besprechungen und Kurzanzeigen," *Die Neueren Sprachen*, NF, XVIII (February, 1969), 96–98.

27 "Besprechungen," *Anglia*, XXCIX (1971), 276–79.

28 "Hemingway: Jeden Tag Geschichte," *Der Spiegel*, XXI (September 4, 1967), 130–32.

29 "Journalismus, unvergilbt: Ernest Hemingways *49 Depeschen*," *Die Zeit*, October 10, 1961, Lit. Sec., p. 3.

30 *Ibid.*

31 "Ein Reporter namens Hemingway," *Süddeutsche Zeitung*, September 13–14, 1969, p. 115.

32 "Er begann als Reporter in Toronto," *Die Welt der Literatur*, November 6, 1969, pp. 4–5.

33 "Ernests Kram: Reportagen des legendären Hemingway," *Christ und Welt*, September 19, 1969, p. 13.

34 "Reise abwärts," *Der Spiegel*, XXIII (April 14, 1969), 169–70.

35 "Hemingway," *Universitas*, XXIV (1969), 801–7.

36 "Die Zerfransung der Literatur," *Allgemeine Zeitung: Mainzer Anzeiger*, August 6, 1971, p. 2.

37 Nicolaisen, "Buchbesprechungen," p. 154.

38 "Two War Novels: A Critical Comparison," *Revue de Littérature Comparée*, XL (1968), 390–406. Professor Liedloff has resided in the United States for the last fifteen years and consequently I did not feel that his article was representative of the recent German response to Hemingway. In "Two War Novels" he argues convincingly that *A Farewell to Arms* is superior in technique, but *All Quiet on the Western Front* is "a substantially more comprehensive war novel."

39 "Bedeutungsschichten in Ernest Hemingways *The Old Man and the Sea*," *Amerikanische Erzählungen von Hawthorne bis Salinger*, ed. Paul Buchloh, *et al.*, Kieler Beiträge zur Anglistik und Amerikanistik, VI (Neumünster, 1968), 224–33.

40 *Ibid.*, pp. 235–38.

41 *Ibid.*, pp. 240–41.

42 "Gekreuzigt im Ring: Zu Hemingways *The Old Man and the Sea*," *Deutsche Vierteljahrsschrift*, XLI (1967), 258–82.

43 *Der Alte Mann und das Meer: Versuch einer Analyse* (Munich, 1964), pp. 54–57.

44 Wittkowski, pp. 258–69.

45 *Ibid.*, pp. 270–82.

46 "Hemingway: *Wem die Stunde schlägt*," *Süddeutsche Zeitung*, April 17–18, 1971, n. pag.

47 Bondy, "Hemingway: *Wem die Stunde schlägt*," n. pag.

48 *Ibid.*

49 Leicht, "Hemingway: *Wem die Stunde schlägt*," n. pag.

50 Ruth J. Kilchenmann, *Die Kurzgeschichte: Formen und Entwicklung*, Sprache und Literatur, XXXVII (Stuttgart, 1967), pp. 10–11.

51 *Ibid.*, pp. 142–47.

52 "Die Disziplin als ethisches Motiv und stilistisches Prinzip in den Kurzgeschichten Ernest Hemingways," Diss. Munich 1963, p. 8.

53 "Hemingways Erzählperspektiven," Diss. Saarbrücken 1964, p. 265.

54 "Erzählende Kurzprosa in Amerika: Ein Überblick," *Amerikanische Erzählungen von Hawthorne bis Salinger*, p. 63.

55 An example is Herbert Henss's "Eine verbindende Interpretation auf der Oberstufe als Teil des Themenkomplexes 'Amerika': Edgar Allan Poe, 'The Masque of the Red Death,' Ernest Hemingway, 'A Clean, Well-Lighted Place,' " *Die Neueren Sprachen*, LXVI (1967), 327–38. In linking the stories of Poe and Hemingway for analysis, Henss was admittedly imitating Hans Galinsky's "Beharrende Strukturzüge im Wandel eines Jahrhunderts amerikanischer Kurzgeschichte (dargelegt an E. A. Poes 'The Masque of the Red Death,' und Ernest Hemingways 'The Killers')." Henss's study, a procedural guideline for teachers of literature in secondary schools, offers little that is new to the understanding of "A Clean, Well-Lighted Place," but it illustrates the Germans' continued faith in the methods of new criticism.

56 The concept of time as a structuring principle was perhaps articulated most successfully by Emil Staiger in *Die Zeit als Einbildungskraft des Dichters* (Zürich, 1939) and *Grundbegriffe der Poetik* (Zürich, 1946). Other influential studies emphasizing the treatment of time and variations in point of view are Günter Müller's *Die Bedeutung der Zeit in der Erzählkunst* (Bonn, 1947) and *Erzählzeit und erzählte Zeit* (Bonn, 1948); Wolfgang Kayser's *Das sprachliche Kunstwerk: Eine Einführung in die Literaturwissenschaft* (Bern, 1951); Franz Stanzel's Die *typischen Erzählsituationen im Roman* (Stuttgart, 1955); and Eberhart Lämmert's *Bauformen des Erzählens* (Stuttgart, 1955). Similar studies in English which have attracted considerable attention in Germany are Percy Lubbock's *The Craft of Fiction* (London, 1921); E. M. Forster's *Aspects of the Novel* (London, 1927); René Wellek and Austin Warren's *Theory of Literature* (New York, 1949); and Wayne Booth's *The Rhetoric of Fiction* (Chicago, 1961).

It is in university dissertations that the critical theories propounded in the preceding studies first appeared in German Hemingway criticism. Among the earliest of these is Matthias W. Stickelmann's "View-Point und Zeitstruktur als Basis morphologischer Interpretation. Eine Darstellung am Roman Gerhart Hauptmanns und Ernest Hemingways," Diss. Bonn 1955. Rather than emphasize the Hemingway legend and the heroic code, which many of the better-known critics were doing in the 1950's, Stickelmann focused his attention on the text of one of Hemingway's novels, *For Whom the Bell Tolls*. His most interesting findings concern the proportionate number of pages dealing with direct narration, dialogue, monologue and secondary episodes.

A similar approach is followed by Lothar Fietz in "Wandlungen der Form im Romanwerk Ernest Hemingways: Untersuchung zum Wesen des Fiktiven," Diss. Tübingen 1960. Fietz examined the function of time in Hemingway's novels, and traced the changes in point of view, which, he claimed, corresponded to Hemingway's search for immediacy and objectivity. A third dissertation which employs the methods of new criticism to examine Hemingway's fiction is Hanspeter Dörfel's "Hemingways Erzählperspektiven," completed under the direction of J. V. Hagopian at the University of Saarbrücken in 1964. Dörfel's contention, based on a systematic examination of eight variations in point of view in the novels and short stories, is that Hemingway's development is marked by a steady decrease in his objective-behavioristic method of narration and a corresponding increase in his reliance upon abstract reflection. Dörfel, like many younger German critics, arrived at the conclusion most frequently expressed by American critics: that Hemingway's best work was done very early in his career.

57 "Die Darstellung des Kampfes bei Stephen Crane, Hemingway, Faulkner und Britting," *Amerikanische Erzählungen von Hawthorne bis Salinger,*" pp. 112–54.

58 *Ibid.,* pp. 113–28.

59 *Ibid.,* pp. 137–54.

60 "Hemingways 'My Old Man' und Faulkners 'Barn Burning': Ein Vergleich," *Amerikanische Erzählungen von Hawthorne bis Salinger,* pp. 188–97.

61 *Ibid.,* pp. 199–200.

62 *Ibid.,* pp. 204–19.

63 An unpublished study which follows an approach similar to that of the Kiel critics in examining Hemingway's short stories is Reinhold Winkler's "Lyrische Elemente in den Kurzgeschichten Ernest Hemingways: Eine Untersuchung der Textstruktur," Diss. Erlangen-Nürnberg 1967. Winkler discussed "Hemingway's lyrical point of view" in selected short stories and subjected the texts to a linguistic analysis.

64 "Hemingway's 'Cat in the Rain' and Joyce's *Ulysses,*" *Literatur in Wissenschaft und Unterricht,* III, No. 1 (1970), 28–30.

65 "Ernest Hemingway's 'The End of Something': Its Independence as a Short Story and Its Place in the 'Education of Nick Adams,' " *Studies in Short Fiction,* IV (1967), 152–53.

66 *Ibid.,* pp. 155–65.

67 As quoted by Hans-Joachim Kann in "Übersetzungsprobleme in den deutschen Übersetzungen von drei anglo-amerikanischen Kurzgeschichten: Aldous Huxley's 'Green Tunnels,' Ernest Hemingways 'The Killers' und 'A Clean, Well-Lighted Place,' " Diss. Mainz 1968, p. 7.

68 "Verräter, Brückenbauer, Waisenkinder," *Übersetzen: Vorträge und Beiträge vom Internationalen Kongress Übersetzer in Hamburg 1965,* ed. Rolf Italiaander (Frankfurt, 1965), p. 72.

69 Dörfel, "Hemingways Erzählperspektiven," p. 33, n.

70 "Die nicht mehr gefüllte Leere," p. 17.

71 "Journalismus, unvergilbt," Lit. Sec., p. 3.

72 As quoted by Kann in "Übersetzungsprobleme," p. 138. The reference is to Longyear's "Linguistically Determined Categories of Meanings. A Comparative Analysis of Meaning in 'The Snows of Kilimanjaro' in English and German," Diss. Michigan 1961.

73 *Ibid.*

74 "Ernest Hemingway's Knowledge of German," *Jahrbuch für Amerikastudien,* XV (1970), p. 231.

75 "Hemingway and Faulkner: 'The End of Something,' " *The Southern Review,* IV (1968), 459.

76 "Hemingway In Our Time," *Yale Review,* LVIII (1969), 321.

77 Braem, "Die nicht mehr gefüllte Leere," p. 17.

SELECTED BIBLIOGRAPHY

BOOKS

Asselineau, Roger, ed. *The Literary Reputation of Hemingway in Europe*. New York, 1965.

Astre, George Albert. *Ernest Hemingway in Selbstzeugnissen und Bilddokumenten*. Rowohlt Monographien, No. 73. Reinbek b. Hamburg, 1961. Published originally as *Hemingway par lui-même*. Ecrivains de Toujours, 46. Paris, 1959.

Bab, Julius. *Amerikas Dichter*. Berlin, 1949.

Baden, Hans Jürgen. *Literatur und Selbstmord*. Stuttgart, 1965.

Baker, Carlos. *Ernest Hemingway: A Life Story*. New York, 1969.

————, ed. *Ernest Hemingway: Critiques of Four Major Novels*. New York, 1962.

————, ed. *Hemingway and His Critics: An International Anthology*. New York, 1961.

————. *Hemingway: The Writer as Artist*. Princeton, 1952.

Ballenger, Sara E. *The American Novel in Germany (1945–1957)*. Unpublished Doctoral Dissertation, Indiana University, 1959.

Bennett, E. K. *A History of the German Novelle*. 2nd ed., rev. and continued by H. M. Waidson. Cambridge, 1961.

Bentz, Hans W. *Ernest Hemingway in Übersetzungen*. Frankfurt am Main, 1963.

Bibliographie der deutschen Zeitschriftenliteratur, Leipzig: Dietrich, various dates.

Bibliographie der fremdsprachigen Zeitschriftenliteratur, Osnabrück: Dietrich, various dates.

Blöcker, Günter. *Literatur als Teilhabe: Kritische Orientierungen zur literarischen Gegenwart*. Berlin, 1966.

————. *Die neuen Wirklichkeiten*. Berlin, 1957.

Breitenkamp, Edward. *The United States Information Control Division and Its Effect on German Publishers and Writers*. Grand Forks, 1953.

Buchloh, Paul, *et al.*, eds. *Amerikanische Erzählungen von Haw-*

thorne bis Salinger. Kieler Beiträge zur Anglistik und Amerikanistik, VI. Neumünster, 1968.

    pp. 9–88: "Erzählende Kurzprosa in Amerika: Ein Überblick," by Peter Freese, Dietrich Jäger, Horst Kruse and Peter Nicolaisen.

    pp. 112–154: "Die Darstellung des Kampfes bei Stephen Crane, Hemingway, Faulkner und Britting," by Dietrich Jäger.

    pp. 187–223: "Hemingways 'My Old Man' und Faulkners 'Barn Burning': Ein Vergleich," by Peter Nicolaisen.

    pp. 224–241: "Bedeutungsschichten in Ernest Hemingways *The Old Man and the Sea*," by Paul Buchloh.

Doderer, Klaus. *Die Kurzgeschichte in Deutschland.* Wiesbaden, 1953.

Duroche, Leonard L. *Aspects of Literary Criticism in Present-Day Germany, with Special Reference to the Thought of Martin Heidegger.* An Unpublished Doctoral Dissertation, Stanford University, 1965.

Eppelsheimer, Hanns W. *Bibliographie der deutschen Literaturwissenschaft.* Frankfurt am Main, various dates.

Fenton, Charles A. *The Apprenticeship of Ernest Hemingway: The Early Years.* New York, 1954.

Feyerabend, Willy. *Die Erotik im amerikanischen Roman.* Stuttgart, 1959.

Fiedler, Leslie. *Love and Death in the American Novel.* New York, 1960.

————. *Waiting for the End.* New York, 1964.

Frahne, Karl E. *Eine Einführung in die Literatur Nordamerikas: Von Franklin bis Hemingway.* Hamburg, 1949.

Grenzmann, Wilhelm. *Weltdichtung der Gegenwart,* 3rd ed. rev. Bonn, 1961.

Hagopian, John, and Dolch, Martin, eds. *Insight I: Analyses of American Literature.* 3rd ed. Frankfurt am Main, 1967.

Hanneman, Audre. *Ernest Hemingway: A Comprehensive Bibliography.* Princeton, 1967.

Helmich, Wilhelm. *Wege zur Prosadichtung des 20. Jahrhunderts.* Braunschweig, 1960.

Hemingway, Ernest. *Across the River and Into the Trees.* New York, 1950.

————. *By-Line: Ernest Hemingway.* Ed. William White. New York, 1967.

————. *A Farewell to Arms.* New York, 1929.

————. *A Moveable Feast.* New York, 1964.

————. *For Whom the Bell Tolls.* New York, 1940

————. *The Fifth Column and the First Forty-nine Stories.* New York, 1938.

————. *Islands in the Stream.* New York, 1970.

————. *The Old Man and the Sea.* New York, 1952.

————. *The Sun Also Rises.* New York, 1926.

Hemingway, Leicester. *My Brother, Ernest Hemingway.* Cleveland, 1962.

Hewett-Thayer, Harvey W. *American Literature as Viewed in Germany, 1818–1861.* Chapel Hill, 1958.

Holthusen, Hans E. *Der unbehauste Mensch: Motive und Probleme der modernen Literatur.* Munich, 1952.

Hotchner, A. E. *Papa Hemingway: A Personal Memoir.* New York, 1966.

Hüllen, W., Rossi, W., Christopeit, W., eds. *Zeitgenössische amerikanische Dichtung.* 2nd ed. Frankfurt am Main, 1964.

Jens, Walter. *Deutsche Literatur der Gegenwart.* Munich, 1961.

————. *Moderne Literatur und moderne Wirklichkeit.* Württemberg, 1958.

Joesten, Joachim. *German Periodicals in 1947.* New York, 1947.

————. *The German Press in 1947.* New York, 1947.

Kermode, Frank. *Continuities.* London, 1968.

Kilchenmann, Ruth J. *Die Kurzgeschichte: Formen und Entwicklung.* Sprache und Literatur, XXVIII. Stuttgart, 1967.

Killinger, John. *Hemingway and the Dead Gods: A Study in Existentialism.* Lexington, 1960.

Klein, Johannes. *Geschichte der deutschen Novelle von Goethe bis zur Gegenwart.* 4th ed. Wiesbaden, 1960.

Kopp, Richard. *Der Alte Mann und das Meer: Versuch einer Analyse.* Munich, 1964.

Lämmert, Eberhard. *Bauformen des Erzählens.* Stuttgart, 1955.

Lania, Leo [pseudonym of Hermann Lazar]. *Hemingway: eine Bildbiographie.* Munich, 1960. (a) Translated into English by Joan Bradley. *Hemingway: A Pictorial Biography.* New York:

Viking Press, 1961. (b) London: Thames & Hudson, 1961. (c) Translated into Spanish by Emilio Donato. *Hemingway: Biografía ilustrada*. Barcelona, 1963. (d) Translated into French by Claire Guinchat. Paris, 1963.

Lennartz, Franz. *Ausländische Dichter und Schriftsteller unserer Zeit*. Stuttgart, 1955.

Lewis, Robert W. *Hemingway on Love*. Austin, 1965.

Link, Franz H., ed. *Amerika: Vision und Wirklichkeit*. Frankfurt am Main, 1968.

Lüdeke, Henry. *Geschichte der amerikanischen Literatur*. Bern, 1952.

McCaffery, John, ed. *Ernest Hemingway: The Man and His Work*. Cleveland, 1950.

Mönnig, Richard. *Amerika und England im deutschen, österreichischen und schweizerischen Schrifttum der Jahre 1945–1949: Eine Bibliographie*. Stuttgart, 1951.

Mucharowski, Hans-Günter. *Die Werke von Ernest Hemingway: Eine Bibliographie der deutschsprachigen Hemingway-Literatur und der Originalwerke. Von 1923 bis 1954*. Hamburg, 1955.

Mummendey, Richard. *Die schöne Literatur der Vereinigten Staaten von Amerika in deutschen Übersetzungen: eine Bibliographie*. Bonn, 1961.

Pongs, Hermann. *Im Umbruch der Zeit*. 2nd ed. Göttingen, 1956.

Price, Lawrence M. *The Reception of United States Literature in Germany*. Chapel Hill, 1966.

Rang, Bernhard. *Der Roman*. 2nd ed. Freiburg, 1954.

Ross, Lillian. *Portrait of Hemingway*. New York, 1961.

Russell, Bertrand, *et al. The Impact of America on European Culture*. Boston, 1951.

Schirmer, Walter F. *Geschichte der englischen und amerikanischen Literatur*. 4th ed. rev. Tübingen, 1967.

Schmidt, Adalbert. *Literaturgeschichte: Wege und Wandlungen moderner Dichtung*. Stuttgart, 1957.

Schulze, Martin. *Wege der amerikanischern Literatur*. Frankfurt am Main, 1968.

Sieburg, Friedrich. *Nur für Leser: Jahre und Bücher*. Stuttgart, 1955.

Skard, Sigmund. *American Studies in Europe.* 2 vols. Philadelphia, 1958.

Springer, Anne. *The American Novel in Germany.* Hamburg, 1960.

Straumann, Heinrich. *American Literature in the Twentieth Century.* 3rd ed. rev. New York, 1965.

Stresau, Hermann. *Ernest Hemingway.* Berlin, 1958.

Timpe, Eugene P. *American Literature in Germany, 1861–1872.* Chapel Hill, 1958.

Verzeichnis amerikanischer Bücher in deutscher Übersetzung erschienen in Deutschland seit 1945. Frankfurt am Main, 1951.

Vollmer, Clement. *The American Novel in Germany, 1871–1913.* Philadelphia, 1917.

Weeks, Robert P., ed. *Hemingway: A Collection of Critical Essays.* Englewood Cliffs, 1962.

Wellershoff, Dieter. *Der Gleichgültige: Versuche über Hemingway, Camus, Benn, und Beckett.* Berlin, 1963.

Wiegler, Paul. *Geschichte der fremdsprachigen Weltliteratur.* Munich, 1949.

Young, Philip. *Ernest Hemingway.* New York, 1952.

Zuckmayer, Carl. *Als wär's ein Stück von mir.* Wien, 1966.

Zuther, Gerhard. *Eine Bibliographie der Aufnahme amerikanischer Literatur in deutschen Zeitschriften 1945–1960.* Munich, 1965.

ARTICLES

A., A. "Dichtung als Imagination," *Die Kommenden,* XVII (May 10, 1963), 12–13.

"Als ob." Anon., *Der Spiegel,* XVI (February 7, 1962), 84–85.

Andersch, Alfred. "Amerikanische Anarchisten," FH, VI (1951), 76–767.

Arnold, Fritz. "Hemingway und der Tod," NDH, IV (August, 1957), 461–62.

B., G. "Wollen Sie den Stierkampf erlernen?" WS, XXVII (1958), 276–78.

Bab, Julius. "Der Schreck am Kilimandscharo," *Die Zeit* (February 4, 1954), p. 4.

Baden, Hans Jürgen. "Der alte Mann und die See," *Zeitwende*, XXIV (1952–1953), 555–57.

Baker, Carlos. "A Myth in the Making," *New York Times Book Review* (May 23, 1965), pp. 42–43.

———. "Hemingway," *Saturday Review*, XLIV (July 29, 1961), 10–13.

Barrett, William. "Introspektion in Amerika," *Monat*, V (November 1952), 148–54.

Baur, Joseph: "Ein Stück Epos," *Welt und Wort*, VIII (1953), 81–82.

"Begegnung in Afrika." Anon., *Die Zeit* (November 4, 1954), p. 4.

Bender, Hans. "Ortsbestimmung der Kurzgeschichte," *Akzente*, IX (1962), 205–25.

Bentley, Eric Russell. "German Writers in Exile 1933–1945," *Books Abroad*, XVIII (1943), 313–17.

Bergholz, Harry. "Book and Music Publishing in Post-War Germany," *Modern Language Journal*, XXIV (1950), 616–25.

Berndt, Ernst. "Neue Dichtung in Amerika," *Das Goldene Tor*, II (1957), 151–57.

"Big Brother." Anon. *Der Spiegel*, XVI (July 4, 1962), 63–64, 65.

Blanke, Gustav. "Der amerikanische Schriftsteller und die Gesellschaft. Zum amerikanischen Roman des 20. Jahrhunderts," NS, IV (1955), 153–64.

Blöcker, Günter. "Der Augenblick der Wahrheit," *Merkur*, XI (1957), 1094–96.

———. "Der Unbesiegte," *Monat*, V (1952–1953), 228–30.

Blumenberg, Hans. "Die Peripetie des Mannes. Über das Werk Ernest Hemingways," *Hochland*, XLVII (1955–1956), 220–33.

Boekhoff, Hermann. "Ein neuer Hemingway," WM, XCII, No. 12 (1951–1952), 82.

———. WM, XCIII, No. 11 (1952–1953), 85.

Bondy, Barbara. "Auf der Suche nach dem verlorenen Hunger," *Süddeutsche Zeitung* (June 26–27, 1965), p. 88.

———. "Hemingway ante portas," *Süddeutsche Zeitung* (November 19–20, 1966), p. 78.

———. "Schlafsack-Gespräche," under the heading "Hemingway: *Wem die Stunde schlägt*," *Süddeutsche Zeitung* (April 17–18, 1971), n. pag.

Bonosky, Phillip. "The Background to American Progressive Literature," ZAA (Ost), IX–X (1961), 253–60.

Borch, Herbert von. "Hemingway," *Universitas*, XXIV (1969), 801–07.

Braem, Helmut M. "Blick zurück in Rührung," *Stuttgarter Zeitung* (September 11, 1965), p. 20.

————. "Journalismus, unvergilbt: Ernest Hemingways *49 Depeschen*," *Die Zeit* (October 10, 1969), LIT. Sec., p. 3.

————. "Die nicht mehr gefüllte Leere: Hemingway kopiert eigene 'wahre Sätze,' " *Die Zeit* (October 15, 1965), p. 17.

————. "Der weisse, weise Jäger Hemingway," DR, LXXXII (1956), 91.

Brumm, Ursula. "Christus in der amerikanischen Literatur," NDH (December, 1958), 790–800.

————. "Hemingways neuer Roman," WS, XX (1950), 49–50.

Brüning, Eberhard. "The Spanish Civil War (1936–1939) and the American Novel," ZAA, XI–XII (1963), 42–55.

Bühler, Barbara. WM, XCII, No. 8 (1951–1952), 85.

Carstensen, Broder. "Evelyn Waugh and Ernest Hemingway," ASNS, CXC (1954), 193–203.

————. "Das Zeitmoment und einige charakteristische Motive in Ernest Hemingways Kurzgeschichte 'The Killers,' " JAS, IV (1959), 180–90.

"Clausewitz," *Die Welt* (April 3, 1962), p. 7.
    The article relates a discovery made by Professor William White of Detroit. The one-page story attributed to Hemingway in *The Secret Agent's Badge of Courage* (a collection of eight detective stories edited by Kurt Singer), is made up of borrowed paragraphs from *Men at War*, a collection of war stories which Hemingway edited in 1942. The brief chapter headings, also borrowed from *Men at War*, come originally from General Carl von Clausewitz's book *Vom Kriege*.

Clements, Robert. "The European Literary Scene," *Saturday Review*, XLVIII (August 7, 1965), 21–22.

Cousins, Norman. *Saturday Review*, XLIV (July 29, 1961), 11.

Cowley, Malcolm. "Hemingway at Midnight," *New Republic*, CXI (August 14, 1944), 190–95.

————. "A Portrait of Mister Papa," *Life*, XXV (January 10, 1949), 86–101.

————. "U.S. Books Abroad," *Life*, XXI (September 16, 1946), 2, 4, 6, 8, 11.

Daiber, Hans. "Der alte Mann und Kapitän Ahab," DR, LXXIX (1953), 618–20.

Damp, Waldemar. "Individuum und Gesellschaft in Hemingways Romanen," *Wissenschaftliche Zeitschrift der Ernst-Moritz-Arndt-Universität Griefswald*, XVI (1967), 189–92.

————. "Zu Ernest Hemingway als weltliterarischen Phänomen," *Wissenschaftliche Zeitschrift der Ernst-Moritz-Arndt-Universität Greifswald*, XIV (1965), 445–49.

"Das nie Gedruckte." Anon., *Der Spiegel*, XII (September 17, 1958), 53–54.

"Der alte Mann und das Meer." Anon., *Der Spiegel*, VI (August 20, 1952), 33.

"Der grosse Killer." Anon., *Der Spiegel*, VIII (November 3, 1954), 36–38.

Dierlamm, Gotthilf. "Der moderne amerikanische Roman als Spiegelbild geistigen Austausches zwischen USA und Europa," *Sprache und Literatur Englands und Amerikas*, ed. Carl A. Weber. Tübingen, 1952, pp. 169–79.

Dietrich, Max. "Ernest Hemingway," *Hochland*, XXX (1933), 89–91.

Doderer, Klaus. "Die angelsächsische Short Story und die deutsche Kurzgeschichte," NS, II (1953), 417–24.

Dörfel, Hanspeter. "Der alternde Hemingway: A. E. Hotchners zweifelhafter Freundschaftsdienst," *Die Zeit* (December 2, 1966), p. VI.

"Dunkles Lachen." Anon., *Der Spiegel*, XI (December 18, 1957), 61–62.

Effelberger, Hanns. "Probleme der modernen amerikanischen Literatur," NS, VI (1957), 318–24.

Einsiedel, Wolfgang von. "Ein Komet verblasst," *Merkur*, IV (1950), 1220–25.

"Ernest Hemingway." Anon., DR, LXXXVIII (July, 1961), 713–14.

Erval, Francois. "Amerikanische Erfolge in Paris," *Magnum*, Heft 43 (1962), 50–52.

F., E. "Romane—Stories—Erinnerungen," NA, IV (1949), 350–52.

Fadiman, Clifton. "Ernest Hemingway: An American Byron," *Nation*, CXXXVI (January 18, 1933), 63–64.

Fallada, Hans. "Ernest Hemingway oder Woran liegt es?" *Literatur*, XXXIII (September, 1931), 672–74.

———. "Gespräch zwischen Ihr und Ihm über Ernest Hemingway: *In Our Time*," *Literatur*, XXXV (October, 1932), 21–24.

Fietz, Lothar. "Modern Writers: Ernest M. Hemingway," *Praxis des neusprachlichen Unterrichts*, II (1964), 245–50.

Frank, Armin P. "American Literature in Germany," *College English*, XXVII (1966), 497–98.

Franzen, Erick. "Der alte Mann und das Meer: Anmerkungen zu Hemingways neuem Buch," *Neue literarische Welt*, IV, No. 6 (1953), 3–4.

Frey, John R. "America and Her Literature Reviewed by Postwar Germany," AGR, XX (1953–1954), 4–6.

———. "Gruppe 47," *Books Abroad*, XXVI (Summer, 1952), 237–39.

———. "Postwar German Reactions to American Literature," *Journal of English and Germanic Philology*, LIV (1955), 173–94.

Fritzsch, Robert. "Der Hemingway'sche Held und die Frau," *Welt und Wort*, XIII (1958), 197–201.

Fussell, Paul. "Thornton Wilder and the German Psyche," *Nation*, CLXXXVI (May 3, 1958), 394–95.

Galinsky, Hans. "American Studies in Germany," *American Studies in Transition*, ed. Marshall W. Fishwick. Philadelphia, 1964, pp. 232–52.

———. "Beharrende Strukturzüge im Wandel eines Jahrhunderts amerikanischer Kurzgeschichte (dargelegt an E. A. Poes 'The Masque of the Red Death' und Ernest Hemingways 'The Killers')," *Amerikanische Dichtung in der höheren Schule*, ed. Hans Galinsky et al. Berlin, 1961, pp. 4–45.

———. "Understanding Twentieth Century America Through Its Literature: A German View," *Midcontinent American Studies Journal*, VIII (1967), 58–69.

Geismar, Maxwell. "Betrachtungen von und über Hemingway," AR, V (1949), 118–21.

George, Manfred. "Ernest Hemingways Nachlass," *Universitas,* XVI (1961), 1129–31.

————. "Filme unserer Zeit: Hemingway-Verfilmung in Hollywood," *Universitas,* XIII (1958), 105–06.

Gerlach, Erika. "Stephen Crane: Hemingways grosser Lehrmeister," *Weltstimmen,* XXIV (1955), 449–54.

"German Writers of Today." Anon., *Books Abroad,* XXI (Summer, 1947), 283–84.

"Germany's Most Representative Writers." Anon., *Books Abroad,* XXIII (Winter, 1949), 30.

Geyh, Karl W. "Prophetisches in Dichtungen und Kunstströmungen," *Welt und Wort,* I (1946), 141–42.

Glaser, Martha. "Dichtung am Rande des Christentums," *Zeitwende,* XXIII (1951–1952), 529–30.

Görres, Ida. "Zwei Bücher: Ein Vergleich," FH, II (1947) , 856–63.

Grenzmann, Wilhelm. "Ernest Hemingway und seine Dichtung," *Universitas,* XXI (1966), 903–13.

Gronke, Erich. "Das jüngste Buch Hemingways," ZAA, II (1954), 119–23.

Grözinger, Wolfgang. "Erzähler, Denker, Träumer," *Hochland,* LXVI (1953–1954), 181–91.

————. "Roman zwischen Dichtung und Reportage," *Hochland,* XLIV (1951–1952), 552–58.

"Grosses Tamtam." Anon., *Der Spiegel,* VIII (February 3, 1954), 25–27.

Günther, Alfred. WS, XVII (1946), 40–43.

H., R. "Wo ist Afrika?" *Gegenwart,* IX, No. 24 (1954), 768–69.

————. "Bücher von Heute," *Gegenwart,* IV, No. 8 (1949), 20–21.

————. "Tauromachie," *Gegenwart,* XII, No. 8 (1957), 244–45.

Haas, Rudolf. "Zum Todesmotiv im Werk Hemingways," NS, VIII (1959), 455–65.

Hagopian, J. V. "Style and Meaning in Hemingway and Faulkner," JAS, IV (1959), 170–79.

" 'Häng dich auf, tapferer Hemingstein!' " Anon., *Der Spiegel,* XXV (August 23, 1971), 96–97.

Hansen-Löve, Friedrich. "Ein Fazit Hemingways?" *Welt und Wort,* VII (1952), 947–48.

Happel, Nikolaus. "Äusserungen Hemingways zur Darstellung der Wirklichkeit und Wahrheit," ASNS, CXC (1954), 204–13.

————. "Chapter V aus Hemingways Kurzgeschichtenband *In Our Time*," ASNS, CXCI (1955), 324–25.

————. "Ein Beitrag zur 'discipline' in Hemingways Stil," NS, VI (1957), 583–87.

————. "Stilbetrachtung an *The Old Man and the Sea*," NS, V (1956), 71–78.

Hartung, Rudolph. "Zur Situation unserer Literatur," *Welt und Wort*, I (1946), 107–10.

Haveland, Hans. "Die Lockung Afrikas," WM, XCVI, No. 10 (1955), 92–93.

Heise, Hans–Jürgen. "Ernests Kram: Reportagen des legendären Hemingway," *Christ und Welt* (September 19, 1969), p. 13.

Heiseler, Bernt von. "Erzähler des Auslands," *Zeitwende*, XXI (1949–1950), 50–57.

Heissenbüttel, Helmut. "Versuch über den Ruhm Hemingways," DR, LXXXIX, No. 1 (1963), 50–56.

Heitzenröther, H. "Der alte Mann und das Bier," NDL, I (May, 1953), 211.

Heller, Peter. "Phantasie und Phantomisierung zur zeitgenössischen amerikanischen Prosa," *Merkur*, X (1956), 917–22.

————. "Unterschiede in der Denkart amerikanischer und deutscher Intellektueller," NDH, V (October, 1958), 620–32.

Helwig, Werner. "Als ihm die Stunde schlug," *Merkur*, XXI (1967), 596–98.

Hemingway, Ernest. "Rede an das deutsche Volk" (1938), *Die Weltbühne*, I (August 25, 1946), 135–36.

According to a prefatory note, Hemingway delivered this speech over short wave to the German Freedom Broadcasting Station, in November, 1938. Partially reprinted under the title "An das wirkliche Deutschland" in *Neue Deutsche Literatur*, IV (July, 1956), 32. Reprinted also in *Die Weltbühne*, XVI (July 19, 1961), 910–11.

"Hemingway: Der alte Mann und die Kritik." Anon., *Der Spiegel*, VI (December 10, 1952), 29.

"Hemingway-Biographie: Vertrauen verletzt." Anon., *Der Spiegel*, XX (January 24, 1966), 93–94.

"Hemingway: Die grünen Hügel Afrikas." Anon., WS, XXIV (1955), 194–96.

"Hemingway: Jeden Tag Geschichte." Anon., *Der Spiegel*, XXI (September 4, 1967), 130–32.

"Hemingway-Manuskripte: Keine Widerrede." Anon., *Der Spiegel*, XXI (May 29, 1967), 144.

Hensel, Georg. "Filmtod eines Schriftstellers: 'Schnee am Kilimandscharo' in Technicolor," *Neue literarische Welt*, IV, No. 6 (1953), 3.

Henss, Herbert. "Eine verbindende Interpretation auf der Oberstufe als Teil des Themenkomplexes 'Amerika': Edgar Allan Poe, 'The Masque of the Red Death,' Ernest Hemingway, 'A Clean, Well-Lighted Place,' " NS, LXVI (June, 1967), 327–38.

Hermand, Jost. "Probleme der heutigen Gattungsgeschichte," *Jahrbuch für Internationale Germanistik*, II, No 1 (1970), 85–94.

Hertel, Leo. "Who Are the Favorite Writers in Germany?" *Books Abroad*, XXIV (Summer, 1950), 251–52.

Hoffmann, Gerhard. " 'The Gambler, the Nun, and the Radio': Untersuchung zur Gestaltungsweise Hemingways," GRM, XLVI (1964), 421–29.

———. "Kontrast und Parallelität in den Kurzgeschichten Ernest Hemingways," *Anglia*, LXXXIII (1965), 199–224.

Hohoff, Curt. "Das religiöse Problem in der erzählenden Literatur," *Hochland*, XLII (1949–1950), 178–87.

Höllerer, Walter. "Die kurze Form der Prosa," *Akzente*, IX (1962), 226–45.

Holthusen, Hans. "Hemingways Darstellungskunst: Zur deutschen Ausgabe des Buches *Die Grünen Hügel Afrikas*," *Universitas*, X (1955), 257–60.

Horvay, Fred. "Book Publishing in Germany in 1946," *Monatshefte*, XXXIX (1947), 134.

Howe, Irving. "Der Nachkriegsroman in Amerika," *Universitas*, VI (1951), 1199–1208.

Hüllen, Werner. "Gespräche ohne Verstehen: Versuch einer Deutung von Ernest Hemingways Kurzgeschichten 'A Day's Wait' und 'Cat in the Rain,' " NS, VI (1957), 432–39.

Huppert, Hugo. "Der Sieger geht leer aus . . . : Ein Nachruf auf Ernest Hemingway," *Die Weltbühne*, XVI (July 19, 1961), 911–16.

Jaesrich, Helmut. "Tod in Venedig," *Der Monat*, III (1950), 93–95.

Jantz, Harold. "Amerika im deutschen Dichten und Denken,"

Deutsche Philologie im Aufriss, ed. Wolfgang Stammler. 3 vols. Berlin, 1954, pp. 309–71.

Jens, Walter. "Marginalien: Zum Tode Ernest Hemingways," *Merkur,* XV (1961), 797–800.

Joachim, Hans A. "Romane aus Amerika," NR, XI (September, 1930), 396–409.

Joerden, Rudolf. "Zu einem neuen Buche von Ernest Hemingway," *Bücherei und Bildung,* I (1948–1949), 81–85.

Joho, Wolfgang, "Ernest Hemingway und der spanische Krieg," *Ost und West,* III (September, 1949), 90–95.

Jones, John A. "Hemingway: The Critics and the Public Legend," *Western Humanities Review,* XIII (Autumn, 1959), 387–410.

Kaiser, Herbert. "Hemingways *The Sun Also Rises* in deutscher Übersetzung," *Lebende Sprachen,* III–V (1958–1960), 25–26.

Kandler, Wolfdietrich. "Der alte Mann und das Meer," *Weltstimmen,* XXXII (1953), 1–4.

Kann, Hans-Joachim. "Besprechungen und Kurzanzeigen," NS, NF, XVIII (February, 1969), 96–98.

———. "Ernest Hemingway's Knowledge of German," *Jahrbuch für Amerikastudien,* XV (1970), 221–32.

Karasek, Hellmuth. "Ein Reporter namens Hemingway," *Süddeutsche Zeitung* (September 13–14, 1969), p. 115.

Kaschkin, I. "Inhalt-Form-Inhalt," *Sowjetwissenschaft,* XII (1964), 688–708.

Kipphoff, Petra. "Hemingways Lyrik," *Die Zeit* (August 13, 1965), p. 10.

Kirchner, Englebert. "Der Tod des Soldaten," FH, VI (1951), 442–45.

———. "Die überwundene Niederlage," FH, VIII (1953), 74–76.

———. "Short Story," FH, V (1950), 507–09.

Klie, Barbara. "Bevor die Sonne Aufgeht: Zum Tode von Ernest Hemingway," *Christ und Welt* (July 7, 1961), p. 13.

Knapp, Friedrich. "Realismus in der zeitgenössischen Literatur," *Welt und Wort,* II (1947), 157–59.

Knight, Arthur. "Hemingway into Film," *Saturday Review,* XLIV (July 29, 1961), 33–34.

Knöller, Fritz. "Hemingways Weltbild und Werkform," *Welt und Wort,* VII (1952), 411–12.

Koeppen, Wolfgang. "Wie David vor Saul: Zum Tode Ernest Hemingways," *Frankfurter Allgemeine* (July 4, 1961), p. 16.

Krannhals, Hanns von. *Welt und Wort*, IV (1949), 248.

Kranz, H. B. "Literatur und Literaturwissenschaft," *Universitas*, VIII (1953), 70–71.

Krebs, Karl. "Die amerikanische Kurzgeschichte in der Schule," NS, V (1956), 306–08.

Kruse, Horst. "Ernest Hemingway's 'The End of Something': Its Independence as a Short Story and Its Place in the 'Education of Nick Adams,'" *Studies in Short Fiction*, IV (1967), 152–66.

————. "Hinrich Kruses *Weg un Ümweg* und die Tradition der Short Story Ernest Hemingway," GRM, XLIII (1962), 286–301.

————. "Hemingway's 'Cat in the Rain' and Joyce's *Ulysses*," *Literatur in Wissenschaft und Unterricht*, III, No. 1 (1970), 28–30.

Lang, Hans-Joachim. "Kunst und Wirklichkeit in der Short Story," *Die Pädagogische Provinz*, XIII (1959), 398–404.

Lange, Victor. "Notes on the German Literary Scene 1946–1948," *Modern Language Journal*, XXXIII (1949), 3–15.

————. "We Are Utopia," *Modern Language Journal*, XXXV (1951), 169–78.

Lania, Leo. "Hemingway," *Welt und Wort*, XVI–XVII (1961), 240.

Lebowitz, Alan. "Hemingway In Our Time," *Yale Review*, LVIII (March, 1969), 321–41.

Ledig-Rowohlt, H. M. "Der Tod am Morgen," *Die Zeit* (July 7, 1961), p. 12.

Leicht, Robert. "Von den Schönheiten eines Bürgerkriegs," under the heading "Hemingway: *Wem die Stunde schlägt*," *Süddeutsche Zeitung* (April 17–18, 1971), n. pag.

Leisi, Ernst. "Der Erzählpunkt in der neueren englischen Prosa," GRM, VI (January, 1956), 40–51.

Lennig, Walter. "Ein literarischer Jux," NDH, IV (December, 1957), 846–47.

Lepiorz, Gerhard. "Ernest Hemingway: *For Whom the Bell Tolls*," NZ, II (1950), 483–85.

Levin, Harry. "Some European Views of Contemporary American Literature," *American Quarterly*, I (Spring, 1949), 264–79.

Liedloff, Helmut. "Two War Novels: A Critical Comparison," *Revue de Littérature Comparée*, XLII (1968), 390–406.

Lilje, Hanns. "Gnadenlosigkeit und Gnade im Werke Hemingways," *Zeitwende*, XXIV (1953), 5–13.

———. "Von Hemingway zu Graham Green," *Sonntagsblatt*, III, No. 11 (1950), 7.

Link, Franz. "Tale," "sketch," "essay" und "short story," NS, VI (1957), 345–52.

Lorbe, Ruth. "Die deutsche Kurzgeschichte der Jahrhundertmitte," *Der Deutschunterricht*, IX, No. 1 (1957), 36–54.

Lubbers, Klaus. "Aufgaben und Möglichkeiten der Rezeptionsforschung," GRM, NF, XIV (1964), 292–302.

Lüdeke, Henry. "American Literature in Germany: A Report of Recent Research and Criticism—1931–1933," *American Literature*, VI (May, 1934), 168–75.

Maier, Hansgeorg. "Bei Hemingway wie bei Rilke: Über die Gefahren der Selbstnachahmung," *Die Zeit* (February 22, 1951), p. 3.

Mann, Klaus. "Ernest Hemingway," *Neue Schweizer Rundschau*, XXIV (1931), 272–77.

Marcuse, Ludwig. "German Intellectuals Five Years After the War," *Books Abroad*, XXIV (Autumn, 1950), 346–51.

Meidinger-Geise, Inge. "Stimmen am Ufer: Zum Werke von Ernest Hemingway und Thomas Wolfe," *Die Erlanger Universität*, IV, No. 11 (1950), 2.

Meindl, Dieter. "Besprechungen," *Anglia*, XXCIX (1971), 276–79.

Menck, Clara. "Muster der Short Story," *Welt und Wort*, VI (1951), 382–83.

Mertner, Edgar. "Zur Theorie der Short Story in England und Amerika," *Anglia*, LXV (1941), 188–205.

Meyer, Heinrich. "The Novel Today: Death or Transmutation? A Symposium," *Books Abroad* (Summer, 1958), 239–40.

Miller, Perry. "Das Amerikabild des amerikanischen Romans und sein Einfluss auf Europa," *Universitas*, VIII (1953), 457–60.

Morgan, Bayard Q. "Book Notes from Germany," *Books Abroad*, XXIV (Spring, 1950), 131–33.

———. "The Literary Underground in Germany," *Books Abroad*, XXII (Autumn, 1948), 358–60.

Mösslang, Monika. "Er begann als Reporter in Toronto," *Die Welt der Literatur* (November 6, 1969), pp. 4–5.

Motekat, Helmut. "Gedanken zur Kurzgeschichte," *Der Deutschunterricht*, IX, No. 1 (1957), 20–35.

Mueller, Gustav. "Die amerikanische Selbstkritik im modernen Roman," *Universitas*, XLV (1959), 511–20.

Müller, Bastian. "Die 'Verlorene Generation' und wir," *Welt und Wort*, I (1946), 173–75.

Müller, Erika. "Hemingway hinter der Mattscheibe," *Die Zeit* (July 27, 1950), p. 5.

Neumann, John. "Ein Gespräch mit Ernest Hemingway: 'Ich packe dieses Herz bei den Hörnern . . . ,'" *Die Literatur*, I (June 15, 1952), 1.

Niedermayer, F. "Spanien in der Literatur," NA, XII (1957), 369–72.

Nicolaisen, Peter. "Buchbesprechungen," *Literatur in Wissenschaft und Unterricht*, I (1968), 154–55.

Opitz, Kurt. "Negative 'Bilanz'? German Literary Reconstruction," *Books Abroad*, XXXVII (Summer, 1963), 275–79.

Oppel, Horst. "American Literature in Postwar Germany: Impact or Alienation?" NS, V (1962), 1–10.

―――. "Hemingway's *Across the River and Into the Trees*," NS, I (1952), 473–86.

Pächter, Heinz. "Die Heimkehr des 'Entfremdeten' Sohnes," WW, VIII (1953), 521–27.

Papajewski, Helmut. "Die Frage nach der Sinnhaftigkeit bei Hemingway," *Anglia*, LXX (1951), 186–209.

―――. "Krisenbewusstsein und Existenzanalyse in der neueren amerikanischen Literatur," JAS, I (1956), 58–69.

"Papas Fiesta." Anon., *Der Spiegel*, XIV (November 9, 1960), 75–78.

"Personalien." Anon., *Der Spiegel*, VIII (December 1, 1954), 40.

Pick, Robert. "Mit europäischen Augen: Amerika im Spiegel der europäischen Literaturkritik," *Der Monat*, II (1950), 658–64.

Pieritz, Hilde. "Ernest Hemingway und sein Werk," *Hefte für Büchereiwesen*, XVI (1932), 313–16.

Piontek, Heinz. *Welt und Wort*, IX (1954), 413.

Plimpton, George. "Gespräch mit Ernest Hemingway," *Merkur*, XIII (1959), 526–44.

Politzer, Heinz. "Der neue Hemingway," NR, LXII, No. 1 (1951), 136–39.

Pongs, Hermann. "Die Anekdote als Kunstform zwischen Kalendergeschichte und Kurzgeschichte," *Der Deutschunterricht,* IX, No. 1 (1957), 5–20.

————. "Hemingway und die Einfalt als Grundwert der Dichtung," NDH, I (1954–1955), 706–11.

Prause, Gerhard. "Ernest Hemingway," *Welt und Wort,* VI (1951), 49–51.

"Privatissima Hotchneriana." Anon., *Die Welt der Literatur* (December 22, 1966), p. 9.

Pusey, William. "The German Vogue of Thomas Wolfe," *Germanic Review,* XXIII (1948), 131–48.

Randall, David A. " 'Dukedom Large Enough': II. Hemingway, Churchill, and the Printed Word," *Bibliographical Society of America Papers,* LVI (1962), 246–353.

Redman, Ben R. "The Champ and the Referees," *Saturday Review,* XXXIII (October 28, 1950), 15–16, 38.

Reich-Ranicki, Marcel. "Verräter, Brückenbauer, Waisenkinder," *Übersetzen: Vorträge und Beiträge von Internationalen Kongress Übersetzer in Hamburg 1965.* Ed. Rolf Italiaander. Frankfurt am Main, 1965. Pp. 69–73.

"Reise abwärts." Anon., *Der Spiegel,* XXIII (April 14, 1969), 169–70.

Richter, Werner. "Hemingway und die Helden," DR, LXXXI (1955), 54–56.

Rohlinger, Rudolf. "Ernest Hemingway," *Das Auditorium,* I, No. 7–8 (1947), 40–41.

"Romane im Safe." Anon., *Der Spiegel,* IX (November 23, 1955), 59–60.

Ross, Werner. "Die amerikanische Literatur als Typus," *Hochland,* LV (1962–1963), 163–67.

————. "Der amerikanische Roman der Gegenwart," *Hochland,* XLVI (1953–1954), 153–63.

Sahl, Hans. "Hemingways Spätwerk," *Universitas,* XX (1965), 1151–54.

Schmied, Wieland. "Der Tod war sein Thema: Ernest Hemingway, Mann ohne Dämmerung," *Wort in der Zeit,* VII (1961), 2–5.

Schnabel, Ernst. "Die amerikanische Story," *Nordwestdeutsche Hefte*, I, No. 3 (1946), 25–28.

Schönemann, Friedrich. "Das amerikanische Buch in Deutschland," *Die Lebenden Fremdsprachen*, III (1951), 167–70.

Schönfelder, Karl-Heinz. "Amerikanische Literatur in Europa: Methodologisches zu geschmacksgeschichtlichen Überlegungen," *Wissenschaftliche Zeitschrift*, VII (1957–1958), 571–81.

Schulz, Franz. "Der nordamerikanische Indianer und seine Welt in den Werken von Ernest Hemingway und Oliver La Farge," *Mainzer amerikanistische Beiträge*, VII (1964), 1–192.

Schulz, Hanfried. "Wer ist Ihr Lieblingsautor?" *Panorama*, IV (August, 1960), 6.

Schwerin, Christoph. *Aufbau*, XIII (1957), 667.

––––––. DR, LXXXIII (1957), 852–53.

––––––. "Hemingways Parodie," DR, LXXXIV (1958), 403–04.

Sieburg, Friedrich. "Bücher von heute," *Gegenwart*, IV (March 1, 1949), 19–20.

––––––. *Die Zeit* (December 2, 1954), p. 14.

––––––. "Tod in Venedig," *Gegenwart*, VII, No. 1 (1952), 24.

Soupault, Philippe. "Bildnis Hemingways wie er es selbst sah," *Sinn und Form*, XIII (1961), 661–63.

St., d. "Haben und Nichthaben," *Gegenwart*, VI, No. 12 (1951), 21.

Stammler, Heinrich. "Der Kriegsroman der heimatlosen Linken Amerikas," *Merkur*, V (1951), 295–99.

Stelzmann, Rainulf. "Religiöse Sehnsucht im amerikanischen Roman," SZ, CLXIX (1961), 201–12.

Straumann, Heinrich. "Amerikanische Literatur in Europa: Eine geschmacksgeschichtliche Überlegung," *Anglia*, LXXVI (1958), 208–16.

Stresau, Hermann. "Ernest Hemingway: Von der Kunst des Weglassens," DUZ, XII, No. 23–24 (1957), 24–26.

t., w. s. "Ein Vortrag über Hemingway," *Börsenblatt für den Deutschen Buchhandel* (Leipzig), CXVI, No. 5 (1949), 39.

Torga, H. R. "Ein amerikanischer Byron–heute," *Neues Europa*, No. 6 (1948), pp. 40–41.

Trilling, Lionel. "Ein Amerikaner in Spanien," *Monat*, I, No. 5 (1949), 90–93.

Tumler, Franz. "Die Wirklichkeit des Schriftstellers," *Zeitwende*, XXVI (1955), 66–67.

U., B. "Umschau," *Aufbau*, XII (1956), 738–39.

Uhlig, Helmut. "Sollte Hemingway verboten werden?" *Die Literatur*, I (July 1952), 6.

Unseld, Siegfried. *"An Diesem Dienstag*: Unvorgreifliche Gedanken über die Kurzgeschichte," *Akzente*, II (1955), 139–48.

Urbach, Ilse. "Nachts wecken mich Bücher," *Die Welt* (March 7, 1953), p. 17.

Viator, Paul. "Perspektive zu Hemingway," WW, IV (1949), 144–45.

Volbracht, Adolf. "Wiederbegegnung mit amerikanischer Prosa," *Aufbau*, IV (1948), 712–14.

"Von den Löwen träumen." Anon., *Gegenwart*, IX, No. 3 (1954), 69.

W., G. "Die Stimme Amerikas, amerikanische Kurzgeschichten," *Aufbau*, XII (1956), 739.

Waggoner, Hyatt H. "Hemingway and Faulkner: 'The End of Something,' " *The Southern Review*, IV (1968), 458–66.

Wandruszka, Mario. "Strukturen moderner Prosa," *Der Deutschunterricht*, IX, No. 3 (1957), 89–104.

Warren, Robert Penn. "Hemingway," AR, III (1947), 89–104.

Waugh, Evelyn. *Tablet*, CXCVI (September 30, 1950), 290, 292.

Weiskopf, F. C. "German Publishers Have Their Problems," *Books Abroad*, XXI (Winter, 1947), 9–11.

"Wem die Stunde schlägt." Anon., *Der Spiegel*, XV (July 12, 1961), 45–52.

Werner, B. E. "Rückkehr ins kleine Leben," *Deutsche Allgemeine Zeitung* (July 27, 1932), n. pag.

West, Ray B., Jr. "The Sham Battle over Ernest Hemingway," *Western Review*, XVII (Spring, 1953), 234–40.

White, William. "Books About Hemingway Abroad," *American Book Collector*, XVIII (April, 1968), 23.

————. "Hemingway Hunting in Scandinavia," *American Book Collector*, XVI (January, 1966), 22–24.

————. " 'The Old Man and the Sea' as a German Textbook," *Bibliographical Society of American Papers*, LX (1966), 89–90.

————. "Why Collect Ernest Hemingway—or Anyone?" *Prairie Schooner*, XL (1966), 232–46.

Wiegenstein, Roland. "Film und Hemingway," *Hier und Heute*, I, No. 3 (1951), 19.

Wittkowski, Wolfgang. "Gekreuzigt im Ring: Zu Hemingways *The Old Man and the Sea*," *Deutsche Vierteljahrsschrift für Literaturwissenschaft und Geistesgeschichte*, XLI (1967), 258–82.

Wohlgemuth, Rolf. "Ernest Hemingway," *Colloquium*, II, No. 10 (1948), 16.

Wolf, G. SZ, CXLVI (1950), 315–16.

Wolpers, Theodor. "Die amerikanische *short story* in der Schule: Gesichtspunkte und Vorschläge für eine representative Auswahl," NS, V (1956), 286–304.

Zahn, A. "Der fünfzigjährige Hemingway," HM (Ost), I (1948), 455–56.

"Die Zerfransung der Literatur." Anon., *Allgemeine Zeitung: Mainzer Anzeiger* (August 6, 1971), p. 2.

GERMAN DISSERTATIONS ON HEMINGWAY

Berendt, Hans Dietrich. "Die Short Stories von Ernest Hemingway: Entstehung, Form und Stil," Diss. Bonn 1957.

Brandstätter, Dieter F. "Das Problem des Krieges im Werk Ernest Hemingways: Ein Beitrag zur Interpretation der amerikanischen Prosadichtung zwischen den Kriegen (1920–1940)," Diss. Kiel 1951.

Damp, Waldemar. "Individuum und Gesellschaft in Hemingways Romanen," Diss. Greifswald 1964.

Dörfel, Hanspeter. "Hemingways Erzählperspektiven," Diss. Saarbrücken 1964.

Fietz, Lothar. "Wandlungen der Form im Romanwerk Ernest Hemingways: Untersuchungen zum Wesen des Fiktiven," Diss. Tübingen 1960.

Gräf, Gerhard. "Amerikanische Syntax der Gegenwart bei Hemingway," Diss. Jena 1956.

Hillebrand-Stadie, Christine. "Die Disziplin als ethisches Motiv und stilistisches Prinzip in den Kurzgeschichten Ernest Hemingways," Diss. Munich 1963.

Kann, Hans-Joachim. "Übersetzungsprobleme in den deutschen Übersetzungen von drei anglo-amerikanischen Kurzgeschichten:

Aldous Huxley's 'Green Tunnels,' Ernest Hemingways 'The Killers' and 'A Clean, Well-Lighted Place,' " Diss. Mainz 1968.

Krotz, Friedrich Wilhelm. "Wesen und Funktion der Jagd im Werke Ernest Hemingways," Diss. Freiburg i.B. 1963.

Raethel, Gerd. "Selbstmorde und Selbstmordversuche amerikanischer Schriftsteller: Von Poe bis Hemingway," Diss. Munich 1966.

Saremi, Aazam. "Die Rezeption der Werke und der Persönlichkeit Ernest Hemingways in der Sowjetunion," Diss. Leipzig 1966.

Schulz, Franz. "Der nordamerikanische Indianer und seine Welt in den Werken von Ernest Hemingway und Oliver La Farge," Diss. Mainz 1964. Published in *Mainzer amerikanistische Beiträge*, VII. Munich: Hueber, 1964.

Schulze, Martin. "Ernest Hemingway: Werden und Wesen seiner Kunst," Diss. Halle 1960.

Skulima, Loni. "Sprachliche Studien zu Hemingway," Diss. Heidelberg 1949.

Stickelmann, Matthias W. "View-Point und Zeitstruktur als Basis morphologischer Interpretation: Eine Darstellung am Roman Gerhart Hauptmanns und Ernest Hemingways," Diss. Bonn 1955.

Winkler, Reinhold. "Lyrische Elemente in den Kurzgeschichten Ernest Hemingways: Eine Untersuchung der Textstruktur," Diss. Erlangen-Nürnberg 1967.

GERMAN TRANSLATIONS OF HEMINGWAY'S COLLECTED SHORT STORIES

Männer (Men Without Women, 1927). Berlin: Rowohlt, 1929. 256 pages.

In unserer Zeit (In Our Time, 1925). Berlin: Rowohlt, 1932. 184 pages. Reissued: Hamburg: Rowohlt, 1958.

Der Schnee von Kilimandscharo und andere Erzählungen ("The Snows of Kilimanjaro" and three other short stories). Stuttgart: Rowohlt, 1949. 144 pages, Illustrated. Same: Zürich: Steinberg-Verlag, 1949. 200 pages.

49 Stories (First 49, 1938). Hamburg: Rowohlt, 1950. 468 pages.

Preface by Hemingway on pp. 5–6, trans. from the *First 49*. Berlin: Aufbau-Verlag, 1965. Gütersloh: Bertelsmann Lesering, 1965.

Das Ende von Etwas und andere Kurzgeschichten ("The End of Something" and five other short stories). Stuttgart: Reclam, 1951. 77 pages. Afterword by Kurt W. Marek, on pp. 74–77.

Der Unbesiegte: 2 Erzählungen ("The Undefeated" and "The Short Happy Life of Francis Macomber"). Munich: R. Piper, 1952.

Schnee auf dem Kilimandscharo ("The Snows of Kilimanjaro"). Hamburg: Rowohlt, 1952. 56 pages. Biographical note on Hemingway, p. ii.

Erzählungen (*The Fifth Column and First 49*, 1938). Berlin: Deutsche Buch—Gemeinschaft, 1954. 375 pages.

Die Hauptstadt der Welt ("The Capital of the World" and three other short stories). Munich: Langen-Muller, 1955. 67 pages.

Männer ohne Frauen (*Men Without Women*, 1927). Hamburg: Rowohlt, 1958. (Rororo, 279.) 142 pages. Berlin: Aufbau-Verlag, 1966.

Der Sieger geht leer aus (*Winner Take Nothing*, 1933). Hamburg: Rowohlt, 1958. (Rororo, 280).

Um eine Viertelmillion—Die Killer ("Fifty Grand," "The Killers"). Freiburg im Breisgau: Hyperion-Verlag, 1958.

Der Unbesiegte ("The Undefeated"). Hannover: Fackelträger-Verlag, 1959. 60 pages. Illustrated with 28 black-and-white drawings by Picasso. Same: Gütersloh: Bertelsmann Lesering, 1961.

Schnee auf dem Kilimandscharo ("The Snows of Kilimanjaro" and five other short stories). Hamburg: Rowohlt, 1961. 148 pages.

Sämtliche Erzählungen (Collected stories and *The Old Man and the Sea*). Hamburg: Rowohlt, 1966. 480 pages.

Each of the above volumes was translated by Annemarie Horschitz. Following World War II her name was changed to Horschitz-Horst.

GERMAN TRANSLATIONS OF HEMINGWAY'S INDIVIDUAL WORKS

Fiesta (*The Sun Also Rises*, 1926). Berlin: Rowohlt, 1928. 312 pages. Translated by Annemarie Horschitz. Reissued: Hamburg: Rowohlt, 1950. (Rororo, 5.) 181 pages. Same: Gütersloh: Bertelsmann Lesering, 1960. 318 pages.

In einem anderen Land (Farewell to Arms, 1929). Berlin: Rowohlt, 1930. 368 pages. Translated by Annemarie Horschitz. Reissued: Hamburg: Rowohlt, 1951 (Rororo, 216.) Same: Zürich: Steinberg-Verlag, 1948. 360 pages. Berlin: Volksverband der Bücherfreunde, 1949. Berlin: Deutsche Buch-Gemeinschaft, 1952. Berlin: Aufbau-Verlag, 1957. Zürich: Buchclub Ex Libris, 1957. Stuttgart: Deutscher Bücherbund, 1963.

Wem die Stunde schlägt (For Whom the Bell Tolls, 1940). Stockholm: Bermann-Fischer, 1941. 560 pages. Translated by Baudisch. Same: Vienna: Bermann-Fischer, 1948. 550 pages. Berlin: Suhrkamp, 1948. 544 pages. Zürich: Büchergilde Gutenberg, 1949. Frankfurt am Main: S. Fischer, 1951. Berlin: G. B. Fischer, 1958. 582 pages. Gütersloh: Bertelsmann, 1955. Vienna: Deutsche Buch-Gemeinschaft, 1959. Frankfurt am Main: Fischer-Bücherei, 1961.

Über den Fluss und in die Wälder (Across the River and Into the Trees, 1950). Hamburg: Rowohlt, 1951. 340 pages. Translated by Annemarie Horschitz-Horst. Same: Zürich: Steinberg-Verlag, 1952. 282 pages. Berlin: Aufbau-Verlag, 1957. Stuttgart: Stuttgarter Hausbücherei, 1958. Zürich: Buchclub Ex Libris, 1959. Hamburg: Deutsche Hausbücherei, 1960. Berlin: Deutsche Gemeinschaft, 1964.

Haben und Nichthaben (To Have and Have Not, 1937). Hamburg: Rowohlt, 1951. 279 pages. Translated by Annemarie Horschitz-Horst. Reissued: 1964. (Rororo, 605.) Same: Frankfurt am Main: Büchergilde Gutenberg, 1957. Zürich: Buchclub Ex Libris, 1958. Düsseldorf: Deutscher Bücherbund, 1960. Gütersloh: Bertelsmann Lesering, 1967.

Der alte Mann und das Meer (The Old Man and the Sea, 1952). Hamburg: Rowohlt, 1952. (Rororo 328.) 128 pages. Translated by Annemarie Horschitz-Horst. Same: Steinberg-Verlag, 1954. 126 pages. Stuttgart: Europäischer Buchklub, 1955. Berlin: Deutsche Buch-Gemeinschaft, 1956. Hamburg: Asmus Verlag, [1961]. 160 pages. Illustrated by Fran Masereel. Berlin: Aufbau-Verlag, [1962].

Die grünen Hügel Afrikas (Green Hills of Africa, 1935). Hamburg: Rowohlt, 1954. 249 pages. (Rororo, 47.) Translated by

Annemarie Horschitz-Horst. Same: Gütersloh: Bertelsmann Lesering, 1962.

Tod am Nachmittag (Death in the Afternoon, 1932). Hamburg: Rowohlt, 1957. 376 pages, including 81 illustrations. Translated by Annemarie Horschitz-Horst.

Die Sturmfluten des Frühlings (The Torrents of Spring, 1926). Hamburg: Rowohlt, 1957. 136 pages. Translated by Annemarie Horschitz-Horst. Same: Zürich: Steinberg-Verlag, 1957.

Paris—ein Fest fürs Leben (A Moveable Feast, 1964). Hamburg: Rowohlt, 1965. 256 pages. Translated by Annemarie Horschitz-Horst. Foreword by Hemingway on pp. 5–6.

49 Depeschen (By-Line: Ernest Hemingway, 1967). Hamburg: Rowohlt, 1969. Contains 49 of the original 77 items edited by William White. Translated by Ernst Schnabel and Elizabeth Plessen.

Inseln im Strom (Islands in the Stream, 1970). Hamburg: Rowohlt, 1971. 445 pages. Translated by Ernst Schnabel and Elizabeth Plessen.

INDEX

For references to Hemingway's writings, see under Hemingway, Ernest: NONFICTION, NOVELS, SHORT STORIES. H is used throughout for Hemingway.